GEORGIA

GETTING STARTED GARDEN GUIDE

**Grow the Best Flowers, Shrubs, Trees,
Vines & Groundcovers**

Brimming with creative inspiration, how-to projects, and useful information to enrich your everyday life, Quarto Knows is a favorite destination for those pursuing their interests and passions. Visit our site and dig deeper with our books into your area of interest: Quarto Creates, Quarto Cooks, Quarto Homes, Quarto Lives, Quarto Drives, Quarto Explores, Quarto Gifts, or Quarto Kids.

First published in 2013 by Cool Springs Press, an imprint of The Quarto Group, 100 Cummings Center, Suite 265-D, Beverly, MA 01915, USA.
T (978) 282-9590 F (978) 283-2742 QuartoKnows.com

Cool Springs Press titles are also available at discount for retail, wholesale, promotional, and bulk purchase. For details, contact the Special Sales Manager by email at specialsales@ quarto.com or by mail at The Quarto Group, Attn: Special Sales Manager, 100 Cummings Center, Suite 265-D, Beverly, MA 01915, USA.

Library of Congress Cataloging-in-Publication Data

Glasener, Erica.
  Georgia getting started garden guide : grow the best flowers, shrubs, trees, vines & groundcovers / Erica Glasener and Walter Reeves.
    p. cm.
  Includes bibliographical references and index.
  ISBN 978-1-59186-571-1 (softcover)
  1. Gardening--Georgia. 2. Plants, Ornamental--Georgia. I. Reeves, Walter. II. Title.

  SB453.2.G4G585 2013
  635.09758--dc23
                                        2013021176

Acquisitions Editor: Billie Brownell
Design Manager: Brad Springer
Layout: Danielle Smith
Cover photo: Dency Kane

GEORGIA

GETTING STARTED GARDEN GUIDE

Grow the Best Flowers, Shrubs, Trees, Vines & Groundcovers

Erica Glasener & Walter Reeves

COOL
SPRINGS
PRESS

DEDICATION & ACKNOWLEDGMENTS

Dedication

To my husband, Daryl, and my daughter, Georgia, for their love, patience, and support in all that I do.

And to my mother, Carol L. Reinsberg, my best editor, for her nurturing spirit and loving guidance.
E.G.G.

To my grandmother "Bubber"—the first gardener I knew who gardened for love.

And to my parents, Frank and Frances, who fell in love as a result of their mutual interest in raising healthy plants and a healthy family.
W.R.

Acknowledgments

Like a seed, this book could not have come to fruition without the care and knowledge of many individuals and groups. Many friends also indirectly contributed to this book. We thank them all for their suggestions and support. In particular we thank the late Roger Waynick and Billie Brownell of Cool Springs Press, for their intuition that this book would be useful for Georgia gardeners.

Erica especially thanks all the gardeners she's visited not only in Georgia but around the country as the host for *A Gardener's Diary*. She also thanks her fellow plant lovers who not only share plants but valuable information.

The intriguing questions a garden "expert" is asked bring the best opportunities for that "expert" to learn more about plants, pests, and gardening. Walter thanks his neighbors Gus and Lisa Callaway, Carl and Laura Greenberg, and "Mr. Kim" and "Mrs. Kim" Cody, plus all of his radio listeners, for the many fascinating gardening questions they've posed.

CONTENTS

WELCOME TO GARDENING

IN GEORGIA

Georgia gardeners are a courageous bunch, working in conditions ranging from the tundra on Brasstown Bald to the tropics of the Okefenokee Swamp. Plants that look wonderful on the pages of garden catalogs wither in our summer heat. Garden solutions that are "guaranteed to prevent disease" may turn out to be miserable failures in our humidity. And never forget the insects! Do gardeners in other parts of the country ever have to pick off Japanese beetles while standing on a fire ant mound?

Native-born Georgia gardeners (and those who have adopted our state) are not dismayed by these challenges, realizing that in many ways Georgia is a plant paradise.

With careful planning and our long growing season, diligent gardeners can have landscape interest throughout the year—from the early-blooming snowdrop bulbs to late-blooming sasanqua camellia. Winters are relatively mild and short, and abundant sunshine and adequate rain (usually) are the norm.

Becoming a Successful Georgia Gardener

So, stuck between garden misery and garden marvels, how does one become a successful Georgia gardener? How does one un-learn growing methods from other regions? The solution is simple: Discover the plants and garden techniques that are best suited to this state. For example, a hosta that the plant catalog says will tolerate five hours of afternoon sunshine—well, five hours of Georgia's afternoon sun will quickly reduce it to compost! Try a shadier spot instead.

Once you decide on the plants you want to grow, you must find the garden tricks necessary to meet the challenges presented by Georgia's soil type, heat, and humidity. Use the wisdom passed down by generations of Georgia gardeners, and combine it with the latest research on the best ways to help a plant flourish. That is exactly what this book is all about: the what, where, when, how, and why of Georgia gardening. You'll learn the best ways to make good soil, discover the tricks that thwart pests, and—best of all—you'll acquire the skills needed to cultivate plants that are proven performers in our area.

We have gardened for many years, both professionally and as a hobby. Gardening is relaxing, intriguing, and nurturing. It is an activity that is both profoundly simple and universally complex.

This book will introduce you to the wealth of ornamental plants that are suited for Georgia gardens. Whether you garden in Atlanta or Savannah, you will find every category of plant you need for a complete residential landscape. Every plant in this book has either been personally grown by us or has been observed growing—strong and healthy—in gardens throughout the state. Some grow best in northern Georgia, some flourish only in southern Georgia, and some require experimentation with location. Vegetables and fruits have not been included in this book, since that topic would demand another whole volume!

Beginning gardeners are offered this bit of advice: *If you haven't moved a plant three times, it's probably not yet in the right place.*

Take comfort in the words of those who remind us: *"Don't say we can't grow it, just say we don't yet know what it needs."*

Start with a Firm Foundation: Georgia Soil

Before you consider the light, drainage, and exposure of your favorite garden spot, spend a little time learning about the soil, nutrients, and common plant pests.

Roots can crack a house foundation or break up a sidewalk, but plant roots are actually quite tender. When you put a plant in the soil, whether it is bermudagrass or a baby oak, the roots will grow in the direction with the least resistance. Roots grow in the areas of soil that offer moisture, oxygen, and nutrients.

Plants prefer to grow in soil that is a blend of clay, sand, and organic matter. The water and oxygen required by roots are plentiful in such an environment, and the nutrients are available throughout. But few gardeners are blessed with perfect soil. The clay soil so abundant in northern Georgia tends to have lots of moisture, but little oxygen. The sandy soil prevalent along the coast has lots of oxygen but holds little water and has few nutrients. The quickest way to improve your soil is to add coarsely textured material in the form of compost or other organic matter.

Amendments
Organic Matter

Organic matter is found in manure, compost, and other materials. Ground pine bark is a common soil amendment sold throughout the state of Georgia. Gardeners in the southern part of the state use ground peanut hulls. Peat moss is readily available, but it doesn't persist in our soil as long as coarser materials do. You may purchase organic soil amendments, but if you learn how to produce your own from good compost, or if you find a good source of manure, you can have an unlimited supply of free organic matter for your landscape.

Compost

Ever wonder why good gardeners wax eloquent about manure and compost? It's because either material, when added to a garden, can double the size and vigor of the plants. Some gardeners swear they achieve triple success when they add one of these

Make sure to make space and time to enjoy your garden!

amendments to their ordinary soil. You might say that successful gardeners don't have green thumbs, they have black thumbs . . . from all of the organic matter they handle!

The reason compost is superior to any other source of organic matter is that it is alive. Compost is the decomposed remains of leaves, lawn clippings, pruned branches, and discarded stalks. The billions of fungi, bacteria, and other living creatures in compost are important parts of any healthy soil. Unfortunately, if you are gardening in a spot that is hard and bare, the soil has very little life in it. Plants growing in hard soil can be made beautiful, but they require more fertilizer and water to keep them looking their best.

Compost is the lazy gardener's friend. It contains billions of living creatures that help roots absorb water and nutrients. These tiny garden helpers can take over some of the tasks of fertilizing and watering your plants.

Making compost never has to be complicated. Mother Nature has been composting for millions of years, and she never used a pitchfork or compost bin or expensive compost starter. Some gardeners choose to compost on a large scale, lugging bags of their neighbors' leaves up the street to dump on their compost piles. Others just throw their own leaves and clippings onto a pile and let nature take its course. Either method is fine. But the forming of compost does take time. It takes approximately six months and a 30-gallon bag of yard trimmings to manufacture 1 cubic foot of compost. Mixing and turning a compost pile once a month can make the process go a bit faster.

Hardy geraniums planted *en masse* create a stunning border.

Many gardeners find it easier to buy soil amendments at a garden center. But how much of this supplemental material does one need to make a difference in the soil? Dr. Tim Smalley, professor of horticulture at the University of Georgia, recommends spreading a layer of organic matter 3 inches thick over a garden flower bed and then mixing it with the soil underneath. In practical terms, that's 2 cubic feet of soil conditioner for every 8 square feet of flower bed. You can see why some composters are caught "borrowing" their neighbors' leaves at night!

The organic matter should be mixed to a depth of 6 to 8 inches in the soil. With the addition of organic matter, the soil will loosen, and it will stay loose for years. Oxygen will penetrate to where the roots are growing. The organic matter will absorb excess water and hold it in reserve for the plant to use when drier times come.

Water Smarts

It seems simple enough to water an outdoor plant, but most gardeners either over- or under-water their charges. Proper watering is accomplished differently in different parts of the state. Sandy soil drains so well that water must be applied twice a week during a blistering summer. Clay soil holds too much water. Plants in clay soil must be watered less often, or they will succumb to root rot.

The amount of water to use also differs among plants. A shallow-rooted fern might need ¼ gallon of water applied every other day. A densely rooted lawn requires 600 gallons per 1,000 square feet every week. A new tree might require 5 gallons twice a week for one month, and afterwards only need watering when a drought occurs.

Your own observations are best for determining when and how much to water. Here are some tips to get you started:

- Put a hose at the base of a newly installed plant and thoroughly soak the rootball once a week.
- Use shallow cans to measure the amount of water applied by a lawn sprinkler. Put six cans in the area being irrigated and run the system for an hour. Then measure the depth of water in all of the cans. When the average depth of water is 1 inch, you know the grass root zone has been well irrigated. Applying an inch of water may take longer than an hour—it all depends on your hose, your sprinkler, and your water pressure.
- Water container plants until the water runs out the bottom. Do not water again until the top inch of soil is dry.
- If summer restrictions limit your watering, determine which plants would cost the most to replace, and water them first. It makes more sense to save a specimen maple tree than to keep $10 worth of petunias alive.
- An inexpensive water timer and a few soaker hoses can be a gardener's best irrigation friends. Weave the soaker hose among your plants and set the timer to apply the amount you need.

Mulch

If a plant's roots are subjected to a long Georgia drought, even the toughest plant in the finest soil will suffer. Mulching will help you avoid this problem. Mulch acts like a blanket. It keeps moisture in the soil, and it prevents plant roots from becoming too hot or too cold. Georgia's millions of pine trees give us two of the best mulches in the world, pine straw and pine bark chips. Other good mulches include shredded fall leaves, wood chips, and shredded hardwood. For the best results apply a 1- to 2-inch layer of mulch on top of the soil around all of your plants.

Fertilizing Facts

Plants need three nutrients in order to grow well—nitrogen, phosphorus, and potassium. When you buy a bag of fertilizer, you will see three numbers on the label. These numbers indicate the amounts of nitrogen, phosphorus, and potassium in the fertilizer. The numbers represent the percentage of each nutrient in the mixture. For example, a bag of 10-10-10 fertilizer contains 10 percent nitrogen (N), 10 percent phosphorus (P), and 10 percent potassium (K). The other 70 percent is just inert filler.

Each nutrient serves a function in the overall good health of a plant. So how do you know which fertilizer to buy when your garden center offers dozens of combinations of the three nutrient numbers? Just look at the numbers on the bag and remember: up, down, and all around.

Up: Nitrogen promotes leaf growth. That's why lawn fertilizer has a high nitrogen percentage. A common turf fertilizer is a 16-4-8, but some brands have even more nitrogen than this. Grass leaves are mowed and removed constantly, so nitrogen is needed to help grow more of them.

Down: Phosphorus is important for the growth of roots and is very important for flower, seed, and fruit formation. That's why so-called "starter fertilizers" and "bloom fertilizers" have a high percentage of phosphorus.

All Around: Potassium increases overall cell health. When your plant is under stress from drought or from cold, adequate potassium helps the plant withstand the crisis.

It is not necessary to buy a different fertilizer for each of the plant types you have in your landscape. You really can't hurt a plant by applying the wrong fertilizer. Your perennials won't be damaged by the application of "azalea fertilizer." The lawn won't be hurt if you fertilize it with 10-10-10. There may be some situations in which one type of fertilizer is marginally better; for example, a "slow-release turf fertilizer" might be especially desirable for some types of grass. But you can do quite well with the purchase of just three main types of fertilizer: 16-4-8 for your lawn, 6-12-12 for new plants, and 10-10-10 for everything else.

Soil Testing

How do you know what amount of fertilizer to apply? How much nutrition does your soil already hold? Do you need any lime? To find out the answers, you need to perform a soil test.

There are two ways to test your soil. You can purchase an inexpensive gardener's test kit with simple chemicals and test tubes and do it yourself, or you can take some of your soil to your local county Extension office (see page 225) for a low-cost analysis.

Do-it-yourself test kits are economical and simple to use. To use one, mix your soil with water, then add a few drops of indicator chemical that will cause the water to change color. If you feel confident that you can match the color of the water with the colors on the small color wheel that is provided, you can determine which nutrients you need to add to your soil.

If you don't trust your powers of analysis, you might want to compare your conclusions with those of the University of Georgia Soil Testing Laboratory through your county Extension office. Having soil tested by the Extension office is a simple process. Collect several scoops of dirt from different areas of your yard and mix them together.

The Extension office needs just one cup of this soil mixture for the test. Put the soil in a bag, take it to an Extension office, and tell the Extension agent what you intend to grow in it. The soil will be shipped to a laboratory in Athens. Within ten days, you will receive a report describing the nutrients present in your soil, the amounts in which they are present, and specific recommendations for correct fertilizer use.

Johnny Jump-ups

Japanese maple surrounded by green and flowering plants.

The Value of Lime

Though lime does not offer plant nutrients (aside from calcium, which plants need in small amounts), it does help plants absorb nutrients more efficiently. Georgia soils, particularly in the northern half of the state, tend to be acidic. In an acidic soil, plant roots can't collect the nitrogen, phosphorus, and potassium they need to function. Lime makes soil less acidic.

Soil acidity is measured in numbers from 1 to 14 on what is called the pH scale. Most plants prefer soil that has a pH of 6.0 to 6.5. A hard, clay subsoil may have a pH of 4.5. It takes a lot of lime to move the pH up to 6.5. Your soil test will determine the pH of your soil and the amount of lime it needs.

Controlling Pests and Diseases

The same conditions that make our gardens so beautiful also make Georgia a happy homeland for insects and disease. A long growing season means that insect populations have time to explode each year. Our high humidity and warm temperatures are perfect for the growth of fungi and bacteria.

It cannot be said often enough that a healthy plant is the best defense against pests. A plant that grows vigorously can quickly overcome insect damage. A plant that is not stressed by its environment can resist disease spores. Many of the plants included in this book were chosen because of their strong resistance to insects and disease. If you follow the recommendations about the proper placement of your plants and how to care for them, your garden will rarely need pesticides. If you choose from the plant varieties recommended, you will also have genetic allies in your fight against pests and disease.

Organic vs. Inorganic Gardening

I am literally the product of an organic garden. My mother purchased a small farm in order to grow vegetables using chicken manure for fertilizer. She had read that "trace-mineralized vegetables" would help her combat her incipient diabetes and her constant feeling of lethargy. She met my father—the local chicken farmer—at a housewarming party. They raised five healthy children on a diet of home-grown vegetables, whole wheat flour, and all the well water we could drink.
　　—Walter

If you find pests attacking your plants, what should you do? Is the problem bad enough to use a pesticide? Which pesticide should you use? Should you rely on synthetic chemicals, or should you choose pesticides made from organic sources? These questions trouble all of us. Some gardeners prefer to use only organic pesticides. Others are more pragmatic, sometimes using synthetic pesticides, occasionally preferring organic ones, but always striving to use the smallest amounts possible in every case.

There is no single correct answer to the question: Which is best—organic or inorganic gardening? Synthetic pesticides for home gardeners have been repeatedly tested for safety by their manufacturers and by the federal government. Scientists, and those who advise us on environmental matters, have declared that the prudent use of approved pesticides offers fewer health risks than would be encountered if pesticides were avoided completely and our food supply, thus, endangered.

Organic gardening does not always completely eliminate pesticide use, as it sometimes calls for the use of pesticides that come from organic sources. These organic pesticides may have risks higher or lower than synthetic ones. Fortunately, new gardening products with fewer risks appear on the market every year.

The choice between an "organic" or an "inorganic" landscape is yours alone to make. You must decide whether the convenience of using synthetic pesticides offsets the hard work and constant vigilance required to completely eliminate their use.

The Name Game

Gardeners may wonder why they need to know the scientific names of plants. The answer is simple: You want to make sure the plant you purchase for your own garden has the same characteristics you admired (and coveted) in your neighbor's garden. It's true that scientific names, which are derived from Latin or Greek, can be long and hard to pronounce. But unlike a common plant name, which often is applied to two very different plants, a scientific designation is specific and unique.

When I moved to Georgia, I wondered what it was that people were fondly calling a "wild honeysuckle." Was it the weedy vine or the blooming bush with which I was familiar? It turned out to be neither! These native gardeners were referring to their native azaleas as "wild honeysuckle." When I design a landscape, I don't specify plants by their common names. What if I were to recommend "sweet box" and my client planted a boxwood instead of *Sarcococca hookeriana*?

—Erica

Throughout this book, plants are identified both by their scientific and common names. A plant's scientific name consists of the genus (the first word) followed by an epithet. For example, all maples belong to the genus *Acer*. The epithet (for example, *rubrum*) identifies a specific kind of maple. *Acer rubrum* is a red maple. The genus and epithet are always italicized, and the genus name begins with a capital letter, while the epithet is written in lowercase.

A third word in the name may refer to a special variety of the plant, called a cultivar. The cultivar name is important because it designates a superior selection known for bigger blooms, better foliage, or some other noteworthy characteristic. A cultivar name is distinguished by the use of single quotation marks, as in the name *Acer rubrum* 'October Glory'. Most cultivars must be propagated by division or cuttings, because they may not come true from seed.

A scientific name can change, but this happens only rarely, and there are certain rigid rules that apply to the practice of plant nomenclature. It is much easier to track down a wonderful plant if you know the full scientific name. Armed with knowledge of both scientific and common names, you will be able to acquire the best plants for your Georgia garden.

Cold-Hardiness Zones

In this book, for questions of hardiness, refer to the map and compare the information there to the label your plant comes with when you purchase it. Zones refer to the United States Department of Agriculture cold-hardiness zones (see the map on page 21). Years of collecting weather data have resulted in a map that divides the country into zones of minimum temperatures. These zones help gardeners identify those plants that will grow best in certain areas.

The minimum winter temperatures that plants can tolerate may not be the main concern of a gardener who wants to grow plants in Georgia's hot, humid summers. It is only recently that scientists have made vigorous efforts to evaluate the ability of plants to withstand summer heat. The plants recommended in this book are good performers in most parts of Georgia.

Just remember, there is a wide range of weather conditions throughout the state. A plant suited for the Piedmont region may languish in a coastal garden, and a plant that thrives in a coastal garden may not do well in the Piedmont. On the other hand, you might be able to create a spot in your landscape that replicates conditions in another part of the state. Plants don't know geography—they only know whether or not they are happy in the site you've chosen!

The location of a plant in your garden, the soil type, and the soil drainage are all factors that affect plant hardiness. As noted earlier, simply moving a plant to another location may result in improved growth and long-term survival. Try to give your plant what you think it needs—but don't hesitate to move it if it is suffering.

Learn by Doing

With these few tips, you now have an overview of the basic information needed to become a gardener. To obtain the truly valuable skills of gardening, you will have to practice the 4-H Club motto: Learn by Doing. So don your old jeans, take up your shovel, and dig!

If you keep your heart and mind open to the nuances of nature, you will cultivate more than just pretty flowers and strong trees. Both your plants and you yourself will grow in your beautiful garden. Fayetteville nurseryman Steven Stinchcomb may have said it best: *"Some people are just gardeners in their heads, and some people become gardeners in their hearts."*

Good gardening!

Japanese iris

How to Use *Georgia Getting Started Garden Guide*

Each entry in this guide provides you with information about a plant's particular characteristics, its habits, and its basic requirements for vigorous growth, as well as our own personal experience and knowledge of it. You will find such pertinent information as mature height and spread, bloom period and seasonal colors (if any), sun and soil preferences, planting tips, water requirements, fertilizing needs, pruning and care, and pest information. Each section is clearly marked for easy reference.

Sun Preferences

We realize that sunshine intensity differs across your landscape and garden. Compare the noon sunshine in Valdosta to the noon sunshine in the mountains of Blairsville—they're radically different! Some plants grow successfully in more than one range of sun, which will be indicated by more than one sun symbol. Note: Afternoon sun is stronger than morning sun, and a site with afternoon sun exposure is more apt to stress certain plants.

Full Sun Coast: unfiltered sunshine for 6 or more hours per day; Mountains: unfiltered sunshine from morning to night; Elsewhere: unfiltered sunshine for 8 or more hours.

 Part Sun Coast: all day sunshine filtered through tall pine or hardwood (e.g., oak, maple); Mountains: 5 hours of direct sunshine between sunrise and noon. Otherwise, direct sun for part of the day or partial sun (as under high pine trees) all day.

 Part Shade Coast: filtered sun as under a sweet gum, maple for one-half day. Mountains: 3 hours of direct sunshine between sunrise and noon. Otherwise, sun for one-half day.

 Full Shade Coast: all day shade under low, evergreen trees (e.g., live oak or magnolia); Mountains: occasional direct sunshine during the day or dappled shade under low, deciduous trees (e.g., dogwood, redbud, or crabapple); Elsewhere: a site that is in dappled shade (as under hardwoods) all day.

Additional Benefits

Many plants offer benefits that further enhance their appeal. The following symbols indicate some of the more notable additional benefits:

 Native–Native to Georgia and the Southeast

 Attracts Beneficial Insects–such as ladybeetles and butterflies

 Drought-tolerant–Typically does not need supplemental water after establishment

 Seasonal Color–from blooms, bark, or foliage

 Attracts Birds–Birds feed on seeds or berries or use leaves for nesting

Companion Planting and Design

In this section, we provide suggestions for companion plantings and different ways to showcase your plants.

Try These

This section describes those specific cultivars or varieties that we have found to be particularly noteworthy. Or, we sometimes suggest other species that are also good choices. Give them a try . . . many times we mention favorite plants we just couldn't bear to leave out of the book.

USDA Cold-Hardiness Zones

The United States Department of Agriculture (USDA) has developed a map of cold-hardiness zones across the United States.

It is based on minimum average temperatures experienced over several years. Each variation of 10°F represents a different zone, indicated by colored bands on a map. Because plants vary in their tolerance for cold, it is important to choose those that are suitable for your region of Georgia. Consult this map to learn the zone in which you live. Remember your zone when you buy plants at a nursery. Most of the plants in this book will perform well throughout the state. Though a plant may grow well in zones other than the recommended zone, it is best to select plants labeled for your part of Georgia, or warmer.

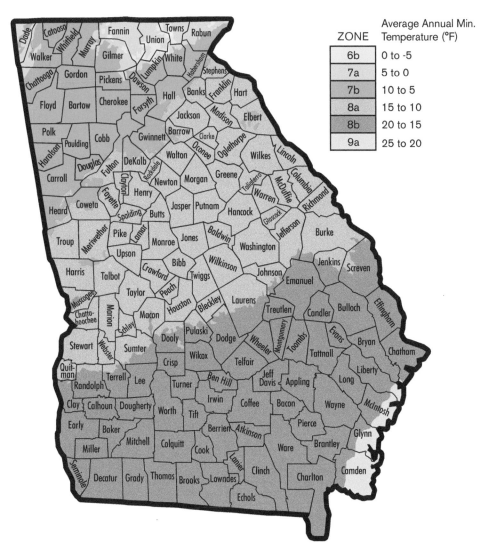

ZONE	Average Annual Min. Temperature (°F)
6b	0 to -5
7a	5 to 0
7b	10 to 5
8a	15 to 10
8b	20 to 15
9a	25 to 20

USDA Plant Hardiness Zone Map, 2012. Agricultural Research Service, U.S. Department of Agriculture. Accessed from http://planthardiness.ars.usda.gov.

ANNUALS
FOR GEORGIA

While perennials may provide the framework for the flower garden, annuals act as the weavers and binders, tying everything together and bridging the gap between seasons. Imagine a shade garden without colorful begonias or a sunny border without petunias. And what would summer be like without sunflowers, or winter without violas?

What Is an Annual?

An annual is defined as any plant that completes its natural life cycle—from germinated seed through growth, flower, and seed production to death—in a single growing season. For this reason, USDA winter-hardiness zones are not provided for annuals. In Georgia, gardeners have many annuals to choose from that will add a long season of color to the garden with a minimum amount of effort and cost. Some annuals bloom almost continuously from spring until frost. Other annuals reward us by reseeding freely, providing free plants for the following year.

Many annuals are easy to grow from seed. Depending on the individual type, they may be sown directly in the garden where they will grow to maturity or started indoors and then transplanted to the garden after they have been hardened off (slowly introduced to outside temperatures).

Zinnia 'Crystal Orange' and Lantana 'Lola'

Getting the Most from Your Annuals
Soil & Fertilizing

As with all types of plants, the secret to growing the most beautiful annuals is to start with good soil. Many of the annuals recommended in this book will tolerate less-than-ideal conditions, such as poor soil and drought. However, ornamental plants—with a few exceptions—produce better growth and more flowers if they are planted in a soil that is well drained and amended with organic matter.

Unlike perennials, annuals complete their entire life cycle in one growing season, and thus benefit from regular applications of fertilizer. Liquid fertilizer is fine. Applied once every month at the recommended rates (as directed on the label), fertilizer encourages vigorous plants and more blooms.

To prolong the flowering of many annuals, gardeners should know about deadheading. This is the practice of removing spent flowers before they have a chance to set seed. The plant will respond to deadheading with bushier growth and more blooms. Shearing back is when whole tops of plants are cut off with clippers, scissors, or even hedge trimmers. If your plants are looking puny, it's worth a try. Cut off the top third of the plant, just above the point where the woody part of the plant turns into flowering stems. This is also a good time to apply a dose of water-soluble fertilizer.

Another technique that prolongs the show that annuals provide is to stagger the sowing of seeds. For example, sowing sunflower seeds at two-week intervals will ensure that you have blooms from early summer until frost.

After a frost has killed the remaining annuals in the garden, it's time to clean up any leaf litter or debris. This will reduce the chances of overwintering pests or disease spores.

Container Growing

Here are a few things to remember when you grow annuals in containers:

- Mix in some slow-release fertilizer when you first plant in your container. (Refer to the fertilizer label for recommended amounts.) Fertilize once a month with a liquid fertilizer.
- Containers will need regular watering; depending on the particular plants, some may need watering twice a day.

Starting Seeds Indoors

One of the best ways to get a jump on the season is to start seeds indoors. This will allow you to have plants ready to transplant into the garden as soon as the frost-free date has come and gone. Always use clean pots. If using old pots, wash them with soap and water to prevent disease problems. Using sterile potting mixes and clean pots is the best way to avoid damping-off, a soil-borne fungus that can wipe out a flat of seedlings in no time.

Now, let's get started!

Annual Larkspur

Consolida ajacis

Botanical Pronunciation
Con-SOL-id-a ah-JAY-siss

Bloom Period and Seasonal Colors
Summer to frost, blooms in white, blue, lilac, pink, rose, salmon, carmine

Mature Height × Spread
1 to 5 ft. × 3 ft.

For gardeners who lust after the giant Pacific hybrid perennial delphiniums that flourish in cooler climates, annual larkspur offers a satisfying alternative for Georgia gardens. More delicate than its cousin, larkspur is easy to grow from seed sown in fall, and rewards us when it's happy by reseeding freely, year after year. Growing 1 to 5 feet tall, the blossoms come in white and blue or shades of blue, lilac, pink, rose, salmon, or carmine. The deeply cut, ferny foliage enhances the flowers and is never messy. Some strains have lots of vertical stems, while others send out many horizontal branches. Great for meadows, cut flowers, arrangements, and drying, larkspur looks at home in a cottage garden or a large, formal border.

When, Where, and How to Plant

Direct sow seeds in the fall or early spring in soil that has been tilled and raked. Cover lightly with pine straw or not at all, as they need light to germinate. For a big impact, plant larkspur in clusters or mix with poppy seed, which has the same requirements. Plant groups 6 to 8 inches apart. You will get the best results from soil that is light and fluffy. Prepare the soil in advance by hand digging or with a tiller. Mix one-third organic matter, one-third coarse sand, and one-third existing soil. Water using a sprinkler with a delicate spray. Once seeds germinate and seedlings are at least 3 inches high, apply a thin layer of mulch (1 inch) to help control weeds. Plant quart- or gallon-sized containers in spring. They resent transplanting, so be gentle with the roots.

Growing Tips

While larkspur is germinating, keep the soil lightly moist. Once it is growing, water weekly while it is in flower. When plants are 1 foot high, apply a liquid fertilizer, such as 20-20-20. This should be enough to get larkspur through the summer.

Regional Advice and Care

Larkspur is low maintenance. Except for watering, it is carefree. While larkspur does not suffer from any serious pest or disease problems, it should be noted that all parts of the plant—especially the seeds—are poisonous if eaten. Once larkspur finishes blooming, don't cut off the dead flowers. Leave the seed pods to turn brown and ripen, then collect them to use next year or leave them to reseed on their own.

Companion Planting and Design

Larkspur is perfect for wildflower gardens, meadows, or cottage gardens. Its spiky form looks great in combination with orange and red poppies or pink and white cosmos. In cottage gardens, larkspur contrasts nicely with old-fashioned roses. For the best impact, plant in large clusters.

Try These

Popular seed mixtures include the Dwarf Hyacinth series, Dwarf Rocket series, and Giant Imperial Series. Give some to your friends and they will be delighted with the results.

Begonia

Begonia hybrids, cvs., and spp.

Botanical Pronunciation
Bee-GOAN-ya

Bloom Period and Seasonal Colors
Flowers on some varieties and ornamental foliage with others, late spring until frost in pink, red, orange, white

Mature Height × Spread
6 in. to 2 ft. × 6 in. to 2½ ft.

Native to tropical climates, there are many different types of begonia. Wax begonias (*B.* × *semperflorens-cultorum*) have long been popular as bedding plants for the shade garden, for edging, in containers, and in window boxes. A profusion of flowers from spring until frost and the ability to thrive in the heat of Georgia summers make this annual popular with homeowners and commercial landscapers. Sun-resistant varieties include the 'Cocktail' hybrids and the dwarf types. The colorful flowers are especially showy against shiny bronze foliage. Wax begonias cannot survive frost, but they are easy to overwinter as houseplants. If you have limited space for growing plants indoors, take stem cuttings of your favorite types and root them in a small container. Some hybrids offer striking foliage that looks good for months.

When, Where, and How to Plant
Plant begonia bedding plants after the last frost date (around April 15) and after the soil has warmed. Plant in bright light or dappled shade for the best results, although they will grow in direct sun. A soil rich in organic matter is ideal, but wax begonias will grow in most soils provided the site is not soggy. Avoid planting directly under trees with lots of root competition. Plant normal bedding plants 8 to 12 inches apart and extra-dwarf types 4 to 6 inches apart. In containers, provide adequate drainage, as they resent being in constantly wet soil. Plant hybrids with colorful foliage in containers with other annuals or on their own.

Growing Tips
Add a shovelful of compost to the planting hole, making sure the soil is moist but well drained. Fertilize with liquid fertilizer once every two weeks for the best results. Water on a regular basis. Begonias do not like dry soil.

Regional Advice and Care
Allow seeds to dry on the plant before collecting them to store. Propagate by leaf cuttings, division of rhizomes or bulbs (depending on the type of begonia), or direct sow begonia seed after the frost-free date.

Companion Planting and Design
With their striking foliage, hybrid begonias like *Begonia* 'Escargot' with its spiral leaf pattern of pewter, chocolate, and green curling into the center like a snail provide a dramatic centerpiece in the shade. Combine begonias with caladiums, ferns, and other begonias for a long season of color. There are also dark leaf and colorful variegated selections of Rex begonias like 'China Curl' with leaves that have spirals of silver and chocolate brown.

Try These
Begonia 'Bonita Shea' is a compact selection with clusters of small flowers (white to pink) and reddish green leaves (with red undersides). It will grow in full sun or part shade. For drama *Begonia boliviensis* 'Bonfire' offers 2-inch-long orange-red flowers and handsome angel-wing-type foliage, forming 2-foot-wide clumps that bloom for months.

California Poppy

Eschscholzia californica

Botanical Pronunciation
es-SHOLT-zee-uh kal-ih-FOR-nik-uh

Bloom Period and Seasonal Colors
Spring to summer flowers and ferny foliage

Mature Height × Spread
18 in. × 9 in.

Native to California and the Southwest, California poppies in the southern U.S. offer bright cup-shaped flowers, single, semi-double and double forms, in shades of yellow, orange, white, and pink. A drought-tolerant species, the flowers glow in the landscape from mid-spring to early summer. The bluish green ferny foliage is a bonus, and after it finishes flowering, this tidy annual disappears in the landscape. When it is happy, it will reseed and appear next year. It looks great in the wildflower garden or flower border with early bulbs and gray-foliaged perennials or biennials like cardoon. It is a good option for coastal gardens with sandy soils. The flowers have a spicy scent. Glorious in the day, they close up at night or on cloudy days.

When, Where, and How to Plant
Sow seeds in fall or very early spring. The ideal time to sow seeds is when the soil temperatures are 60°F to 70°F. Prepare the soil by adding a ½-inch layer of organic matter and a layer of coarse sand, then tilling or digging it in to a depth of 6 to 8 inches. Cover the seeds thinly with ¹⁄₁₆ of an inch of soil. Water lightly on a daily basis until seeds germinate and then only once a week. Don't let soil get soggy. Plant in a site that receives full sun and is well drained. Once established, California poppies can tolerate a fair bit of drought.

Growing Tips
For the best results, sow seeds directly where you want them to grow because the seedlings are difficult to transplant. If you sow them in pots, use peat pots so that you can transplant the peat pots directly and not disturb the developing roots of the poppies. Rake out the soil before you sow the seeds but don't apply fertilizer. As long as the soil is well drained and has a small percentage of organic matter, your poppies will be happy. Cover very lightly with straw or pine straw. Use a water breaker attachment when you water so that you have a delicate spray and don't wash the seeds away.

Regional Advice and Care
Once seeds germinate you can thin them out and encourage the strongest seedlings. After they flower, let them set seed and watch the seedpods ripen on the plant stems. You can then collect the pods when they are brown and dry and store them in a cool dry place. Sow seed in fall or early next spring in an area where you would like them to grow.

Companion Planting and Design
California poppies add welcome color to the garden in spring and early summer. Combine them with bulbs, cardoon, and ornamental grasses like muhly grass, pennisetum, *Miscanthus* selections, and the pineapple plant, *Eucomis*.

Try These
Look for 'Red Chief' or 'Rose Chiffon'.

Coleus

Solenostemon scutellarioides

Botanical Pronunciation
sol-en-oh-STEM-on skew-tell-ar-ee-OH-ih-deez

Bloom Period and Seasonal Colors
Foliage in all colors and combinations; attractive from summer until frost

Mature Height × Spread
9 in. to 3 ft. × 1 to 3 ft.

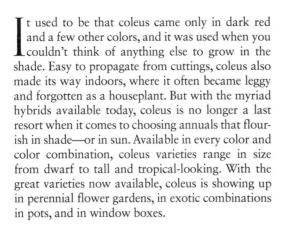

It used to be that coleus came only in dark red and a few other colors, and it was used when you couldn't think of anything else to grow in the shade. Easy to propagate from cuttings, coleus also made its way indoors, where it often became leggy and forgotten as a houseplant. But with the myriad hybrids available today, coleus is no longer a last resort when it comes to choosing annuals that flourish in shade—or in sun. Available in every color and color combination, coleus varieties range in size from dwarf to tall and tropical-looking. With the great varieties now available, coleus is showing up in perennial flower gardens, in exotic combinations in pots, and in window boxes.

When, Where, and How to Plant

Plant coleus after the fear of frost has passed. Bedding plants can be installed beginning in spring and well into summer. Coleus prefers a moist, well-drained soil. If the coleus is growing in a pot, be sure to use a soil mix that is moisture retentive and well drained. Site particular varieties according to their needs (e.g., shade, sun, trailing, tall, or dwarf). Coleus can be propagated from stem cuttings and overwintered indoors or in a greenhouse.

Growing Tips

If you grow coleus in containers, add a slow-release fertilizer to the planting mix or apply a liquid fertilizer, such as 20-20-20, once a month. Apply liquid fertilizer once a month to bedding plants as well. Water container-grown plants when soil is dry to the touch, and water those planted in the ground once a week.

Regional Advice and Care

Coleus is a fast grower. Many varieties send out lots of branches, making them appear almost like miniature shrubs. Pinch plants and flower buds back regularly—monthly or more often—to keep plants full and bushy. Coleus may be attacked by mealybugs, which look like tiny white cotton balls, usually at the node where the leaf and stem meet. Blast them off with a stream of water from the hose or use insecticidal soap.

Companion Planting and Design

There is a coleus for almost every type of garden, whether you have a large sunny flower garden, a woodland area, or space only for containers. There are even trailing varieties that grow beautifully in hanging baskets. Chartreuse types complement annuals, such as the magenta *Petunia integrifolia* and the black sweet potato vine, *Ipomoea* 'Blackie'. They also look good with ornamental grasses. Striped and mottled coleus blends nicely with evergreen ferns. In a shade garden, coleus adds easy-care seasonal color when planted with perennials, such as autumn fern.

Try These

For a bright chartreuse coleus with serrated leaves try 'Wasabi'. It holds its color in part sun and is heat tolerant too. For shade, 'Kong Scarlet' grows 18 to 20 inches tall and has dark red and green leaves.

Common Sunflower

Helianthus annuus

Botanical Pronunciation
hee-lee-AN-thus AN-yoo-us

Bloom Period and Seasonal Colors
Flowers from summer until frost

Mature Height × Spread
2 to 14 ft. × 2 to 3 ft.

Gardeners and artists alike have long been inspired by sunflowers. Historically, they were grown not for their ornamental flowers, but rather for edible seed and seed oil. Yet there's nothing quite as magical as a field of sunflowers with their cheerful yellow faces that follow the sun. Upon close examination, each face is unique and charming. Many hybrids are available today in a range of sizes. 'Sunspot Dwarf' is perfect for containers with its single, golden, 10-inch flowers on 2-foot stems. 'Kong', a giant, grows to 14 feet tall with 6- to 8-inch yellow blooms. All varieties make great cut flowers, and some produce seed that is particularly appealing to birds. Sunflowers will bring beauty to your garden and a smile to your face.

When, Where, and How to Plant
Sunflowers are easy to grow, and by staggering plantings, you can have blooms throughout the summer. Once the threat of frost is past and soil temperatures have warmed, sow sunflower seeds directly where you want them to grow and prick out the weakest seedlings after sprouting. These sun worshipers will turn their faces toward the sun when young. If you start them indoors, sow seeds in peat pots to avoid disturbing the roots when you transplant them. Sunflowers tolerate drought and heat, but sitting them in moist, well-drained soil amended with some organic matter ensures the best flower production. Certain varieties need lots of room, so plant accordingly. If you have a problem with rabbits or other creatures looking for tasty young seedlings, plant extra seeds so that you won't be disappointed.

Growing Tips
When sunflowers are grown commercially, farmers till the soil, then water and fertilize regularly. Even if you're growing only a few sunflowers, you will get bigger and better blooms if you do the same. Water once a week and fertilize once a month with a water-soluble fertilizer.

Regional Advice and Care
Once sunflowers finish blooming, don't be too quick to cut down the withering stalks. If the birds don't eat them first, spent flower heads left to dry on the plant produce masses of seed, which can be used for decorations or stored for next year's crop. Sunflowers do not suffer from any serious insect pests or disease problems. Deer and rabbits, though, find the plants very tasty.

Companion Planting and Design
Use large types to create a screen, as a bold accent in the flower or vegetable garden, or as a background. Smaller sunflowers make great cut flowers and add splashes of yellow, orange, red, rust, or white to the garden.

Try These
For a dramatic effect, 'Kong' reaches 12 feet tall and has yellow blooms that are 4 to 6 inches across. 'Buttercream' makes a great cut flower, with coloring described as French vanilla. Its blooms are 4 to 6 inches across on 4½- to 5-foot-tall plants.

Cosmos

Cosmos spp. and cvs.

Botanical Pronunciation
KOS-mus

Other Name Mexican aster

Bloom Period and Seasonal Colors
Flowers in late summer to fall

Mature Height × Spread
2½ ft. to 8 ft. × 3 ft.

For drought-resistant beauty, cosmos is hard to beat. This adaptable annual blooms for weeks, and once established, requires very little moisture. In fact, if the soil is too rich, plants may become tall and lanky. Deeply divided, feathery foliage adds to the overall fine texture of cosmos. Thriving in full sun, the bold flowers seem to dance in the breeze. Cosmos produces masses of 2- to 3-inch-wide flowers. Depending on the variety, blooms may be yellow, white, pink, rose, lavender, or crimson. The heights vary from 2½ feet to 8 feet tall. For bright summer and fall blooms, or for cut flowers, cosmos is a winner. This champ of a plant attracts butterflies and hummingbirds too.

When, Where, and How to Plant
For the earliest blooms, sow seeds indoors two to three weeks before the last frost date (around April 15). Sow them into individual peat pots, and then transplant the pots directly into the garden soil. Plant cosmos seeds outdoors in spring after the fear of frost has passed and the soil has warmed. To extend the bloom season, sow a second batch of seeds two weeks after you sow the first. Cosmos needs full sun and seems to thrive with neglect. An average, well-drained garden soil is best. If you plant in a meadow, prepare the soil first by tilling or—at a minimum—removing any weeds. Lightly cover seeds with ¹⁄₁₆ inch of soil. You can sow a few seeds in the same spot, and then thin out the weaker seedlings as they start to grow.

Growing Tips
Fertilize young seedlings with a diluted solution (three-fourths the strength of the recommended rate for annuals) of water-soluble plant fertilizer. Water young plants until they are about 8 inches high. Once established, cosmos will thrive even during periods of drought.

Regional Advice and Care
Remove spent flowers to encourage a longer bloom time. If the soil is too rich, plants may become tall and lanky and require staking. Cosmos is sometimes attacked by spider mites that can leave the leaves looking bleached and speckled. Control the mites with an insecticidal soap or spray with a horticultural oil.

Companion Planting and Design
Plant cosmos wherever you want brilliant color. Use them for masses of color in the formal garden, as a cut flower, or in the cottage garden with other annuals and perennials. Light and airy, they are beautiful in combination with gray- and silver-foliaged plants, such as lamb's ear and *Artemisia,* or with spiky flowers, such as *Liatris* or *Iris.*

Try These
The selection 'Sea Shells' has fluted petals in shades of white, pink, rose, and carmine. The 'Bright Lights' selection offers semidouble flowers in vibrant shades of orange and yellow.

Diamond Frost™ Euphorbia

Euphorbia hypericifolia 'Inneuphdia'

Botanical Pronunciation
yoo-FOR-bee-uh hy-PER-ee-see-FOH-lee-uh

Bloom Period and Seasonal Colors
White flowers summer to frost, apple green foliage

Mature Height × Spread
12 to 18 in. × 2 ft.

This annual occupies many top ten lists of go-to plants for its performance in southern gardens. A "good doer," Diamond Frost™ thrives despite heat and humidity. It reminds one of baby's breath but is much more satisfying to grow. In the garden it looks delicate: mounds of airy white flowers and thin apple-green foliage—but this is one tough beauty. Once established, it requires only a minimum of water and no deadheading of faded blooms—it will pump out flowers until frost. Perfect for filling in gaps in the flower garden, it provides a soothing effect and looks good with other white flowers. It's also an excellent filler plant in hanging baskets. Good news for north Georgia gardeners: Diamond Frost™ is almost completely deer-proof.

When, Where, and How to Plant

Plant Diamond Frost™ in the flower garden after the frost free date (April 15). Give it room to spread; 12-inch spacing should be fine. A location with a well-drained soil that receives full sun is ideal, but it will also grow and flower in part shade. Plant it with perennials and other annuals or use it to make a transition from one group of colors to another. If you plant it in decorative pots or hanging baskets, make sure the containers have drainage holes.

Growing Tips

Once plants are established, they should require very little supplemental watering. Adding compost to the soil before you plant or using liquid fertilizer every month will help ensure you get the most out of your plants both in the garden and in containers. If they do dry out, give them a light trim plus a watering, and in no time they should be lush and full. In containers, make sure to give them room to spread.

Regional Advice and Care

Because they are self-cleaning, you don't have to worry about deadheading or pruning. In one Atlanta garden, during a particularly hot, dry summer, Diamond Frost™ thrived and bloomed until well past Thanksgiving. If you decide to overwinter plants indoors in a sunny window, cut them back by one-third in late summer, dig up the plant, and pot it up in a container. This annual is also moderately salt tolerant and it is reported to be able to withstand salt spray if it is 30 or more feet away from the source. If you have a skin reaction to the milky sap of poinsettias (also a euphorbia), wear gloves when handling this plant.

Companion Planting and Design

Combine Diamond Frost™ with other white flowers like *Phlox paniculata* 'David' and gray foliage like that of lamb's ears, *Stachys* 'Helen Von Stein'. Use it as a groundcover with roses and other shrubs.

Try These

Euphorbias are great drought-tolerant plants. Perennial types include *Euphorbia characias* 'Tasmanian Tiger', 'Glacier Blue', and *E.* 'Blackbird' with dark red-purple leaves on stiff 24-inch stems.

Fan Flower

Scaevola cvs.

Botanical Pronunciation
Skave-O-la

Bloom Period and Seasonal Colors
Summer until frost blooms in purple, blue, white
or mauve

Mature Height × Spread
8 to 12 in. × 36 in.

When it blooms, fan flower looks like a low mound covered with a profusion of tiny, purple-blue fans marked with yellow. Some say the flowers look more purple in color, but many describe them as blue. For long-season bloom (from late spring until frost) and easy care, this Australian transplant is one of the top ten annuals for Georgia gardens. In the most southern parts of the state it may be perennial. In fact, the hotter it gets, the more fan flower seems to thrive. *Scaevola* offers unusual flowers that bloom over a long period of time. Its diminutive blooms make it adaptable to many types of gardens and containers. With its sprawling habit, it is also suited to the rock garden.

When, Where, and How to Plant
Plant bedding plants in spring after the fear of frost has passed and the soil has warmed (late April or early May). Fan flower needs full sun or part-shade in a well-drained soil, whether in the ground or in a decorative container. Good drainage is essential. If needed, add coarse sand (about one-third of the overall mix) to the soil. When you plant, dig a hole as large as the container that the plant is growing in. Drench the soil after planting. Overwinter plants in a cold frame, greenhouse, or sunny window.

Growing Tips
Fertilize fan flower with a liquid fertilizer once a month. Water bedding plants once a week until established; that is, when they are blooming

and putting out new growth. Water established plants during periods of drought (no rain for two weeks or longer). Container-grown plants should be watered when the top ½ inch of soil is dry to the touch. Mulch plants—both in the garden and in containers—to keep the soil from baking in full sun.

Regional Advice and Care
Although you don't need to deadhead, if plants get leggy, cut them back to encourage a flush of vigorous new growth. If you purchase plants in full bloom, cut them back by half to encourage bushier plants. Prune them back in midsummer if they get too leggy. Fan flower suffers from no serious pest or disease problems.

Companion Planting and Design
Plant fan flower in containers with other annuals and perennials, in window boxes, in hanging baskets, or as a seasonal groundcover in the flower border. Let it weave itself between other annuals and perennials. It will also trail over a wall. For a striking combination, plant fan flower with the magenta-flowered *Petunia integrifolia*. Lamb's ear, lotus vine, variegated vinca, and small petunias all make good companions. Fan flower also looks good with yellow sunflowers or lantana.

Try These
'Whirlwind Blue' or 'Whirlwind White', both prolific bloomers, are heat and drought tolerant.

Globe Amaranth

Gomphrena globosa

Botanical Pronunciation
Gom-FREE-na glo-BOH-suh

Other Name Gomphrena

Bloom Period and Seasonal Colors
Summer until frost in red, pink, purple, lilac, and white

Mature Height × Spread
1 to 2 ft. × ½ to 1 ft.

An old-fashioned favorite, globe amaranth blooms all summer in Georgia gardens. In autumn, when many annuals look tired and worn out, it blooms and blooms some more, until the plants are finally killed by a hard frost. The flowers (red, pink, purple, lilac, and white) hold their color well, not only in the garden, but also in fresh and dried flower arrangements. All this dependable annual requires is lots of sun and well-drained soil. It doesn't seem bothered by wind or rain. Whether you use it as edging, in groups throughout the garden, or for cut flowers, globe amaranth adds interesting texture. The increase in the variety of colors and sizes available has made this tough annual well suited for all styles of gardens.

When, Where, and How to Plant
Plant young bedding plants after the last frost (around April 15). Globe amaranth likes hot sun and moist, well-drained soils. Seeds can be sown in clumps where you want them in the garden and thinned out as they develop; however, they are slow to develop, so this may not be practical. Amending the soil is not necessary unless it is heavy clay. For clay soils, till in some organic matter to improve the drainage and overall health of the soil. Mix together one-third organic matter, one-third coarse sand, and one-third of the existing soil. Planted closely in a pot, globe amaranth makes a beautiful living bouquet.

Growing Tips
Globe amaranth requires no special care or fertilizer, but it will respond to monthly fertilizer applications of liquid 20-20-20 during summer. Water once a week until plants are established (with healthy foliage and lots of buds), and thereafter, once a month. Globe amaranth tolerates a good bit of drought, but container-grown plants will benefit from watering when the soil's surface is dry to the touch.

Regional Advice and Care
If you want to dry flowers, harvest them just after they are fully open. Hang them upside down to dry in a dry cool place and they will hold their color for years. Globe amaranth does not suffer from any serious pest or disease problems, but mildew can attack drought-stressed plants. Taller varieties benefit from staking or being cut back one-fourth to one-third of their height in midsummer.

Companion Planting and Design
Plant globe amaranth in the flower garden for a long season of color. Use shorter varieties for edging or in containers. Larger types make beautiful cut flowers. The dark fuchsia-colored selection looks wonderful in combination with purple-foliaged plants, such as *Alternanthera* 'Wave Hill'. It also makes a good companion for heat-lovers, such as lantana and scaevola and for perennials, such as *Verbena* 'Homestead Purple'.

Try These
The Woodcreek series offers colors in shades of purple, silver, white, and pink; the plants grow 2 to 2½ feet tall.

Joseph's Coat

Alternanthera ficoidea

Botanical Pronunciation
al-ter-nan-THER-uh fy-KOY-dee-uh

Other Name Calico plant

Bloom Period and Seasonal Colors
Colorful foliage (red, green, white, pink, burgundy—depends on cultivar) summer until frost

Mature Height × Spread
6 to 15 in. × 1½ ft.

When it comes to gardening in shade, finding plants that provide color can be a challenge. Often foliage and not flowers must prevail. Joseph's coat is a shade star, with brilliant foliage that brightens the woodland or shady corner for months. If you grow it in sun, protect it from the hottest part of the day. Plant it as an alternative to impatiens or combine it with hardy ferns, caladiums, and begonias. Popular in Victorian times, modern selections display colorful green leaves that are blotched, mottled, and variegated with a multitude of colors (red, orange, white, copper, yellow). Joseph's coat is also great for containers in the shade. Combine it with tender ferns like 'Rita's Gold' or as an accent with a conifer.

When, Where, and How to Plant

If you want to grow this annual from seed, start them indoors in mid-March. Wait until the frost-free date has passed (around April 15) to transplant seedlings to the flower garden or into containers with other annuals and perennials. Prepare the soil before planting by adding a 1-inch layer of organic matter and mixing it in to a depth of 6 to 12 inches. After you plant, water and mulch plants to help control weeds. Plant in a moist well-drained soil in part shade for the most colorful foliage. For quick coverage, site plants on 4 inch centers.

Growing Tips

Apply liquid fertilizer every two weeks to plants in the ground and in containers. Water plants in the landscape once a week during the hot summer months (unless there is rain). For containers, water daily, or more often during extreme heat. To determine if containers need water, the top ½ inch of the soil should be dry to the touch. Saturate plants completely so that water rushes out of holes in the bottom or sides of the container they are growing in.

Regional Advice and Care

If plants get leggy, pinch or cut them back, and they should recover quickly. Overwinter it as a houseplant, making sure it gets plenty of bright light, and you'll have a jump on next spring.

Companion Planting and Design

Combine Joseph's coat with caladiums, begonias, autumn fern, or hellebores. In containers they look good on their own or with ferns like 'Rita's Gold' and its chartreuse foliage. This annual has an upright habit and is easy to maintain in a clipped formal hedge or as a mass. Use it as a low border in flower beds, in containers, or window boxes.

Try These

Try the selection 'Grenadine' with its hot pink foliage and burgundy veins; 'Partytime', which has green-and-pink foliage; and 'Cognac', with bronze leaves.

Mini Petunia

Calibrachoa cvs.

Botanical Pronunciation
Kal-a-bra-KO-a

Other Name Million Bells™

Bloom Period and Seasonal Colors
Flowers summer to frost in a wide range of colors

Mature Height × Spread
6 to 10 in. × indefinite

For Southern gardeners that love petunias but have been frustrated by those that melt in the heat and humidity, *Calibrachoa* is the perfect solution. Once established they will tolerate brief periods of drought, and hummingbirds are drawn to the blooms. The flowers look like miniature petunias and come in a range of brilliant colors. These workhorses pump out blooms all summer until frost and don't need deadheading. The leaves also aren't sticky like some of the old-fashioned petunias. Vigorous, disease resistant, and beautiful, all in one plant! Whether you grow them in hanging baskets, in containers with succulents and other drought-tolerant plants, or in the flower border with other annuals and perennials, *Calibrachoa* offers a big bang for your bucks!

When, Where, and How to Plant

Plant *Calibrachoa* in the spring after the frost-free date. Select a site that receives full sun and make sure the soil drains well. Plant it in the ground, in containers, window boxes, or hanging baskets. Add a shovelful of compost and some coarse sand to the planting mix or to the soil in the garden. This will help ensure that the roots don't get waterlogged.

Growing Tips

Water every other day for a week to help plants get established in the garden. After the first week, water only during periods of drought and then only when the first ½ inch of the soil feels dry to the touch. Too much water will make the roots rot. Fertilize with a liquid fertilizer once a month.

Regional Advice and Care

Apply a ½-inch layer of mulch to your plantings after you plant. This will help reduce weed infestations and keep the soil from getting too hot during summer. If you plant in containers, mix in some slow-release granular fertilizer when you plant. If plants get leggy, prune or pinch them back.

Companion Planting and Design

For a striking combination, plant *Calibrachoa* with large succulents such as agave. The contrast of the bold foliage and the delicate leaves makes for a great container planting. *Calibrachoa* also makes a great hanging basket or container plant. Use it to add seasonal color in the flower garden. For a big splash of color that will last until a hard frost, plant several different selections of different colors in the same area. Combine *Calibrachoa* in hanging baskets with trailing dark green ivy or other vines.

Try These

There are numerous selections to choose from in the new Superbell series from Proven Winners. Coralberry Punch™ is a beauty. The deep peach-colored flowers are marked with a dark burgundy center. There are also Superbells Red™, Superbells, Lavender, Blackberry Punch, Yellow, and Plum.

Moss Rose

Portulaca grandiflora

Botanical Pronunciation
Porch-yew-LA-ka gran-da-FLOR-a

Other Name Portulaca

Bloom Period and Seasonal Colors
Blooms summer to frost in rose, red, yellow, white, and striped (flowers open during the day and close at night)

Mature Height × Spread
6 to 8 in. × 24 in.

Moss rose offers Georgia gardeners colorful blooms for hot, dry spots where few other flowers survive. Native to Brazil, this succulent grows happily along the Georgia coast and throughout the state—as long as it gets lots of sun and heat. Left undisturbed in the garden, it will reseed freely, offering an ongoing source of plants in many colors, including those with single or double flowers. With its fleshy, needlelike leaves, *Portulaca* resembles moss plants clumped together. Finding annuals that hold up in Georgia summers without constant watering is a challenge—moss rose answers that challenge beautifully. It is a reliable choice for bright summer color that survives even in the cracks of sidewalks or along driveway edges. It is also great for hanging baskets, and the double-flowered selections look like tiny roses.

When, Where, and How to Plant

Sow seeds indoors six to eight weeks before the last frost date. Once seeds have germinated, thin out the seedlings and transplant them to small pots. Harden them off before planting in the garden once the fear of frost is passed and the soil has warmed. Seeds may also be sown directly in the garden once the soil temperature has warmed in early spring. Bedding plants should also be installed after the soil has warmed. Moss rose likes hot, dry, sunny spots. Plant it in a well-drained soil that is not too rich in organic matter; sandy soils are fine too.

Growing Tips

Moss rose is a low-maintenance annual. It is fairly drought resistant. If there is no rain, water once every two weeks.

Regional Advice and Care

These carefree plants will continue to produce blooms all summer long without deadheading. They do not suffer from any serious pest or disease problems. If plants are left undisturbed in the garden, they will reseed freely, offering interesting combinations of flower colors each year. If plants get scraggly, cut them back (by half) in midsummer and they should fill out nicely.

Companion Planting and Design

Plant *Portulaca* in rock gardens, flower garden beds, containers, or window boxes. Because it is low and spreading, let it trail over a wall or use it as an edging plant creeping along a stone walkway. Plant this creeper as a filler next to perennials that only bloom for a short time. Fairly drought tolerant, moss rose is a good companion for other succulents, such as sedum, hardy cactus, or ornamental grasses. It makes a good groundcover on a sunny bank, with bright flowers from early summer until frost.

Try These

There are many cultivars available, in both single- and double-flowering forms, and in every color from the brightest magenta to the softest melon. The Yubi™ series offers flowers in a wide range of colors.

Narrowleaf Zinnia

Zinnia angustifolia

Botanical Pronunciation
ZIN-e-ah an-GUS-ta-folia

Bloom Period and Seasonal Colors
Summer until frost, white, orange, pink, red, yellow, single and double flowers

Mature Height × Spread
6 to 12 in. × 18 to 24 in.

This small vigorous zinnia is an upright, compact annual or tender perennial native to parts of the United States and Mexico. Unlike its cousin, *Zinnia elegans,* grown for cut flowers, this plant is disease resistant and easy to grow. It's drought tolerant and happy in both humid and arid climates. The brilliant flowers, cup-shaped and 2 to 4 inches in diameter, cover the plant and bloom for months. This zinnia thrives despite the heat and humidity of Georgia summers. With its mounding and spreading habit, it makes a colorful mass in the flower border, in containers, or hanging baskets. And, you don't have to deadhead this beauty. Selections come in single and double forms, in white, yellow, orange, red, and pink blooms.

When, Where, and How to Plant
Start seeds indoors in late April or early May. These plants resent having their roots disturbed, so sow seeds directly into peat pots. If you sow them in the garden, wait until the frost-free date has passed. Plant transplants or bedding plants in the garden once the soil has warmed (usually in early May). Space them on 1-foot centers as they can spread up to 2 feet across. This zinnia does best if planted in a moist, well-drained soil that has been amended with organic matter. It also needs full sun and warm temperatures. Dig a hole at least 2 inches larger than the pot it is growing in. For mass plantings, rototill a large area so that the soil is easy to plant in.

Growing Tips
Zinnia loves long, hot days and will tolerate some drought. Water plants once a week in the garden and once daily if they are planted in containers. It is true that the better the soil is, the better the blooms will be. Apply a liquid fertilizer every two weeks during the growing season to keep plants vigorous.

Regional Advice and Care
If the plants get too large for an area, cut them back and they will quickly become bushy again. This should be done in early summer. This long-season bloomer does not need deadheading and does not suffer from any serious pest or disease problems. During hot, dry weather, it may be attacked by spider mites. Control these with insecticidal soap or horticultural oil. A daily blast from a hose will often wash most mites away from the leaves.

Companion Planting and Design
Plant zinnias in the front of borders, in window-boxes, in containers, or in combination with other sun-loving annuals and perennials. For a striking contrast, plant with 'Homestead Purple' verbena, or grow the orange and white forms together. Combine it with purple salvia, petunias, and ornamental grasses.

Try These
Look for the Profusion series or the Zahara series, with both single and double flowered selections.

New Guinea Impatiens

Impatiens hawkeri

Botanical Pronunciation
im-PAY-shuns HAWK-er-eye

Bloom Period and Seasonal Colors
Summer to frost blooms in all colors

Mature Height × Spread
1 ½ to 4 ft. × 1 ½ to 3 ft.

ommon garden *Impatiens walleriana* (busy lizzies) have been a staple of the Southern shade garden for generations, but in recent years downy mildew disease has been a major problem, wiping out impatiens in gardens across the United States. This is a good reason to diversify what you plant in your garden; avoid using the same plant in the same place year after year. If you love impatiens, look for New Guinea impatiens as an alternative; they seem to be less susceptible to this disease problem. The plants tend to be bushy; leaves may be green, bronze, or purple with darker pink or yellow midribs. They will also bloom in sun or shade, and the flowers, single or double, come in a wide range of colors, including orange, red, pink, crimson, lavender, and white.

When, Where, and How to Plant
Install bedding plants once the fear of frost has passed (around April 15). Depending on the variety's needs, site in sun or shade. The secret is to start with a moist, well-drained soil that has been amended with organic matter. This can make the difference between small plants and large robust plants. Work the soil to a depth of 6 inches, using a mixture of one-third coarse sand, one-third organic matter, and one-third existing soil. Space dwarf types 6 inches apart and large varieties 1 foot apart.

Growing Tips
If you have selected a moist, well-drained soil, watered weekly, and fertilized with a liquid fertilizer once a month, you will have small bushes of blooms! Just don't let the soil get too dry or wet in summer.

Regional Advice and Care
If plants get leggy, pinch or cut them back to as low as 6 inches to encourage a bushier, healthier plant. If you touch the ripe seedpods, they will explode and spread seeds. If you don't want volunteers, cut off the seedpods before they ripen. Impatiens may be attacked by slugs. To control them, use a commercial slug bait. Traps, such as the empty half of a grapefruit rind placed upside down, are also effective. Simply dispose of the rind and the slugs it attracts early the next morning. Sadly, Balsam impatiens, *Impatiens balsamina,* and the poison ivy foe jewelweed, *I. capensis,* are also susceptible to impatiens downy mildew.

Companion Planting and Design
New Guinea impatiens is ideal for the semishade garden, at the edge of a woodland where the soil is rich in organic matter and isn't too dry, or in pots that can be moved to wherever a spot of color is needed. Impatiens makes a good companion for ferns and hostas on the sunny edge of a woodland or in pockets of a semishade garden.

Try These
For vigor and large flat flowers, look for the Paradise series, including 'Paradise True Red', with dark green leaves and rich red flowers.

Pansy

Viola × wittrockiana

Botanical Pronunciation
Vi-O-la wit-rock-e-A-na

Other Name Viola

Bloom Period and Seasonal Colors
Fall to spring blooms in white, lilac, mahogany, blue, rose, yellow, apricot, purple, bicolors

Mature Height × Spread
4 to 8 in. × 9 to 12 in.

In Georgia, particularly in the middle and northern parts of the state, pansies are popular for the flower garden and for containers. Planted in the fall, they bloom for months during the winter, their colorful faces providing cheer on all but the coldest of days. Even when plants look shriveled and wilted from extreme cold, with just a bit of warmth and sunshine, they are quick to recover and continue blooming well into spring. In early spring, they become an elegant carpet for early bulbs, such as tulips. Pansies come in a wide range of colors and sizes. *Viola tricolor* (Johnny-jump-up) often reseeds itself. It delights us by showing up where we least expect it, blooming happily in lawns, beds, and borders.

When, Where, and How to Plant

Plant pansy plants in fall for color through winter and into spring. While they may be available at nurseries in September, early planting leads to stretched-out stems. Early October is a good time to plant because they will have time to establish a strong root system before winter. Pansies like full sun or part shade. They respond well to a cool, moist, moderately fertile soil that is well drained. The larger types will spread and should be planted on 5-inch centers. To encourage vigorous plants, pinch off the flower buds when you first plant them. Summer heat will greatly reduce flowering.

Growing Tips

Fertilize pansies with a liquid fertilizer, such as 20-20-20, once a month during the growing season. For containers, mix in some slow-release granular fertilizer at the time of planting. Water plants once a week if they are planted in the ground and once daily if they are growing in containers.

Regional Advice and Care

If plants get leggy or suffer from stem rot, leaf spots, or anthracnose, just cut them back and they will put out new growth. Deadheading the spent blossoms will encourage more blooms. On occasion, plants may be attacked by downy mildew. To control this problem, avoid overhead watering and water early in the day so that foliage dries out quickly. Once summer heat arrives, it is time to pull out the pansies and replace them with summer-blooming annuals.

Companion Planting and Design

Plant pansies in containers, in window boxes, or in a flower border; or use them as bedding plants. They also provide a lovely carpet for early daffodils. For a different effect, combine them with brightly colored dianthus and edibles such as red mustard greens, lettuce, ornamental cabbage, kale, and parsley.

Try These

The Crystal Bowl series offers flowers that are 2 inches across on 8-inch-tall plants; they are clear-faced, early flowering, heavy bloomers. 'Imperial Antique Shades' and the Sorbet series are also good performers. The Cool Wave™ series spreads up to 30 inches wide. Johnny-jump-ups, *Viola tricolor,* is an old-fashioned favorite that often reseeds freely.

Petunia

Petunia × hybrida

Botanical Pronunciation
Pa-TUNE-ya HI-brid-a

Bloom Period and Seasonal Colors
Summer to frost, blooms in many colors, ranging
from white to deep purple

Mature Height × Spread
8 to 24 in. × 8 to 24 in.

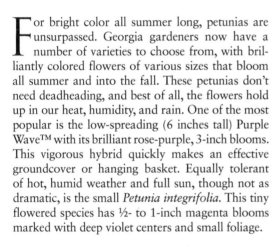

For bright color all summer long, petunias are unsurpassed. Georgia gardeners now have a number of varieties to choose from, with brilliantly colored flowers of various sizes that bloom all summer and into the fall. These petunias don't need deadheading, and best of all, the flowers hold up in our heat, humidity, and rain. One of the most popular is the low-spreading (6 inches tall) Purple Wave™ with its brilliant rose-purple, 3-inch blooms. This vigorous hybrid quickly makes an effective groundcover or hanging basket. Equally tolerant of hot, humid weather and full sun, though not as dramatic, is the small *Petunia integrifolia*. This tiny flowered species has ½- to 1-inch magenta blooms marked with deep violet centers and small foliage.

When, Where, and How to Plant

Start seeds indoors five to six weeks before the last frost date. Install transplants and bedding plants once the fear of frost is past. Most varieties of petunia like full sun. Choose a light, well-drained soil. The species plant is more adaptable to clay soils than the newer hybrids. Space petunias at 8 to 18 inches apart, depending on the variety. Be sure to give groundcover types plenty of room to spread. Space Wave™ series petunias on 2½ - to 3-foot centers, as they can spread to 4 feet.

Growing Tips

Fertilize petunias once a month—whether you grow them in containers or in the ground—with an all-purpose liquid fertilizer. Water on a weekly basis until plants are established; thereafter, water only during periods of drought.

Regional Advice and Care

Many hybrids are bushy types with mounded growth that require no pruning. Cut back long, trailing types if the plants get leggy. Today's hybrids require little deadheading and are better adapted to growing in heat, humidity, and rain. Look for the F1 hybrids; these are the most vigorous of the types offered. Botrytis disease can damage foliage and flowers. If you notice any dieback, prune off the infected parts and then sterilize your pruners with bleach.

Companion Planting and Design

Plant petunias in hanging baskets, window boxes, containers, or in the garden for bright annual color. Hybrids such as 'Purple Wave' make good groundcovers and bloom all summer long. *Petunia integrifolia* is ideal for a spot of intense annual color. Spiky plants and flowers (such as salvia and ornamental grasses) and bold foliage (such as *Perilla frutescens*) make good companions for petunias.

Try These

There are many types of petunias in both single- and double-flowering forms. Look for Surfinia™ trailing petunias and the Shock Wave™ series, which do well in our heat and humidity. For something different, try 'Debonair Black Cherry'. The blooms are dark black with burgundy undertones.

Silver Spurflower

Plectranthus argentatus

Botanical Pronunciation
plek-TRAN-thus r-gen-TATE-us

Other Name Plectranthus

Bloom Period and Seasonal Colors
Fuzzy gray green foliage summer until frost, small flowers in summer

Mature Height × Spread
2 to 3 ft. × 2 to 3 ft.

Although *Plectranthus* produces small tubular bluish white flowers in summer, its foliage (leaves up to 4 inches long) steals the show—soft gray-green and fuzzy. From summer until frost, this Australian native is a standout in the garden, where it glows behind smaller flowers. Silver spurflower gets to be the size of a small shrub and provides a foil for bright flowers. It looks good in containers with other annuals or in the flower garden. In the perennial garden it adds a soothing quality when planted in combination with orange and blue flowers like scaevola and Mexican sunflower. In container gardens it mixes and blends with every color. There are also selections with leaves that are green and white or green and gold.

When, Where, and How to Plant
Plant spurflower after the frost-free date in a site that is well drained. Part shade is ideal, but, provided you supply enough moisture, this annual will grow in full sun. Add a ½-inch layer of organic matter and mix it to a depth of 6 to 8 inches in the area where you plan to grow this annual. Water every few days for the first two weeks and then only as needed (no rain for several weeks) during dry periods. For container gardens, water when the top ½ inch of the soil is dry.

Growing Tips
If you grow *Plectranthus* in a pot, a large substantial container with several drainage holes is best for the health and vigor of the plant. Fertilize with a liquid fertilizer once every two weeks and mix in some slow-release granular fertilizer when you plant up the container.

Regional Advice and Care
This annual is fairly disease resistant. The best way to avoid pest problems is to have robust plants that are well cared for. If you see signs of mealybugs (which looks like white cotton) or scale or mites, treat with insecticidal soap. If plants get leggy, cut them back several inches and they should fill in with new growth quickly.

Companion Planting and Design
Combine *Plectranthus* in containers with annuals like scaevola, *Euphorbia* Diamond Frost™, and narrow leaf zinnias. It also looks good with ornamental grasses and cosmos.

Try These
Plectranthus 'Mona Lavender' is grown for its lavender flowers and dark green leaves—purple underneath and purple stems. Although you may see this plant in full bloom in nurseries in spring, the blooms will fall off with summer heat. They reappear in fall when day length shortens. A variety with green leaves edged in white, *Plectranthus coleoides* 'Vareigata' also makes a good houseplant.

Snapdragon

Antirrhinum majus

Botanical Pronunciation
An-ti-RHIN-um MAY-jus

Other Name Dragon-mouthed snaps

Bloom Period and Seasonal Colors
Early spring to frost blooms in white, yellow, pink, red, maroon, coral

Mature Height × Spread
½ to 3 ft. × 4 ft. depending on the variety

Snaps are favorites of many gardeners, both as cut flowers and in the garden. Individual flowers (which look like snapping jaws) open over a period of more than two weeks, starting at the bottom of the spike and continuing upward. Young plants set out in fall will bloom until hit by a hard frost. They then rest over the winter and start blooming again in early spring once the weather warms up. In the warmest parts of Georgia, snapdragons are perennial. In the rest of the state, during mild spells they will bloom on and off through winter. Snapdragons range from 6 inches to 3 feet tall and come in myriad colors. The Coronette series makes striking accents in the garden, as well as beautiful cut flowers.

When, Where, and How to Plant
Sow seeds indoors after the fear of frost has passed. Don't cover the seeds, as they need light to germinate. After germination (in one to two weeks) thin and transplant seedlings to peat pots. Harden them off before planting in the garden. Move them to a shady spot outside and gradually introduce them to full sun. Install young bedding plants in April or in fall in any soil, as long as it has excellent drainage. If the soil is too rich or fertile, plants will produce lots of foliage and few flowers. Place plants in holes that are larger than their containers. Space them according to variety.

Growing Tips
Snapdragons benefit from regular monthly fertilization during the growing season with a balanced liquid fertilizer. Too much nitrogen can result in lots of foliage and few flowers. Water plants weekly, especially during periods of drought. Containers may need water on a daily basis.

Regional Advice and Care
Deadheading (removing spent flowers) encourages more blooms over a longer period of time. Snapdragon rust (a fungus with orange spots that shows up on the undersides of leaves) can be avoided by selecting rust-resistant varieties, keeping leaf litter at a minimum, and avoiding overhead watering. Snapdragons will often reseed themselves around the garden. To encourage this practice, let some plants set seed. Self-seeding can result in interesting combinations. If snaps show up where they're not welcome, just pull them up.

Companion Planting and Design
Whether grown in containers or in the flower garden, snapdragons make a nice complement to pansies, iris, daylilies, and foxglove. These cheerful flower spikes range in size from dwarfs that only grow 6 to 10 inches tall and are well suited for bedding or edging plants, to the giant snaps that grow 30 to 36 inches tall and make great cut flowers. Use giant snaps in borders or in large groups for cut flowers.

Try These
For cut flowers, the Rocket™ series grows 30 inches tall and comes in more than ten different colors. For semidwarf types, try the Sonnet™ and Liberty™ series.

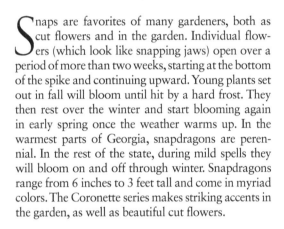

Sweet Alyssum

Lobularia maritima

Botanical Pronunciation
lob-yoo-LAR-ee-uh mar-ah-TEAM-ah

Bloom Period and Seasonal Colors
Spring and fall blooms in many colors, including pink, mauve, purple, white

Mature Height × Spread
4 to 12 in. × 12 in.

Native to southern Europe, sweet alyssum has naturalized throughout much of the United States. It perfumes the air with its tiny, honey-scented flowers from spring until frost. This delicate beauty creeps about the garden, gracefully spreading its seed wherever it finds bare soil. Planted among spring bulbs, its dense clusters of snow-white flowers fill in once the bulbs finish blooming, and its leaves help hide the bulbs' withering foliage. This reseeder comes in many colors, including pink, mauve, purple, and white. Sweet alyssum reaches 1 foot tall at maturity with leaves only ½ to 2 inches long. It's great in containers when combined with bulbs or other annuals. Tough, resilient, beautiful, and easy-to-grow—all reasons to try this popular plant.

When, Where, and How to Plant

Once the fear of frost is past (around April 15), sow sweet alyssum seeds directly in the ground. Do not cover seeds as they need light to germinate. In just 15 to 20 days, seedlings should sprout. For the earliest possible bloom, start seeds indoors in early April. Use a sterile potting mix, keep the seeds uncovered, and keep the air temperature at 65°F to 70°F. However, you will probably have the best results if you start with small, container-grown plants; these may also be planted in spring. If they are leggy when you plant them, shear them back to a couple of inches high, and new foliage and blooms will appear in a matter of weeks. Sweet alyssum thrives in full sun or part shade, and in almost any soil. It tolerates both heat and drought.

Growing Tips

When you first plant seeds or seedlings, water them with a diluted (half-strength) solution of liquid fertilizer. After they become established (usually within a few weeks), water them only when the soil is dry to the touch at ½ inch below the surface. Water using a liquid fertilizer once a month. If you grow sweet alyssum in containers, mix in a slow-release fertilizer at the time of planting.

Regional Advice and Care

About four weeks after sweet alyssum flowers, cut the plants back to half their size; this will help ensure a second crop of blooms. Sweet alyssum has no serious pest or disease problems.

Companion Planting and Design

Plant sweet alyssum between steppingstones, as a carpet under annuals and perennials, in window boxes, and in containers. It makes a perfect filler between small, spring-blooming bulbs, such as species tulips and grape hyacinth. Sweet alyssum attracts bees, so keep it away from any large open areas where people congregate.

Try These

Your first choice for growing sweet alyssum should be 'Snow Princess', a vigorous sterile hybrid cultivar that tolerates extreme heat and offers a long season of bloom; it's perfect for the garden. In hanging baskets it is reported to hang down 4 or 5 feet.

Wishbone Flower

Torenia fournieri

Botanical Pronunciation
Tor-RHEEN–e-ah FOURN-e-rye

Other Name Clown flower

Bloom Period and Seasonal Colors
Summer to frost, flowers come in white, blue,
purple, burgundy, pink, yellow, and two-toned

Mature Height × Spread
8 to 10 in. × 10 to 12 in.

The wishbone flower gets its name from the wishbone-shaped stamens found inside the flower's throat. Reminiscent of a snapdragon, the 1½-inch long, tubular flower is like a small trumpet with a pronounced flare. Both the flowers and seedpods look like tiny Chinese lanterns. This enchanting annual comes to us from Asia, and it adapts to a wide range of growing conditions in our Southern climate. The colorful flowers are a welcome alternative to the impatiens that has long been popular in Georgia gardens. (Note, impatiens have been suffering from downy mildew in recent years. Many gardeners no longer grow them.) When in flower, this profuse bloomer's foliage is barely visible. Plant them in the shade or part sun, and they will delight you for weeks.

When, Where, and How to Plant
Wait until the fear of frost is past and soil temperatures have warmed before sowing seeds in the garden (about late April or early May). The seeds need light to germinate. Plants normally begin to bloom in early July. For earlier blooms, start seeds indoors and transplant young plants to the garden. Wishbone flower will grow in sun or shade, but it likes humidity and moist soil. A moderately fertile soil is best. Plants reseed freely and are easy to move in any stage of development. For bedding plants, dig a hole the same size as the container the plant was growing in.

Growing Tips
Wishbone flower requires no special care, but for maximum blooms, use a liquid fertilizer (such as 20-20-20) once a month during the growing season. Plants respond to regular watering—once a week— especially during periods of drought. If grown in containers with other annuals, water when the soil is dry to the touch.

Regional Advice and Care
Wishbone flower is an old-fashioned plant that blooms in the summer garden with little or no care, but it will thrive with a bit of attention. Occasionally, plants will get leggy. Pinch them back to just above a node where attractive leaves emerge; they should produce new growth in no time. In a spot where plants dry out regularly, the flowers will begin to look worn and faded. If attacked by aphids, just blast them off with a strong spray of water from the hose.

Companion Planting and Design
Plant wishbone flower in the shade garden, in a semi-shady flower border, in containers, or in window boxes. They look great in a mass planting and bloom almost continuously through the summer and until frost. In a green woodland with ferns, they add a bright spot of color. Use them as an alternative for impatiens.

Try These
The hybrid Summer Wave™ series contains plants with flowers in amethyst, blue, and violet.

BULBS
FOR GEORGIA

Bulbs—those treasures that we plant in their dormant stage, ever hopeful that they will burst forth and flower in another season. Whether they are true bulbs, rhizomes, corms, or tubers, they all have certain characteristics in common. Most go through a period of having no foliage, when the root system may completely die away, only to be replaced later by a new one.

During the dormant period, when growth is slowed to a minimum, underground portions of the plant contain stored food, leaves, flowers, and seeds. The dormant stage can be extended if the bulb is dug up while it is still leafless and rootless. Provided the bulb is kept cool and dry, it can be transported great distances with relative ease. Because of this unique characteristic, we are able to import bulbs from all over the world. In Georgia, a great number of these bulbs naturalize as perennials and reward us with flowers year after year.

True Bulbs—Daffodil, Tulip, and Hyacinth

A true bulb may be considered a bud. It has concentric circles of fleshy tissue called scales. The scales contain stored food and energy for the plant during its active growth period. Future flowers are protected by the scales and leaves. At the base of the bulb is a basal plate from which the roots originate. The outer paper covering, called the tunic, keeps the bulb from drying out.

Colorful dahlias edged by ageratum.

Corms—Colchicum, Crocus, and Gladiolus

A corm is a short, enlarged, fleshy underground stem. Like a true bulb, it is usually covered by a tunic, but instead of concentric layers, it is solid. One or more buds give rise to the aboveground leaves, stems, and flowers. The roots come from the base.

Rhizomes—Calla Lily and Bearded Iris

A rhizome is a thickened stem that grows completely or partially underground. Growing points initiate at the tip and along the sides; roots develop from the underside.

Tubers—Anemone, Caladium, and Cyclamen

A tuber is a swollen, underground branch or rootstock that contains a supply of stored food. It has "eyes" or buds from which stems are produced. If you divide tubers, make sure each section has a growth bud.

Tuberous roots—Daylily and Dahlia

The roots store nutrients and grow in clusters, radiating out from a central point. Buds are produced at the base of old stems.

Tips for Cultivating

1. Make sure bulbs are firm and dry. Store them in a cool, dry place until you plant.
2. Plant dormant spring flowering bulbs in the fall and those that bloom in summer or fall in the spring.
3. For fall planting, soil temperatures should be at 60°F. or cooler, usually from October to November or later.
4. Amend the soil with organic matter before you plant.
5. Plant bulbs at a depth that is three times the width of the bulb. Dig individual holes or for a more naturalistic look, plant them in masses.
6. Fertilize after you plant in the fall with a bulb fertilizer.
7. Use golf tees to mark where you plant.
8. Divide bulbs after they flower and when at least one-third of the foliage is yellow or brown. (This may be eight to ten weeks after they flower)
9. If you grow bulbs in containers, follow the same guidelines.
10. For the best effect, plant bulbs like daffodils in combination with perennials like hellebores. This way, when the daffodils finish blooming, the hellebore foliage will mask the dying foliage of the daffodils.

Water bulbs after you plant them. If you water by hand, apply 5 gallons of water for every 10 square feet. This is approximately the amount of water released by a garden hose operating at medium pressure for one minute. This amount of water should penetrate the soil to at least 6 inches. Water when bulbs are actively growing only if there is no rainfall. Apply 1 inch per week.

Baby Cyclamen

Cyclamen hederifolium

Botanical Pronunciation
SIGH-kla-men hed-er-ih-FOH-lee-um

Other Name Hardy cyclamen

Bloom Period and Seasonal Colors
Late summer and fall blooms in rose-pink or white

Mature Height × Spread
3 to 5 in. × 3 to 5 in.

A miniature version of the large florist's cyclamen (*Cyclamen persicum*), baby cyclamen (*C. hederifolium*) charms us with its tiny flowers and foliage. A base of heart-shaped, green-marbled silver and white leaves shows off the tiny rose-pink or white flowers that appear atop 3- to 4-inch stems in late summer to fall. Baby cyclamen is great for a rock garden or naturalized area. Just make sure you place the flowers so that you can appreciate and admire them up close. This cyclamen is vigorous and easy to grow in pots or in the ground. Start them from seed and have flowers in as few as seven months, or start them from container-grown tubers. Once it's established in the garden, baby cyclamen will often self-sow.

When, Where, and How to Plant

Plant container-grown plants (grown from tubers) in spring or fall. Space them about 10 inches apart as they can grow, over time, to the size of a small dinner plate. Select a site that gets protection from hot afternoon sun. A bright woodland location under shrubs or small trees, such as rhododendrons or dogwoods, is ideal. Make sure you plant them where you will remember them even if the leaves are not visible because the leaves appear when the flowers appear and then die away the following summer. Hardy cyclamen likes well-drained soil that has been amended with organic matter or compost. Mix together one-third organic matter, one-third coarse sand, and one-third existing soil. After planting, water well and apply a ½-inch layer of mulch. Take care to avoid mulching directly over the tubers. See page 45 for more planting tips.

Growing Tips

Topdress hardy cyclamen once in spring and once in fall with ½ inch of compost. Water them thoroughly after planting and once a week during the first growing season. After this initial period, check the soil and when the top ½ inch is dry, water thoroughly during the growing season.

Regional Advice and Care

Baby cyclamen requires no special pruning. It suffers from no serious pest or disease problems.

Companion Planting and Design

Plant cyclamen in rock or woodland gardens in combination with ferns and evergreen groundcovers, such as ajuga, or against a backdrop of the Lenten rose (*Helleborus × hybridus*). Small flowering snowdrops (*Galanthus nivalis*), which bloom in winter, make great companions. Under shrubs, such as rhododendrons or camellias, baby cyclamen will be protected from hot afternoon sun and drying winds. Cyclamen also makes a good container plant for shady areas.

Try These

Cyclamen coum blooms in winter and early spring. The deep crimson flowers appear on 4- to 6-inch stems. The round leaves are green on top and rose on the undersides. There are also white- and pink-flowering selections.

Caladium

Caladium bicolor

Botanical Pronunciation
ka-LAY-dee-um BY-kul-ur

Other Name Angel wings

Bloom Period and Seasonal Colors
Foliage from summer until frost in red, rose, pink,
white, bronze, and green combinations

Mature Height × Spread
2 to 4 ft. × 2 ft.

Splendid foliage plants in the summer, caladiums provide a long season of beauty with a minimum amount of effort. Relatives of old-fashioned elephant ears, caladium's flattened tubers quickly grow into lush plants in our humid Georgia climate. The foliage comes in shades of white, red, green, and various combinations of these colors. Some leaves can be one solid color and others can be marked with veins of another color, such as the hybrid 'Candidum' with its large, silvery white leaves and dark green veins. This old-fashioned variety is a strong grower and tolerates direct sun. Dramatic as bedding plants or in containers, there are numerous cultivars available. 'Pink Beauty' has soft pink leaves with a deep green background. 'Red Flash' has red centers and veins with pink and green accents.

When, Where, and How to Plant
Caladiums need warmth and abundant moisture to thrive. If they are set out too early in spring, before soil temperatures warm up, the tubers will rot in no time. The best time to plant is early May once the soil begins to warm, 70°F or warmer. Caladiums thrive in bright, filtered light, but some varieties will tolerate full sun. If planted in too much shade, the colors will not be as brilliant. Caladiums need a well-drained soil, rich in organic matter, and reasonably fertile. The tubers have visible eyes on the tops of the dormant roots, which contain buds of the flower spikes. Cutting off the larger-growing points on the tubers, before they are planted, will result in vigorous plants with more side branching. Because the roots sprout from the tops of the tubers, plant the tubers at least 1 inch deep. Apply a thin layer of mulch after planting. More planting tips are on page 45.

Growing Tips
Make sure caladiums don't dry out, especially when they are getting established. Check daily to see if they need watering. Once caladium leaves begin to flop with the first cool days of autumn, reduce watering. Fertilize with a liquid fertilizer once a month during the growing season.

Regional Advice and Care
Remove the finger-like greenish flowers as they appear. This will help the plant direct all of its energy into growing beautiful foliage. In all but the warmest parts of Georgia, caladiums must be dug up and stored for the winter. After the leaves have died down in fall, lift the tubers and store them in a warm, dry place until next spring. Caladiums do not suffer from any serious pest or disease problems.

Companion Planting and Design
Plant caladiums as bedding plants, in containers, or at the edge of a woodland garden for summer color. Caladiums make good companions for hostas and ferns, such as autumn fern, cinnamon fern, and royal fern. In containers, combine them with colorful coleus and other shade-loving annuals.

Try These
Caladium 'Aaron' has dark green leaves with a white center.

Canna

Canna × generalis

Botanical Pronunciation
KAN-uh jen-er-RAY-liss

Other Name Canna lily

Bloom Period and Seasonal Colors
Mid- to late-summer blooms in pink, orange, red, scarlet, colorful foliage

Mature Height × Spread
1 to 6 ft. × 2 ft.

In Victorian times, cannas were planted for their exotic tropical foliage. Still popular with Georgia gardeners, today there are hybrids that offer both striking flowers and luxuriant foliage. With leaves 2 to 6 feet long, in shades of green, blue-green, bronze, and variegated, cannas make a bold statement in the perennial border, in containers and beds, or as specimens. Canna flowers are usually divided into two groups, the orchid-flowered and the gladiolus-flowered. Both types are robust and free-flowering. The hybrids range in size from the giant 'Red King Humbert', which grows to 7 feet tall, to the dwarf 'Tropical Rose', which only grows to 2½ to 3 feet. From subtle to gaudy, cannas offer an easy way to introduce color into a hot, sunny garden.

When, Where, and How to Plant
Plant canna rhizomes in spring after the fear of frost is over and soil temperatures have warmed, 70°F or warmer. You can start rhizomes earlier in sand or soil and then transplant them outdoors after the frost-free date. Annual types, such as 'Seven Dwarfs Mix', can be grown from seed. Break the hard seed coats, soak the seeds in water, and allow them to swell before planting. Plant canna in full sun or part shade. For best performance, plant them in a soil that is fertile, rich in organic matter, and well drained (except for those cannas that grow naturally in swampy areas). Plant rhizomes 18 to 24 inches apart, or more if you are planting clumps of established plants. Cover the roots with 4 to 6 inches of soil.

Growing Tips
For the best blooms, feed with a liquid fertilizer monthly. If the soil is amended with an abundance of organic matter before planting, established plants will not need to be watered as frequently during the growing season. Cannas are robust plants.

Regional Advice and Care
In the lower two-thirds of Georgia, you may leave canna rhizomes in the ground all winter if they're mulched. Remove the dead leaves after they are killed by frost. When storing rhizomes over winter, wrap the tubers in slightly moist peat moss in a ventilated room at 45°F to 50°F. This will prevent them from drying out. In spring, cut rhizomes so that they contain at least two or three eyes. These are the points from which the new growth (buds, shoots, and roots) generates. If cannas suffer from leaf roller moth (the leaves are rolled up tight like cigars), contact your county Extension office (page 225) for recommended controls. Deadhead any varieties that are not self-cleaning.

Companion Planting and Design
Large varieties make a colorful summer screen. Use both large and dwarf types in containers, as bedding plants, with other annuals, or in the flower border.

Try These
Canna 'Bengal Tiger' has variegated foliage and shocking orange flowers that look wonderful in combination with blue-flowered perennials.

Crocus

Crocus spp. and cultivars

Botanical Pronunciation
KROH-kus

Bloom Period and Seasonal Colors
Late winter, early spring, or fall blooms (by variety) in white, red, yellow, purple, rose, blue

Mature Height × Spread
2 to 3 in. × 3 in.

Harbinger of spring, crocus has long been a favorite of Georgia gardeners. While most bloom in late winter or very early spring, there are also types that bloom in autumn. One of the most vigorous species, *Crocus vernus,* blooms from February to March in shades of white, yellow, lavender, and purple. For autumn flowers, there is *C. speciosus,* with blue-violet flowers. This species increases quickly by seed and division. Crocus produces grasslike foliage, often marked with silver that—depending on the particular type—appears before, during, or after flowering. The flowers, which are either flaring or have cupped petals, are 1½ to 3 inches long. The blooms seem to rise magically out of the earth as the short stems are hidden underground.

When, Where, and How to Plant
In Georgia, plant spring-blooming bulbs after soil temperatures have begun to cool, usually between November and December. Fall-blooming crocus may be planted from late July through August. Plant crocus at a depth of 2 to 3 inches in well-drained soil that is a mixture of one-third organic matter, one-third sand, and one-third clay. Because they are small, planting in groups of ten to twenty bulbs makes a more effective display. Rather than planting individual bulbs, dig out an area, place them in a group, and then cover them with soil. Plant crocus in full sun or partial shade. You can plant them under deciduous trees that will create shade as the season progresses.

Growing Tips
Topdress bulbs in fall after planting rather than putting fertilizer directly in the planting bed. Topdressing annually will ensure healthy bulbs and blooms. For best results, use a slow-release fertilizer. Water when the bulbs are actively growing or blooming.

Regional Advice and Care
For the most part, crocus is free of serious pest and disease problems. However, squirrels and chipmunks can wreak havoc and destroy a planting in no time. *Crocus tommasinianus* is squirrel resistant and spreads easily by seed, making it an ideal candidate to naturalize in the lawn. Divide clumps if needed every three to four years. Don't remove the bulb foliage until at least 50 percent of it is yellowed.

Companion Planting and Design
These gems will grow happily in the lawn, in the front of a perennial border, in a rock garden, or in pots. For a sequence of blooms, plant in combination with other later-blooming bulbs, such as daffodils. Crocus can also be planted among groundcovers such as the tiny blue star creeper or creeping Jenny.

Try These
Keen gardeners love the pale lavender blooms of *Crocus tommasinianus,* also known as Tommies. These tiny gems are 2 to 3 inches tall, and their happy faces smile up at you in late winter when flowers are especially appreciated.

Daffodil

Narcissus spp. and cultivars

Botanical Pronunciation
nar-SIS-us

Other Name Jonquil

Bloom Period and Seasonal Colors
Spring blooms in yellow, white, bicolor

Mature Height × Spread
5 to 20 in. × 5 in.

Some of the best gardeners are confused by the seemingly complicated set of rules for naming daffodils. People will tell you that they don't grow daffodils, they grow jonquils, while others claim that they grow only narcissus. Keep in mind that all daffodils and jonquils belong to the genus *Narcissus*—so in a sense, everyone is right! There are hundreds of varieties to choose from for Georgia gardens, but a few stand out as particularly well adapted and persistent in our climate. Just a drive through the country in early spring will introduce you to some of the more common varieties. All daffodils are poisonous and therefore resistant to pests such as rodents, which will eat other bulbs as fast as you can plant them.

When, Where, and How to Plant
Plant daffodil bulbs in fall when soil temperatures have cooled to about 60°F, usually around the first frost. Plant them in soil that is well drained, in full sun or partial shade. If you plant them near trees, observe the light that filters through the leaves. They should receive at least a half-day of sunlight. A location that receives plenty of moisture when the bulbs are growing but is dry during their dormant season is ideal. As a general rule, plant bulbs at a depth three times the height of the bulb, and space at three times the width of the bulb on center. If you add organic matter, remember that bulbs need 6 to 8 inches of soil underneath for their roots. Also see page 45.

Growing Tips
Topdress bulbs after planting. Bulbs prefer a low nitrogen, moderate-phosphorous, high-potash fertilizer. A slow-release fertilizer with trace elements has been specially formulated for daffodils. For organic nutrients, use cottonseed or bloodmeal for nitrogen; bonemeal for phosphorous and calcium; and wood ashes for potash. Water daffodils when they are actively growing. Mulch to conserve moisture and reduce weeds.

Regional Advice and Care
Daffodils are free of pests and disease, and rodents leave them alone. To avoid basal rot, site them in a well-drained soil shaded from the summer sun. Leave the foliage to ripen (turn yellow) naturally. If you have to store them, make sure bulbs stay dry and have plenty of ventilation. Sweet-smelling paperwhite narcissus is best used for indoor enjoyment and discarded afterward.

Companion Planting and Design
Plant larger types, such as 'Carlton', in large groups. Interplant them with hostas or daylilies that will help mask the foliage as it ripens in early summer. Plant heirloom types, such as *Narcissus pseudonarcissus* ssp. *moschatus,* in areas where they can naturalize without being disturbed. Force miniature types, such as 'Tete-a-Tete', in pots or plant them in the perennial border.

Try These
It's hard to pick one favorite, but many gardeners are partial to heirloom varieties—especially those with white flowers, including 'Thalia' and 'Tresamble'.

Dahlia

Dahlia spp. and cultivars

Botanical Pronunciation
DAH lee-a

Bloom Period and Seasonal Colors
Summer through fall blooms in every color
except blue

Mature Height × Spread
15 in. to 6 ft. × 1 to 5 ft.

Native to Mexico and Central America, dahlias are among the most colorful of the summer bulbs. Introduced to Europe in the early 1800s, there are thousands of cultivars. It's no surprise that these prolific bloomers—which come in every size, form, and color—are a favorite of flower arrangers. When the dog days of summer set in, many perennials and annuals are beginning to fade just as dahlias are coming into their own. They brighten the late-summer garden and dazzle us throughout the fall until frost. Depending on the variety, they grow anywhere from 15 inches to 6 feet tall. The flowers range in size from tiny pompom-types to single flowers as large as a dinner plate. Dahlias add color and fun to the summer garden.

When, Where, and How to Plant
Plant dahlia tubers, seeds, or seedlings in spring once the soil has warmed. Before planting, work organic matter into the soil to at least 1 foot deep. Space large varieties 4 to 5 feet apart and smaller types 1 to 2 feet apart. For large types, place a stake for support in the hole at the time of planting. Place tubers horizontally in the hole with the eye (growing points) pointed toward the stake and cover with 3 inches of soil. Add soil to the hole as the shoots expand over time. Dahlias like full sun, but in the warmest part of the state they need shade during the hottest part of the day.

Growing Tips
Dahlias like regular watering once the shoots emerge. Continue watering while they are in active growth. If you amend the soil with organic matter before planting, there is no need to fertilize. If you do fertilize, use a formula that is high in phosphorous and potassium. Avoid high nitrogen fertilizers, which may cause weak stems.

Regional Advice and Care
There are definite advantages to pinching and thinning dahlias. With tall varieties, remove all but the two strongest shoots. Once they grow and develop at least three sets of leaves, pinch off the tip just above the top set; this will encourage the development of side shoots. Pinching off all buds on the side shoots, except for the terminal bud, will encourage the development of large flowers. Harvest cut flowers in early morning or evening. Place the stems immediately in 2 to 3 inches of hot water. Let the water cool gradually before adding more cool water. Dahlias can develop fungal diseases.

Companion Planting and Design
Dahlias look great on their own or as part of the perennial border. Grow several different varieties to ensure a source of cut flowers from summer through fall. Combine them with roses, coneflowers, ornamental grasses, and sunflowers.

Try These
For the perennial border, try the heirloom *Dahlia* 'Bishop of Llandaff'. It has a semidouble flower with 3½-inch scarlet blooms and dark foliage.

Elephant Ear

Colocasia spp. and cultivars

Botanical Pronunciation
kol-oh-KAY-see-uh

Other Name Taro

Bloom Period and Seasonal Colors
Summer to frost, colorful foliage green, black, spotted, chartreuse

Mature Height × Spread
8 in. to 7 ft. × 1 to 4 ft.

For drama in the summer and fall garden, tropical elephant's ear is a great choice. The heart-shaped leaves (glossy, textured, or variegated) commonly range in size from 6 inches to 24 inches across and even larger. In the garden, with adequate moisture, they can become quite large. *C. esculenta* can have leaves that are 2 feet wide and the plant can attain heights of 3 feet or taller. With upright shiny green leaves that form a "tea cup" that holds water, C. 'Tea Cup' grows to be 6 feet tall. Elephant ear provides a bold contrast in the perennial border, makes great container plants with other annuals, and grows happily in damp soils next to a pond with other aquatic type plants. You can also submerge containers in a pond.

When, Where, and How to Plant
Plant firm bulbs in spring once the soil has warmed up, (late April to early May). Prepare the soil in advance by adding organic matter, a couple of shovels worth, check on the needs of the particular variety, many prefer part shade. If you plant them in full sun, provide a constant supply of water. If you grow them in containers, make sure to allow room for the bulb to grow tall and top heavy; some varieties get to be large plants in a short time. Fertilize with an all-purpose fertilizer once every two weeks during the growing season.

Growing Tips
Apply a ½-inch layer of mulch after you plant to help control weeds and keep the soil from drying out too quickly.

Regional Advice and Care
Elephant's ear adds a tropical quality to your garden with their dramatic foliage and stems. They do best with plenty of moisture. In the garden, some like C. 'Illustris' will spread to form a large clump. Some gardeners experience a skin reaction to the sap of elephant's ear. If you want to increase their winter hardiness, Brent Heath (a nationally known bulb expert) recommends planting bulbs deeper than you normally would so that they are below the freeze line. Alternatively, you can remove the stems and leaves just before the first frost, dig the corms, and keep them indoors in a box filled with shredded newspaper. If you're not worried about keeping them alive during winter, treat them like annuals and try new types next year.

Companion Planting and Design
Plant them with roses, ornamental grasses, in the perennial garden, next to ponds, or in large containers.

Try These
For a big impact *Colocasia* 'Thailand Giant' has leaves that are 5 feet long and 4 feet across. *Alocasia* is a separate genus whose members resemble elephant's ear. *Alocasia* 'Frydek' has dark leaves with white veins. *Alocasia* 'Black Magic' has almost black leaves.

Ginger Lily

Hedychium coronarium

Botanical Pronunciation
hed-EE-kee-um kor-oh-NAR-ee-um

Other Name Butterfly ginger

Bloom Period and Seasonal Colors
Late summer to frost blooms in white

Mature Height × Spread
3 to 6 ft. × 3 ft. or more

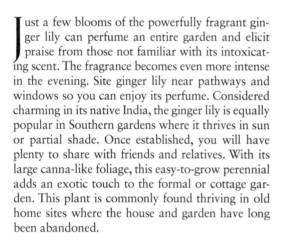

Just a few blooms of the powerfully fragrant ginger lily can perfume an entire garden and elicit praise from those not familiar with its intoxicating scent. The fragrance becomes even more intense in the evening. Site ginger lily near pathways and windows so you can enjoy its perfume. Considered charming in its native India, the ginger lily is equally popular in Southern gardens where it thrives in sun or partial shade. Once established, you will have plenty to share with friends and relatives. With its large canna-like foliage, this easy-to-grow perennial adds an exotic touch to the formal or cottage garden. This plant is commonly found thriving in old home sites where the house and garden have long been abandoned.

When, Where, and How to Plant
Divide and plant rhizomes in early spring, just before growth begins and after the frost-free date has passed. Plant ginger lily in average garden soil and provide plenty of moisture during the growing season. Give the plants some space to spread out. The canes grow 4 to 6 feet tall before producing flowers, and the rhizomes spread quickly to form large clumps up to 3 or more feet across. For best results, plant in full sun or part shade. They will tolerate sun, especially if they are planted in a soil that is moist and rich in organic matter. Don't plant them too deeply. The soil should just cover the thick rhizomes. Apply a 2- to 3-inch layer of mulch. Except for the coldest parts of Georgia, rhizomes should overwinter in the ground.

Growing Tips
Water butterfly ginger weekly during the growing season. Although they will tolerate a wide range of soil types, they will benefit from one that is rich in organic matter. If you have average soil with a good bit of clay, fertilize once or twice during the growing season with a general, all-purpose fertilizer. Follow the directions on the label.

Regional Advice and Care
Ginger lilies love humidity and thrive in Georgia summers, coming to life late in the fall when many other plants are tired and wilted. For best flowering, lift and divide clumps every three or four years. Apply a thick layer of mulch in the fall to protect the roots from freezing. Leaving the dried foliage on plants until the following spring is another way to help plants overwinter.

Companion Planting and Design
Plant ginger lily in a spot where you can appreciate its fragrant flowers in late summer through autumn. Plant them at the back of a flower border, as a focal point in a shrub border, or as a specimen.

Try These
Other ginger lilies to try include red ginger lily, *Hedychium coccineum*, and *Hedychium aurantiacum*, orange ginger lily. Edible ginger, *Zingiber officinale*, can be grown from grocery store roots. It is winter hardy in the lower half of the state.

Rain Lily

Zephyranthes candida

Botanical Pronunciation
ze-fi-RANTH-eez kan-DEE-duh

Other Name Fairy lily

Bloom Period and Seasonal Colors
Late summer to autumn blooms in white

Mature Height × Spread
6 to 12 in. × 6 in.

Some of the best plants in Georgia gardens started out as roadside treasures. The common rain lily, *Zephyranthes candida,* started as a wildflower that blooms throughout much of the South. Undemanding in the garden, it grows in clay or sandy soils as well as in the bog garden. With its grassy foliage and small flowers, it is a choice addition to the perennial border. With every fall rainstorm, clumps seem to burst into bloom. The white starry flowers glisten in the garden and stand out against the dark green, rush-like leaves that persist through the winter. The small bulbs suffer from drying, so it's best to acquire this plant when it's actively growing in a pot. Provide a little extra watering during the summer.

When, Where, and How to Plant
Plant rain lilies when they are actively growing in spring or in fall. They bloom late in the season from July through November. Rain lilies will tolerate full sun or partial shade. For best flowering, plant rain lilies in a moist soil that is rich in organic matter—though they will grow happily in most types of soil. Avoid planting in areas with lots of competition from tree roots. Plant eight to ten bulbs per square foot. If they are growing in a pot, don't plant them any deeper than the depth of the soil in the pot. See page 45 for more planting details.

Growing Tips
Use a liquid fertilizer during the growing season. If rain lilies are planted in heavy clay soils, they benefit from topdressing with compost yearly. A layer of mulch will help keep bulbs cool. Planting them in combination with groundcovers will also help keep the soil cool and moist. Watering the bulbs during periods of drought in summer ensures they won't shrivel up and die before they become established.

Regional Advice and Care
After they are established, they require very little care. Rain lilies suffer from no serious pest or disease problems.

Companion Planting and Design
These tiny wonders are easy to incorporate into the garden and offer delightful flowers at a time when few others compete for attention. Plant them in groups of ten or more for a good display. Site them in areas where you can appreciate the small, colorful flowers in late summer and through the fall. They are beautiful in combination with groundcovers, such as ajuga or evergreen *Vinca minor.* The foliage makes for a good edging plant after it finishes flowering.

Try These
Growing along the Gulf Coast is *Zephyranthes grandiflora.* This pink-flowered subtropical has blooms of over 3 inches across. The showy flowers stand out with a white stigma and yellow anthers. They are a great choice for the garden or in containers.

Siberian Squill

Scilla siberica

Botanical Pronunciation
SIL-uh sy-BEER-ah-kuh

Other Name Wood squill

Bloom Period and Seasonal Colors
Early spring, white, blue, sky blue

Mature Height × Spread
4 to 5 inches × 3 to 4 inches

Early bulbs give us hope and inspiration about the spring ahead of us. Only 4 to 5 inches tall, Siberian squill are charming early-spring bloomers that brighten the dark woodland floor. The bell-shaped flowers are a good choice for an area where you want to naturalize bulbs in filtered sun or shade. And, you don't have to worry about deer or rodents as they don't seem to find these little bulbs appetizing. You can also force them in pots. The selection 'Spring Beauty', which dates to 1939, is still a winner today, producing sky-blue flowers on strong stems, only 5 inches tall, in March or April. They look great in combination with white flowered daffodils. Once you have some success with this bulb, you'll want to add more to your garden.

When, Where, and How to Plant
Plant *Scilla siberica* in the fall, once soil temperatures have cooled (usually in November or later). The perfect setting is a woodland garden in a spot that gets filtered light. Part sun or part shade is ideal, along with a soil amended with organic matter. Tuck them under shrubs in the shade or combine them with other early spring-flowering bulbs.

Growing Tips
Plant bulbs 5 inches deep and 1 to 2 inches apart. Make sure bulbs are firm and get them into the ground before they dry out. For a big impact, plant them in groups of twenty-five or more. Add a ½-inch layer of mulch after you plant and then water well.

Regional Advice and Care
A deciduous woodland that is sunny in early spring and shady by the time summer arrives provides the ideal situation for this minor bulb. This bulb is small enough you can naturalize it in areas of lawn but set the mower on a high height until the foliage ripens off. Use golf tees to mark where bulbs are planted so that you can fertilize in the fall when no foliage is visible. Fertilize on top of the soil (compost will work); never put fertilizer in the hole when you plant bulbs.

Companion Planting and Design
Combine different selections of squills together including white- and blue-flowered forms. Tuck them under trees like dogwoods or shrubs including native azaleas, forsythia, witchhazel, and corylopsis with its soft yellow flowers. Scilla also look good with daffodils (white or yellow selections) that bloom at the same time. Plant Siberian squills in the woodland with ferns, (Japanese painted fern, maidenhair) and hostas, dwarf crested iris, and hardy ginger, *Asarum* species. Other small bulbs that make good bedfellows include *Chionodoxa* and *Ipehion* 'Rolf Feidler', or *Leucojum aestivum,* with white bell-shaped flowers, also known as summer snowflakes.

Try These
Scilla tubergeniana dates to 1931, with pale blue-white flowers with dark midribs. For a different color, *Scilla bifolia rosea* has fragrant, light pink, star-shaped flowers on 4- to 5-inch stems. Other minor bulbs to try include dwarf iris, *Iris reticulata.*

Spanish Bluebells

Hyacinthoides hispanica

Botanical Pronunciation
hy-uh-sin-THOY-deez his-PAN-ih-ka

Other Name Wood hyacinth

Bloom Period and Seasonal Colors
April to May blooms in lavender-blue,
lilac-pink, white

Mature Height × Spread
12 to 16 in. × 12 in.

This heirloom bulb dates to 1601 and adapts well to shady Georgia gardens, where it naturalizes easily in a deciduous woodland or anywhere that it receives plenty of moisture in the spring. In April, the 12- to 16-inch spires are hung with ten to twenty bell-shaped blossoms, each about ¾ inches long. The flowers come in shades of blue, violet, pink, and white. The numerous shiny leaves are about 8 inches long and ½ inch wide. With its lush foliage, it can be used to edge a woodland path in combination with evergreen groundcovers. Deer and rodent resistant, once it gets established, it should bloom for years. The bulbs quickly seed and multiply to form carpets of color under trees or in the perennial border.

When, Where, and How to Plant
Spanish bluebell bulbs should be firm (not mushy) and dry when you plant them. Plant bulbs in autumn in soil that is moist and moderately fertile. This shade-tolerant bulb, a member of the lily family, will also grow in full sun. Cover the bulbs with 3 to 4 inches of soil, and plant them 4 to 5 inches apart or 10 to 12 inches apart, depending on the desired effect. Bell-shaped flowers will appear on 8- to 12-inch stems. Refer to page 45 for additional planting specifics.

Growing Tips
Topdress bulbs in fall after you plant them rather than putting fertilizer directly in the planting bed. Contrary to popular thinking, bonemeal is not a complete fertilizer. For best results, you should use a slow-release fertilizer, such as a bulb booster.

Water once a week during the bulb's active growth period (when foliage, buds, and blooms are visible).

Regional Advice and Care
Remove the dead flower stalks after they finish blooming. Once they finish flowering, let the foliage ripen (turning at least half yellowed). Divide clumps in the fall if they become overcrowded and cease to bloom. Spanish bluebells do not suffer from any serious pest or disease problems.

Companion Planting and Design
Plant Spanish bluebells in a deciduous woodland garden with rhododendrons and azaleas or in combination with other shade-loving perennials, such as hostas and ferns. Plant them near a pond or stream that receives lots of moisture in the spring. Plant them in rows in the cut-flower garden. Spanish bluebells are great for naturalizing and make an effective mass planting. For a colorful combination in the woodland garden, plant Spanish bluebells with ajuga, Japanese painted ferns, *Pulmonaria* species, giant bleeding hearts, and the cardinal flower. For bulb companions, plant them with late daffodils and tulips.

Try These
'Danube' has dark blue flowers. 'Excelsior', an heirloom variety that dates to 1906, has deep violet-blue flowers and is larger than most of the Spanish bluebells. The related English bluebell, *Hyacinthoides non-scripta,* is less suited to the heat and humidity of Southern gardens.

Spider Lily

Lycoris radiata

Botanical Pronunciation
Lye-CORE-is RAID-ee-ah-ta

Other Name Surprise lilies

Bloom Period and Seasonal Colors
September blooms in coral-red or bright red, depending on the source of the bulb

Mature Height × Spread
18 to 22 in. × 12 in.

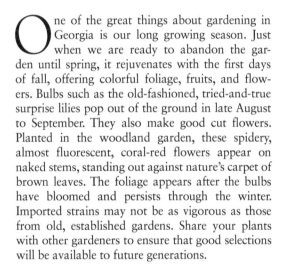

One of the great things about gardening in Georgia is our long growing season. Just when we are ready to abandon the garden until spring, it rejuvenates with the first days of fall, offering colorful foliage, fruits, and flowers. Bulbs such as the old-fashioned, tried-and-true surprise lilies pop out of the ground in late August to September. They also make good cut flowers. Planted in the woodland garden, these spidery, almost fluorescent, coral-red flowers appear on naked stems, standing out against nature's carpet of brown leaves. The foliage appears after the bulbs have bloomed and persists through the winter. Imported strains may not be as vigorous as those from old, established gardens. Share your plants with other gardeners to ensure that good selections will be available to future generations.

When, Where, and How to Plant
The best time to divide and plant *Lycoris radiata* bulbs is in June, but you can plant as late as early fall. Often you will have blooms the same fall, but the bulbs may take a year to settle in before they produce flowers. Surprise lilies have been passed down from generation to generation in Georgia gardens, so we know they will tolerate heavy clay soils. For best results, however, plant them in soil that has been amended with organic matter. A deciduous woodland with lots of leaf litter provides the perfect planting medium. Partial shade is ideal, but they will tolerate full sun. The flowers will last longer if protected from hot afternoon sun and winds. Plant bulbs 3 to 4 inches deep. If you pot them up in containers, make sure the tops are exposed. If the

roots are crowded in the pot, you'll have abundant blooms. After planting, topdress the bed.

Growing Tips
For best results, fertilize in fall each year with an organic or commercial bulb fertilizer. Water when the bulbs are blooming and growing. Once the foliage disappears, cease watering.

Regional Advice and Care
Spider lilies resent being disturbed. When they are divided and replanted, they take at least one season before they are happy and blooming. They are members of the Amaryllis family; therefore, they are pest resistant and not bothered by rodents. Let the foliage wither naturally on its own.

Companion Planting and Design
Spider lilies look wonderful planted in masses or in combination with ferns and other shade-loving perennials. Plant them in the woodland garden in combination with native plants. Tuck them in a bed of ivy to highlight the flowers and help mask the foliage until it dies back in the spring. In the perennial border, combine them with flowers that have hot colors like Mexican sunflower and *Helenium*.

Try These
Called "naked lady," *Lycoris squamigera* sends up pink trumpets on naked stems in mid- to late-summer. The strap-like, gray-green foliage emerges in the spring and dies back just before the flowers appear.

Summer Snowflake

Leucojum aestivum

Botanical Pronunciation
loo-KOH-jum E-stiv-um

Bloom Period and Seasonal Colors
Late spring to early summer, blooms in white

Mature Height × Spread
18 to 24 in. × 12 to 18 in.

Native to the Mediterranean, summer snowflake benefits from excess spring moisture and a long summer baking, making it right at home in Georgia gardens. It grows happily in a range of soil types, including heavy clay and moist sand. Masses of lush green foliage set off the clusters of two to five flowers that spray out from the top about 18 inches high. The bell-like flowers are white and green-tipped and about ¾ inch long. The large-flowered selection 'Gravetye' originated in the garden of the famous English horticulturist William Robinson. Despite its name, summer snowflake begins to bloom in spring and continues for a month or longer. Summer snowflake is a reliable early-blooming bulb that perennializes easily in Southern gardens, blooming for years to come.

When, Where, and How to Plant
Plant them after soil temperatures have begun to cool, usually between November and December. If you have to store them, make sure they stay dry and have plenty of ventilation (a cool basement is good). Because they tolerate lots of moisture, the edge of a pond or stream is an ideal spot to site these lush bulbs. A great bulb for naturalizing, summer snowflakes will also grow in a flower border that is not irrigated. Site these charming bulbs in full sun or shade. Plant them 3 to 4 inches deep, allowing five to six bulbs per square foot.

Growing Tips
Topdress bulbs in fall after planting, rather than fertilizing at planting. Remember, bonemeal is not a complete fertilizer. For best results, use a slow-release fertilizer or bulb booster. Water summer snowflakes on a weekly basis when they are actively growing. While they thrive in moist areas, they don't require excess moisture to perform well.

Regional Advice and Care
Once established in your garden, summer snowflakes will multiply and increase quickly. You can divide them as soon as they finish blooming, or wait until fall when the bulbs are dormant. Let the foliage ripen (when at least half of the leaves turn yellow) before you remove it. Fortunately, rodents do not find this bulb appealing.

Companion Planting and Design
Plant summer snowflakes with ferns, hellebore, and hosta, or with other bulbs that bloom at the same time, such as grape hyacinth and midseason daffodils. In the woodland garden, they make good companions for other shade-tolerant bulbs, such as Spanish bluebell. They also provide a lush groundcover under rhododendron, azalea, viburnum, and other spring-flowering shrubs.

Try These
Another bulb in the amaryllis family is the tiny (only 4 to 5 inches tall) snowdrop, *Galanthus nivalis*. The nodding, three-lobed, bell-shaped, white flowers tipped with green appear in February or earlier.

Tulip

Tulipa spp. and cultivars

Botanical Pronunciation
TEW-li-pa

Bloom Period and Seasonal Colors
Spring flowers various colors

Mature Height × Spread
5 to 20 in. × 12 in.

Growing the classic large hybrid tulips can be challenging in our Georgia gardens. Most of the time there is not enough cold to give them the proper chilling they require in winter. Generally speaking, Darwin hybrid tulips, lily-flowered tulips, and parrot tulips, all typically available in nurseries, should be treated as annuals. The good news is that some of the species tulips persist in our mild climate (except for the coastal areas where it is too warm to grow tulips at all, except as potted plants). While the species plants tend to be smaller and more delicate, they have proven garden worthy and the types recommended here should act like perennials, provided you give them a moist, well-drained soil and plenty of sunshine.

When, Where, and How to Plant
Species tulips should be planted in the fall when the soil temperatures are 60°F or cooler. Sometimes this is not until October or November. Plant them in the rock garden, perennial border, or in pots. Combine them with other small bulbs. Dig out an area and plant a group to make an impact.

Growing Tips
Bulbs should be planted at a depth that is three times the width of the bulb. If the soil is heavy clay, bulbs should be planted half as deep as the standard recommendation. Water heavily after you plant and then don't water again.

Regional Advice and Care
Try to find a location that offers full sun in the winter and early spring but is shaded in summer. This will reduce the chance of pest and disease problems that bulbs are more susceptible to when the soil temperatures are too warm. Remove spent flowers so that plants put energy into making food for next years' flowers instead of seed. Some people use golf tees to keep track of where bulbs are planted when they are dormant and no foliage is visible. Voles (a type of meadow mouse) love to eat tulip bulbs. One way to protect the bulbs is to plant groups of five or six in cages made of one-half-inch mesh hardware cloth with a bottom and four sides and open at the top.

Companion Planting and Design
Combine species tulips like *Tulipa* 'Lady Jane' with other small bulbs like *Ipheion* 'Rolf Fiedler', which has fragrant lavender-blue flowers. Plant them in a deciduous woodland in combination with ferns and other shade-loving perennials.

Try These
Tulipa tarda grows 4 inches tall and has bright yellow flowers with a brownish base. *Tulipa clusiana*, also known as the lady tulip, grows 6 to 12 inches high. *Tulipa sylvestris* has a tendency to spread if planted in a woodsy area.

FERNS & GROUNDCOVERS

FOR GEORGIA

Mondo Grass 'Silver Mist'

Home-building booms have come and gone in Georgia. No matter the era, though, each home comes with a requisite landscape: trees, shrubs, turf, and maybe a spot by the mailbox for flowers.

Decades later, the landscapes around these homes have matured. The maples that were 15 feet tall are now 50 feet tall. The shrubs, planted from 1-gallon pots, are now large, rounded, and mature. Both have encroached on the area once given to the lawn. Shade has caused both grass and smaller shrubs to decline. Larger areas have become devoted to perennial and annual flowers.

If this sounds like your landscape, join the club! Homeowners have discovered that shade, not sun, is a threat to their original landscape. And for many, the love affair with the lawnmower has lost its bloom. The aroma of new-mown grass is still as sweet . . . but that perfume can be enjoyed from 1,000 square feet of turf just as easily as from 10,000 square feet!

Easy Math

One of the mathematical problems facing a professional or amateur landscaper is to determine how much area a site covers as measured in square feet. This is important, whether it be for a lawn or for a bed of seasonal annuals. You calculate the amount of fertilizer to apply or the number of plants to purchase based on the approximate size of a site. Here are some tips to help you solve the measuring problem:

1. You will need several soft drink cans, a pencil, and a piece of paper. Roughly sketch the lawn or flower bed on the paper and divide it into rectangles. Outdoors, put a can on the four corners of each rectangle.
2. Walk from can to can. Count your paces between each can and mark down the figure on your sketch. Assuming your pace is 2½ feet long, multiply the number of your steps by 2½ (or ⁵⁄₂) to find the length of each side in feet.

3. For each rectangle, multiply the length of one short side by the length of one long side. That will tell you the number of square feet in that individual rectangle.
4. Add all of the rectangles together to find the total square feet. Remember, you're not aiming for precision—just get "close!"

There are many more good choices for groundcovers than we have space for in this book. Here is an extensive list of plants for you to investigate and enjoy.

Plants for Shady Sites

Common Name	Botanical Name	Sun Needs
Bear's breeches	*Acanthus mollis*	Full sun, part sun
Begonia	*Begonia grandis*	Part sun, shade
Bleeding heart	*Dicentra* spp.	Part sun, shade
Blue phlox	*Phlox divaricata*	Full sun, part sun
Blue star creeper	*Amsonia tabernaemontana*	Full sun, part sun
Cardinal flower	*Lobelia cardinalis*	Part sun, shade
Carpet bugleweed	*Ajuga reptans*	Full sun, part sun
Cast-iron plant	*Aspidistra elatior*	Part sun, shade
Columbine	*Aquilegia canadensis*	Full sun, part sun
Confederate jasmine	*Trachelospermum jasminoides*	Full sun, part sun
Creeping fig	*Ficus pumila*	Full sun, part sun
Creeping phlox	*Phlox stolonifera*	Part sun
Foam flower	*Tiarella cordifolia*	Part sun, shade
Foxglove	*Digitalis purpurea*	Part sun
Golden pennywort	*Lysimachia nummularia 'Aurea'*	Full sun, part sun
Hellebore	*Helleborus × hybridus*	Part sun, shade
Hosta	*Hosta* spp.	Part sun, shade
Italian arum	*Arum italicum*	Part sun, shade
Japanese ardisia	*Ardisia japonica*	Part sun, shade
Japanese pachysandra	*Pachysandra terminalis*	Part sun, shade
Lily-of-the-valley	*Convallaria majalis*	Part sun
Lungwort	*Pulmonaria* spp.	Part sun, shade
Mazus	*Mazus reptans*	Full sun, part sun
Mexican petunia	*Ruellia brittoniana*	Full sun, part sun
River oats	*Chasmanthium latifolium*	Full sun, part sun
Sedge	*Carex morrowii*	Part sun, shade
Solomon's seal	*Polygonatum* spp.	Part sun, shade
Spiderwort	*Tradescantia virginiana*	Part sun, shade
Spotted dead nettle	*Lamium maculatum*	Part sun, shade
Strawberry geranium	*Saxifraga stolonifera*	Part sun, shade

Autumn Fern

Dryopteris erythrosora

Botanical Pronunciation
dry-OP-ter-iss er-rith-roh-SOR-uh

Other Name Japanese shield fern

Bloom Period and Seasonal Colors
Evergreen foliage in bronze-red turning to green
in summer

Mature Height × Spread
1 ½ to 2½ ft. × 2 to 3 ft.

How can a fern be compared to Rudolph the Red-Nosed Reindeer? To begin with, ferns are among our oldest-known plants. They have developed a special ability to grow and reproduce by rooting wherever conditions are favorable. Ferns do not produce flowers and seeds. They reproduce by spores that are formed on the backside of the fronds. Scattered by the wind, if a spore finds a bit of shade and damp soil, a new fern will appear. Autumn fern gets its scientific name from the red capsules, which contain spores, on the bottom of the fronds. The capsules are called sori. *Erythro* means red. So, it is easy to see why this member of the fern family could be called "Dryopteris the Red-Sori'ed Fern!"

When, Where, and How to Plant

The best time to plant a container-grown autumn fern is spring, but you can install it in the heat of midsummer if it is sited in shade and watered regularly. Find a spot that is in the shade or at least part shade, and dig a hole 2 feet wide and 10 inches deep. Mix in 1 cubic foot (or 5 good shovelfuls) of soil conditioner. Put the fern in the center, and water every other day for a week. Plant 18 inches apart for a massed effect. The rootball is not very large, so transplanting from another spot is easy. Move autumn fern in early to midspring while the fiddle-heads are still emerging.

Growing Tips

A shovelful of compost or fully decomposed manure spread around each clump before spring will supply all the nutrients the plant needs. Once the plant is established, no further care is necessary, other than watering occasionally during summer.

Regional Advice and Care

Autumn ferns can survive with no care if they are planted in partial to deep shade. Autumn fern remains evergreen during most winters. In March, remove any fronds that were damaged by cold.

Companion Planting and Design

One of this fern's most distinctive features is the bronze-red color of the new fronds in spring. This color remains for weeks, changing gradually to green as the frond matures. One of the best places to use this fern is in front of a large landscape stone or a low stone wall where the form and color change can be appreciated. Autumn fern, like other *Dryopteris* species, has sturdy fronds, so you can plant it among more delicate ferns such as lady fern or northern maidenhair fern. The fronds are often used in flower arrangements; you might choose to keep a couple in your landscape for that reason alone!

Try These

Lacy autumn fern, *Dryopteris erythrosora* var. *prolifica,* is a lacy-leafed form of autumn fern. The foliage is more finely cut than that of the common autumn fern.

Christmas Fern

Polystichum acrostichoides

Botanical Pronunciation
pol-IS-tick-um ak-ruh-stik-OH-id-eez

Other Name Dagger fern

Bloom Period and Seasonal Colors
Evergreen foliage

Mature Height × Spread
20 to 28 in. × 24 to 30 in.

Few ferns are completely evergreen, but this one comes close! Christmas fern's name reputedly comes from its use by American settlers in Christmas decorations. This fern is one of the few green plants in a wintry forest. Extreme cold will freeze the fronds back to just a flat green pancake on the ground, but spring will bring silvery green fiddleheads curling up and leaning limply backward from the fern roots. Look for the brown spores on the back of the fronds. You'll notice that some fronds do not have spores on them at all. These are the sterile fronds—they are typically smaller and more erect. The spore-carrying fertile fronds are larger and are able to bend enough to touch the ground at their tips.

When, Where, and How to Plant
Plant Christmas fern in fall or spring so it can establish itself before summer. Early summer is not a bad time for planting as long as new plants are watered occasionally for the first few weeks. Christmas fern will tolerate dry soil and heavy clay that would send other ferns to the compost heap. The clump will grow much larger in moist, loose soil, but a dry pine forest near a lake or stream will often have several seemingly happy clumps of this fern. Dig a hole 2 feet wide and 10 inches deep in a moderately shady spot. Mix in 1 cubic foot (or 5 good shovelfuls) of soil conditioner. Put the plant in the center of the hole, and water every other day for a week. Once established, water during dry spells. It is best transplanted in March.

Growing Tips
Make regular inspection visits during July and August to make sure Christmas fern has not wilted. If the summer is dry, pamper it with 2 gallons of water weekly. Throw some nutritious compost around each clump in early spring.

Regional Advice and Care
A large, mature clump of Christmas fern is composed of several smaller plants. A clump can be dug and carefully divided in spring for planting in other spots or for sharing with friends. This is one of the least fussy ferns you can plant or transplant. No pests affect it.

Companion Planting and Design
Several companion plants grow nicely in the shade with this fern. The bright red cardinal flower, *Lobelia cardinalis,* makes a good companion with the dark green foliage of Christmas fern. Toad lily, *Tricyrtis hirta,* has white blooms with purple spots on its arching stems in September. Partridge berry, *Mitchella repens,* makes a nice, noncompetitive groundcover nearby. Large clumps of Christmas fern can be divided several times and used as a groundcover under oak and dogwood trees.

Try These
Tassle fern, *Polystichum polyblepharum,* is also evergreen, though smaller than Christmas fern. Its fronds and stems are covered in brown fuzz.

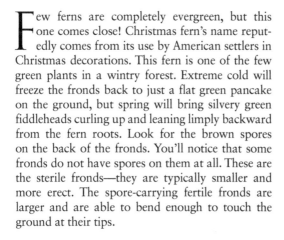

Cinnamon Fern

Osmunda cinnamomea

Botanical Pronunciation
os-MUN-duh sin-uh-MOH-mee-uh

Bloom Period and Seasonal Colors
Deciduous foliage; "cinnamon stick" fronds in late spring

Mature Height × Spread
2 to 5 ft. × 2 to 4 ft.

Cinnamon fern is an excellent plant for a moist site. It grows in practically every swamp in Georgia. The fronds are clustered around, and emerge from, a dark brown, wiry rootstock. This gives the appearance of a large, green badminton shuttlecock when viewed from above. *Osmunda* fiber, harvested from cinnamon fern bogs, was once commonly used as a potting medium for orchids. Fortunately for the ferns, fir bark has supplanted *Osmunda*. The most fascinating time for the fern is in late spring, when light brown "cinnamon sticks" grow above the greenery. These are the fertile fronds of a cinnamon fern; the spores tightly packed on them are scattered by the wind during the summer, perhaps to land on moist, fertile soil nearby.

When, Where, and How to Plant
Plant cinnamon fern in fall or early spring, after the fiddleheads have begun to unfurl. This is a fascinating process for young children, who can follow the daily progress of the young fern. Don't worry that the spot you've chosen for cinnamon fern is too wet! The drainage area of a backyard pond is ideal, though the ferns will also thrive in normal fern habitats—constantly moist, shady, very organic soil. Dig a hole 2 feet wide and 10 inches deep. Mix in 1 cubic foot (or 5 good shovelfuls) of compost or soil conditioner. Put the plant in the center of the hole and water regularly for a week. The rootball is not extensive, so transplanting from another spot is easy.

Growing Tips
A shovelful of compost or decomposed manure spread over the dead fronds in early spring will supply all the nutrients the plant needs. In partial to deep shade, cinnamon fern can survive with no care. If the summer is dry, pamper your fern with a deep watering each week.

Regional Advice and Care
Hail, heavy rain, pets, and errant children can wreak havoc with the brittle fronds. Place your fern out of heavy traffic. No other pests seem to bother it.

Companion Planting and Design
The "cinnamon stick" fertile fronds are striking in flower arrangements, but they disintegrate after a week. Use cinnamon fern as a background for variegated hosta. The contrast between vertical fronds and horizontal leaves is striking. The Atlanta Botanical Garden has several clumps of cinnamon fern near a wooden bridge in their woodland area. In April, the erect fertile fronds draw a crowd of admirers each day. *Lobelia cardinalis,* cardinal flower, and Louisiana iris are also good companions because they thrive in the same environment.

Try These
Osmunda regalis, royal fern, is a close cousin to cinnamon fern. Royal fern fronds do not look like a typical fern, resembling instead the branch of a locust tree. It is quite happy in the same damp spots as its botanical kin.

Creeping Raspberry

Rubus pentalobus

Botanical Pronunciation
ROO-bus pen-tuh-LOH-bus

Bloom Period and Seasonal Colors
Evergreen foliage turning to purple in winter; small summer blooms in white; yellow-orange fruit in fall

Mature Height × Spread
4 to 6 in. × indefinite

Creeping raspberry is a tough, fast-growing, evergreen groundcover that is related to blackberries and strawberries. It is not thorny at all. The dark green, grape-like foliage forms a dense mat and offers the gardener a distinctive choice of evergreen groundcover for a partially shady location. The plant is frost tolerant, but the leaves display purple and red tints during the winter. White flowers are seen in the summer followed by small, bright yellow-orange edible fruit in the fall. It is an excellent choice for weed suppression and great on slopes to prevent erosion. Other uses include planting in containers where the rich foliage can be used to drape over the sides. The woody nature of this plant also makes it a good choice for topiaries.

When, Where, and How to Plant
Plant either in spring or fall. Nursery availability may be more abundant in spring. Part sun or part shade is best, but the vine can tolerate full sun until early afternoon. Rich, well-drained soil is essential. Newly installed plants will not tolerate poorly draining or compacted soil. Established plants root wherever the branches touch the soil. Prepare the planting area by spading in 40 pounds of soil conditioner for every 10 to 15 square feet. Mix to a depth of 6 to 8 inches. Water weekly until established. For fast coverage, space plants 2 to 3 feet apart.

Growing Tips
Broadcast one pint of 10-10-10 fertilizer per 100 square feet in spring. Once established, the plant is fairly drought tolerant. Water deeply but only occasionally during periods of extreme drought or heat.

Regional Advice and Care
Pruning is sometimes needed to keep the plant within bounds. During periods of severe cold, some dieback may occur. Prune away dead sections before new growth occurs in the early spring. Creeping raspberry may be susceptible to bacterial or fungal leaf spots and root rot in poorly draining soil. Leaves from deciduous trees and shrubs should be raked or blown off. The vine seems to be deer resistant. If your patch grows too big, give rooted branches to your neighbors.

Companion Planting and Design
Evergreen groundcovers present somewhat of a dilemma. Their use practically precludes the use of other perennials in the same area. Creeping raspberry can be mixed with shade-tolerant shrubs, such as azaleas, camellias, and rhododendrons, but a great use is as a green cascade trailing over a low stone wall. Since this plant does not climb, it is a better groundcover choice than ivy. It is also attractive for use in containers or attached to a topiary.

Try These
Creeping raspberry is becoming more popular, if only because it is a carefree substitute for the ubiquitous—but invasive—English ivy. The cultivar 'Emerald Carpet' has rounded leaves and was introduced by the University of British Columbia.

Creeping Thyme

Thymus spp.

Botanical Pronunciation
TY-muss

Other Name Mother of thyme

Bloom Period and Seasonal Colors
Depending on cultivar, flowers range from white to pink or light lavender in June and July

Mature Height × Spread
1 to 6 inches × unlimited width

Several species of thyme make low-growing evergreen groundcovers. Some grow taller than others, so check plant labels for the mature size. Don't assume that all thymes are edible. Most of the creeping thymes have a disagreeable taste, unlike culinary types such as lemon thyme, *Thymus × citriodorus* or French thyme, *Thymus vulgaris*. Creeping thyme can be used in rock gardens and is especially attractive when growing between steppingstones or cascading over a retaining wall. When walking down a path planted with thyme you can appreciate its fragrant qualities as you brush against it. Thyme blooms in summer, perhaps more than once, with short white or pink flowers. If any family members are allergic to bee stings, keep in mind that thyme flowers are especially attractive to bees.

When, Where, and How to Plant
Thyme needs full sun, well-drained gritty soil, and good air circulation around it. Add new plants to your garden in spring, after the last frost. Once established, thyme is a hardy perennial that can tolerate most winter weather. Mix a quart of granite dust or gritty sand in the planting area before planting.

Growing Tips
Apply fertilizer at ½ strength at planting. One feeding per year with a time-release fertilizer product is all that's required afterward. A mulch of crushed limestone pebbles looks good and also counteracts the soil acidity that thyme hates. Plant spacing varies according to cultivar. Usually 6 to 12 inches between plants is adequate.

Regional Advice and Care
Given the right conditions, it's remarkable how tough thyme can be. Cold, wet soil will cause thyme's downfall. In mountainous north Georgia, plant near a brick or stone wall that retains the heat of the winter sun. Spider mites occasionally cause problems. The foliage will look slightly mottled in random areas of the plant. Light infestations can be controlled with a daily spray of water in the hot afternoon, so foliage dries quickly. If ants build mounds among the plants, treat with an appropriate garden insecticide. If your plants look ragged after winter, shear them to a couple of inches high in early spring.

Companion Planting and Design
Creeping thyme is an excellent companion in the garden or in containers with other herbs like rosemary and lavender. Use it in the landscape as an evergreen carpet below early spring bulbs, with roses, or in combination with perennials like hardy geranium and lamb's ear. Many kinds of beneficial insects are attracted to thyme flowers. These same beneficial insects provide a unique pest control when they feed on destructive aphids and mites that attack plants in the landscape.

Try These
'Elfin' is the most diminutive of the cultivars. It rarely grows more than an inch tall. Red creeping thyme, *T. praecox* 'Coccineus' has bright, reddish pink flowers that fade to light pink; it blooms throughout the summer.

Epimedium

Epimedium spp.

Botanical Pronunciation
ep-ih-MEE-dee-um

Other Name Barrenwort

Bloom Period and Seasonal Colors
Pink, yellow, orange, lavender, or white flowers
in spring

Mature Height × Spread
10 in. × unlimited (slowly spreading)

A challenge that many gardeners face is "dry shade." It's tough to get plants to grow under mature trees, where root competition is fierce. *Epimedium* offers a solution: not only does it grow, but it will thrive under trees where many other plants languish. Most spread by underground rhizomes. Medium green leaves with heart-shaped leaflets on wiry stems form attractive foliage mounds. This groundcover boasts unique, tiny spurred flowers that appear in early spring before or as new foliage appears. Some *Epimedium* are more persistently evergreen than others, but all will benefit from shearing in winter. This removes tattered foliage that would otherwise detract from the bright flowers. *Epimedium* may also be called "barrenwort."

When, Where, and How to Plant
Plant *Epimedium* in average to rich soil in part shade to full shade, where it is moist but well drained. Amend the soil with compost or peat humus, if needed for heavy clay or sandy areas. Mix a couple of teaspoons of general-purpose fertilizer into the planting hole. After planting, soak the soil; they won't need to be watered again. It likes occasional moisture but is drought tolerant once established. Once established it also does well in very dry shade. Plant it under trees and shrubs or use it to edge garden paths in the shade.

Growing Tips
Epimedium grows fine in just about any woodland type soil; scattering a shovelful of composted manure around it in spring will help it grow and flower better. Once growing, water is only needed after three weeks of hot drought. Make a calendar note to shear old leaves in early January. Warm February days may push out the flowers before you expect them.

Regional Advice and Care
Epimedium spreads underground by creeping rhizomes or from a central crown, depending on the variety. Space 15 inches apart. Plant so that all of the sprouts and rhizomes are covered by about ½ to 1 inch of soil, then mulch lightly. Follow a regular watering schedule during the first growing season to establish a deep, extensive root system. For a neat appearance, remove old foliage before new leaves emerge. Divide clumps every two to three years in early spring.

Companion Planting and Design
Plant barrenwort in combination with hellebores, hosta, ferns, and spring wildflowers. Use it as a groundcover under hydrangea, azalea, and other spring-blooming shrubs. Use it as a groundcover under an allée of trees.

Try These
Epimedium pinnatum ssp. *colchicum* grows to 16 inches tall and has handsome foliage that gets tints of red in the autumn. *Epimedium × versicolor* 'Sulphureum' spreads faster than most. *Epimedium grandiflorum* 'Rose Queen' has small crimson flowers in spring and dark bronze-purple foliage in fall. It can be used in containers.

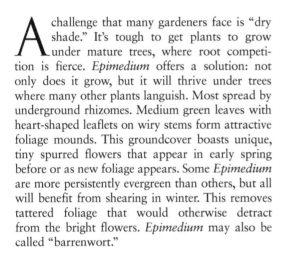

Green and Gold

Chrysogonum virginianum

Botanical Pronunciation
kris-OG-oh-num vir-jin-ee-AN-um

Bloom Period and Seasonal Colors
Evergreen to semi-evergreen foliage; spring blooms in yellow

Mature Height × Spread
6 to 10 in. × 24 in.

Green and gold is a great evergreen to semi-evergreen groundcover that grows in a wide variety of conditions. Native to the southeastern United States, this plant offers the environmentally conscious or native plant gardener a good alternative to other groundcovers. Green and gold makes a cheerful appearance just as the spring growing season is getting under way. The bright yellow flowers seem to glow on the dreariest of days. Don't be fooled by the plant's somewhat gentle appearance. It has no trouble holding its own in the garden. Although not considered to be aggressive, it will spread at a respectable pace if grown in a favorable environment. No matter—pot up surplus plants and give them to gardening friends, who will thank you for your generosity.

When, Where, and How to Plant
Green and gold is best planted in spring or fall, but it will tolerate planting almost anytime. Water summer plantings weekly until established. Green and gold prefers soil that is rich in humus, evenly moist, but well drained. It will grow in poor soils but will not spread as readily. In compacted clay soils, prepare the planting area with equal parts soil conditioner and native soil mixed to a depth of 4 to 6 inches. Partial shade is best, but it can tolerate full sun if adequate moisture is provided. For fast coverage, space container-grown plants 1 to 1½ feet apart.

Growing Tips
If the soil is prepared properly before planting, no supplemental fertilizer is needed. A spring dressing of compost around the edges of the plant should suffice. Once established, supplemental water is usually not necessary. Plants grown in full sun may need weekly watering during heat and drought.

Regional Advice and Care
No pruning is necessary, not even deadheading to remove faded blooms. Plants grow better if they're not buried by leaves dropped from trees and shrubs in the fall. Gently rake or blow to remove leaves when they accumulate. *Chrysogonum* does not seem to be bothered by any pests or disease.

Companion Planting and Design
Gardeners use this plant as a groundcover under shrubs and alongside perennials in partial shade. Because it is well behaved, it makes a good companion for hosta, fern, hellebores, foam flower, and bleeding heart. It also seems to do well planted between steppingstones in full sun. Any location that calls for a sturdy, yet unpretentious groundcover seems to be a good place for green and gold.

Try These
The cultivar 'Eco Lacquered Spider' was developed by Atlanta plantsman Don Jacobs. It is more "running" (some say invasive) in nature and almost spider-like in habit. The leaves also tend to have a shiny, lacquered appearance. Where space is limited, the species plant, which is a clumper, is the best choice.

Japanese Holly Fern

Cyrtomium falcatum

Botanical Pronunciation
sir-TOH-mee-um fal-KAY-tum

Other Name Rochford's holly fern

Bloom Period and Seasonal Colors
Glossy foliage; evergreen except after severe cold

Mature Height × Spread
1 to 2½ ft. × 2 to 3 ft.

Most gardeners know the typical shape of a fern and its lacy fronds. Their mental image is probably not of a plant that is "thick, tough, and leathery," but that is exactly the appearance of a holly fern. The fronds of a holly fern are held upright in a vase-like shape. It really looks nothing like a fern; the aboveground parts are more like holly leaves on a green stem. Like millions of holly shrubs, holly fern can indeed be used as a foundation plant beneath the shady windows of a home! The fronds of a holly fern are coarser than those of a typical fern, so it provides a contrast to plants that have a more refined look.

When, Where, and How to Plant
Plant or move holly ferns in early spring, just after the fiddleheads have unfurled. You can plant container-grown holly fern in midsummer if it is sited in shade and watered deeply once each week for a month. With regular watering, holly ferns can tolerate direct sun for a few hours each day. A holly fern will grow in heavy clay soil, but it prefers a rich, organic site. Mix equal parts soil conditioner and garden soil in the planting bed. They spread very slowly, so holly ferns can be planted 2 feet apart and not become crowded over time. Plant more closely for a massed effect.

Growing Tips
Spread a ½-inch layer of manure or compost over the bed each spring. Soak the soil around the fern weekly during dry weather, when no rain occurs for two weeks in summer. This is especially important if the plant is exposed to full sun for more than two hours.

Regional Advice and Care
In spring, remove any brown fronds that have died during the winter. Most plants will have at least a bit of damage, so many gardeners just shear off all of the foliage in early March. The leathery leaves make holly fern resistant to pests.

Companion Planting and Design
The coarse texture of holly fern's leaves contrasts well with azaleas and hosta. If planted around a backyard pond, the fern will provide winter greenery. As a foundation plant, a holly fern looks very attractive beneath a shady picture window or when edging a low deck. Lady fern (*Athyrium filix-femina*) and northern maidenhair fern (*Adiantum pedatum*) are good companions. Columbine (*Aquilegia canadensis*) provides colorful blooms and a delicate contrast. Holly fern makes an attractive border around large trees or shrub beds. Japanese holly fern tolerates low humidity and is sometimes used as a houseplant.

Try These
Cyrtomium fortunei, the hardiest of the species, offers foliage that is bold but not shiny.

Japanese Painted Fern

Athyrium niponicum 'Pictum'

Botanical Pronunciation
uh-THEE-ree-um nip-PON-ih-kum

Bloom Period and Seasonal Colors
Deciduous foliage; silvery white fronds with a maroon center stripe

Mature Height × Spread
12 to 20 in. × 18 to 30 in.

Gardeners who think of ferns as displaying only varying shades of green are invariably surprised when they see the color of Japanese painted fern. This fern, as it unfurls its silver fronds in spring, is an incomparable beauty! The central stem of each frond has a maroon stripe, while the rest of the blade is silvery white. Despite its delicate appearance, it's a vigorous grower. This fern looks its best when set among or in front of dark green plants. The light color almost demands that it be the center of a shady grouping. The silver color contrasts well with moss-covered, granite rocks or a large log rotting along the edge of your property. Native to Japan, the painted fern has become wildly popular.

When, Where, and How to Plant

The best time to plant a Japanese painted fern is in spring, so it can establish itself before summer. Choose a shady spot that you or others pass by each day. Japanese painted fern usually survives with no care if it is planted in partial to deep shade. Dig a hole 2 feet wide and 10 inches deep. Mix in 1 cubic foot (or 5 good shovelfuls) of soil conditioner. Put the fern in the center, and water every other day for a week. The rootball is not very large, so transplanting from another spot is not problematic.

Growing Tips

If the summer is dry, pamper your fern by soaking the soil to 6 inches deep weekly. Don't allow the soil around the fern to dry out during the summer. A shovelful of compost or decomposed manure spread over the clump each spring will supply all the nutrients the plant needs.

Regional Advice and Care

A mature Japanese painted fern will have several offspring around the base of the original plant. When the fronds have unfurled in early spring, dig and divide the fern. Carefully brush away the soil around the roots and tease the young plants away from the parent. Each group of fronds should have some roots and a few yet-to-emerge fiddleheads. Hot sun or dry soil cause the fronds to become tattered; move the plant to a better site. Though the fern appears delicate, deer seldom browse it.

Companion Planting and Design

The light color of this fern draws the eye directly to its home in the shade, particularly when set against a blue-green hosta or a deep green vinca groundcover. Use it as a border beneath the shade of rhododendrons or a group of camellias. Other good companions include foam flower (*Tiarella wherryi*) and hardy begonia (*Begonia grandis*).

Try These

Although the common Japanese painted fern has attractive light maroon stems, newly emerged 'Burgundy Lace' fronds are a stunning purple with silver stripes along the vein lines and tips.

Mondo Grass

Ophiopogon japonicus

Botanical Pronunciation
oh-fee-oh-POH-gon juh-PON-ih-kus

Bloom Period and Seasonal Colors
Evergreen foliage; summer blooms in lilac;
bright blue seeds in fall

Mature Height × Spread
3 to 10 in. × clumping

M ondo grass and *Liriope* are often confused for each other. Both are members of the lily family, and both have evergreen, grass-like leaves. The easiest way to tell them apart is by their size: Mondo grass leaves are rarely more than ¼ inch wide, while *Liriope* leaves are wider than ¼ inch. A clump of mondo grass is not as tall as *Liriope*. If you observe the two in July, the flowers are a dead giveaway—mondo grass flowers are hidden in the foliage, while *Liriope* flowers stand above the leaves. The seeds are bright blue. Because mondo grass resembles turf grass, and because it is so shade tolerant, it is often substituted for grass in dense shade. As turf, it spreads slowly but requires only one mowing per year.

When, Where, and How to Plant
Mondo grass is easy to plant or transplant anytime. It prefers partial to full shade, and tolerates any kind of soil. If you plant in the middle of summer, water it occasionally to help it through dry weather. Mondo grass grows best in thoroughly loosened soil. To divide, dig a clump and soak it for 30 minutes. Use a hose to wash most of the soil from the roots. Use your fingers and a pair of hand clippers to separate the clump into several divisions. A clump 12 inches in diameter might yield twenty divisions. Divide plants growing in nursery containers into four to six small clumps, and space them 4 inches apart.

Growing Tips
Mondo grass does not require fertilization unless you are trying to speed up its growth. If that is the case, sprinkle 1 pint of 10-10-10 fertilizer over 100 square feet of bed in March and June. Water three times, at weekly intervals, after planting. Further irrigation is not needed.

Regional Advice and Care
Mondo grass may be damaged by winter cold, but the injury is not as noticeable as it is on *Liriope*. To renew a planting, mow or cut it down to 2 inches in February. Avoid mowing during summer. No pests attack mondo grass.

Companion Planting and Design
This plant is very attractive when planted along the edges of a path or around individual steppingstones. It also makes a good filler plant among rocks that surround a backyard pond. Golden creeping Jenny, *Lysimachia nummularia* 'Aurea', provides a colorful chartreuse companion. Mondo grass is a good groundcover under a small Japanese maple. The shade of the maple won't faze the mondo grass, and in November its dark green color provides a contrast to the marvelous red foliage of the maple.

Try These
Dwarf mondo grass, *Ophiopogon japonicus* 'Nana', grows only 2 inches tall and spreads extremely slowly. Black mondo grass, *Ophiopogon planiscapus* 'Nigrescens', has leaves that are almost black. Variegated mondo grass, *Ophiopogon planiscapus* 'Variegata', can be very attractive but may be afflicted with leaf spot in full shade.

Monkey Grass

Liriope muscari

Botanical Pronunciation
lir-RYE-oh-pee mus-KAR-ee

Other Name Liriope

Bloom Period and Seasonal Colors
Evergreen foliage; June blooms in purple, blue, lilac-pink, lavender, white; blue-black berries in fall

Mature Height × Spread
8 to 16 in. × clumping

Most gardeners recognize *Liriope* in an instant. It is used to line sidewalks and to edge flower beds in landscapes from Dalton to Darien. It is also used as a groundcover in shady spots, and offers an alternative to invasive English ivy. *Liriope* produces blue-black berries, which—rumor to the contrary—are not poisonous. No one knows the origin of the common name monkey grass. One wag says it received the moniker because it made monkeys out of the plant experts who tried to trace the name. Adding to the confusion, *Liriope* has at least three pronunciations (do you know them all?). Nonetheless, *Liriope* is an ever-present denizen of Georgia landscapes, referred to by some garden designers as a "vernacular"—or standard—element.

When, Where, and How to Plant

Plant *Liriope* from a pot, or divide and transplant it just about anytime. It tolerates full sun to full shade and every kind of soil. For best growth, plant *Liriope* in thoroughly loosened soil. To divide, dig a clump and soak it in water for 30 minutes. Use a hose to wash most of the soil from the roots. With strong fingers, separate the clump into individual plants. A clump 16 inches in diameter might yield one hundred sprouts. Of course, you can always just slice the clump apart with a shovel!

Growing Tips

Unless you need to accelerate the growth of a bed of *Liriope*, it does not need fertilizer. For a new bed, apply 1 pint of 10-10-10 fertilizer per 100 square feet of area in March, June, and August. Water newly planted *Liriope* once a week for a month. It will never need watering again.

Regional Advice and Care

After a severe winter, *Liriope* will be brown and tattered in early spring. In February, raise your lawnmower to its highest mowing height and cut off all foliage. In a few weeks, dark green sprouts will appear. Rabbits may dine on the leaves in early spring, but plants recover quickly.

Companion Planting and Design

Liriope is commonly used to line walks and beds and is a good substitute for turfgrass in dense shade. *Liriope spicata,* creeping monkey grass, spreads rapidly. It has narrow, light-green leaves. This species can be a good groundcover for a slope, but take care to contain its invasive spread. One way to distinguish between *L. muscari* and *L. spicata* is that creeping monkey grass flowers are not as showy and are white or light lavender. Do not plant creeping *Liriope* where you can't easily control it.

Try These

Liriope is appreciated for its grape hyacinth-like flowers in June. The flowers might be blue ('Big Blue'), lilac-pink ('Christmas Tree'), lavender ('Majestic'), or white ('Monroe's White'). The leaves could also be variegated ('John Burch' and 'Silvery Sunproof').

Periwinkle

Vinca minor

Botanical Pronunciation
VIN-kuh MY-nor

Other Name Dwarf vinca

Bloom Period and Seasonal Colors
Evergreen vine; April blooms in white, blue

Mature Height × Spread
4 to 6 in. × vining to cover large areas

Sometimes the only way to know where a house once existed is by the green patch of periwinkle covering the earth near trees that once shaded a front porch. Periwinkle is a groundcover whose qualities are more appealing than those of English ivy. "Periwinkle-blue" flowers emerge over the ground-hugging leaves in April and then occur sporadically for the rest of the year. *Vinca* can tolerate heavy shade. Periwinkle would receive great praise if it were not so common and easy to grow. Though it can be invasive, it does not climb nearby shrubs. A twice-yearly plucking of wandering shoots is all that's needed to keep it within bounds. Its non-climbing character makes vinca much more appealing than English ivy for covering a shady slope.

When, Where, and How to Plant

Plant container-grown periwinkle in fall or spring. It might be easier and cheaper to transplant from a neighbor's yard if they have some to donate—gardeners almost always do! Periwinkle prefers moist, loose soil, but it tolerates heavy clay or sand. Site plants in soil softened to 8 inches deep. To save money, plant container-grown plants in heaviest shade and try rooting cuttings in brighter sunlight. Root 12-inch cuttings in place by making a 6-inch slit in the soil and burying half of each cutting, leaving 6 inches of stem and leaves exposed. Cuttings root best if planted May through June. Lightly water each day for a month.

Growing Tips

Periwinkle spreads faster if fertilized lightly during the growing season for a couple of years. Apply 1 pint of 10-10-10 fertilizer per 100 square feet in March, June, and August. After establishment, water weekly for a month. No supplemental water is needed thereafter. *Vinca major*, large leaf periwinkle, is much coarser and less tidy than *Vinca minor*. It can be used on isolated steep banks but is too invasive for most gardens.

Regional Advice and Care

Watch for weeds that may pop up while periwinkle is establishing; pull before they become rampant. If rainwater runs through your *Vinca* bed, plants in the wettest part may turn brown and die due to fungal and bacterial diseases. There is no cure other than correcting the flow of water. Rake fallen tree leaves from the vine regularly.

Companion Planting and Design

Periwinkle is often given jobs no other plant can handle. Dark, bare, clay banks or dense shade under a low-growing tree do not faze it. An excellent use is under deciduous trees over an area where early spring-flowering bulbs have been planted. After the bulbs bloom, their fading leaves will be hidden by vinca's foliage.

Try These

Vinca minor 'Alba' has white flowers. 'Sterling Silver' has green leaves edged in white. 'Illumination' leaves have a dark green edge with a solid yellow center.

Saint John's-Wort

Hypericum spp.

Botanical Pronunciation
hy-PER-ee-kum

Bloom Period and Seasonal Colors
Semievergreen to evergreen foliage; summer blooms in yellow

Mature Height × Spread
1 to 5 ft. × 5 ft. (varies by species)

Every Georgia garden has a spot for one (or two or three) Saint John's-wort plants. With more than four hundred species to choose from, you should have no trouble finding one that's right for your landscape. Plants originate from all over the world, including several species native to the southeastern United States. They range in size from groundcovers to low, sprawling shrubs. The Center for Applied Nursery Research in Deering, Georgia, is cross-breeding *Hypericum* species to produce superior varieties. Most *Hypericum* are semi-evergreen to evergreen, and all possess lively, bright yellow flowers. Used as medicinal plants by herbalists, they can often lift your mood with their mere presence in the landscape. Tough and undemanding, Saint John's-wort can be grown by gardeners with even the blackest thumbs.

When, Where, and How to Plant
Saint John's-wort is best planted in fall, but spring or summer plantings will probably thrive if adequate moisture is provided. Spring and summer plantings should be watered once weekly until established. Full sun is best, but Saint John's-wort tolerates partial shade provided the exposure is predominately afternoon sun. Saint John's-wort prefers well-drained soil that contains organic matter. It will grow in rocky or poor soils provided good drainage is present. In compacted clay soils, the planting area should be prepared with a 3-inch layer of compost or soil conditioner applied on the surface and then tilled into the soil to a depth of 6 to 8 inches. Coarse sand or even gravel can be used to further increase drainage in the planting area.

For best coverage, container-grown plants should be spaced 2 feet apart.

Growing Tips
Once established, little—if any—supplemental water is needed. Scatter 1 pound of 10-10-10 fertilizer per 100 square feet over beds (or 1 tablespoon per plant) in early spring.

Regional Advice and Care
Most varieties of Saint John's-wort bloom on the current season's growth. Some benefit from a hard pruning just before new growth in the spring. Removing old blooms is not necessary. When conditions are excessively moist, Saint John's-wort can be susceptible to disease, including leaf spots, rust, and anthracnose. If water is needed, irrigate in the morning so that leaves dry by afternoon.

Companion Planting and Design
The long, flowing branches of several Saint John's-wort species lend themselves to a nice display down a sunny hillside or draping over a retaining wall. *Hypericum* can be used for weed suppression and light erosion control. They also make nice companion plants with other summer-blooming trees and shrubs, such as crapemyrtle and lantana. Reserve a hot, dry location in full sun for these resilient plants.

Try These
Bushy Saint John's-wort (*H. densiflorum*) is native to the eastern United States. 'Creel's Gold' is a good selection. *Hypericum × moserianum* 'Tricolor' has arching stems than can cascade over a wall.

Southern Lady Fern

Athyrium filix-femina

Botanical Pronunciation
uh-THEE-ree-um FY-liks fem-in-uh

Other Name Lady fern

Bloom Period and Seasonal Colors
Deciduous foliage

Mature Height × Spread
1½ to 2 ft. × 2 to 3 ft.

Southern lady fern is one of the most common and reliable ferns for a shady Georgia garden. It spreads by rhizomes underground and is typically found in a colony of several dozen, if not hundreds, of fronds. It grows readily in moist woods and along streams. Given shade and moisture, it adapts easily to almost any situation. Although the coloration is subtle, from a distance the foliage of a grouping of lady ferns will appear to have a red-purple tint. The epithet of the species, *filix-femina,* means "fern-lady-like." The gently arching fronds, moving lazily on a humid Southern day, recall stereotypes of the languid gestures of a visitor to Tara. There are dozens of lady fern varieties, selected for their different frond shapes.

When, Where, and How to Plant
Lady ferns transplant easily in fall or early spring, just after the initial fiddleheads have unfurled. You can plant container-grown lady fern in midsummer, but water often enough to keep the soil moist, yet not soggy. Full to partial shade is important. An hour of scorching sunshine will burn the fronds. Where dogs or children play, fronds break easily, although new foliage will quickly cover the damage. Mix soil conditioner in a two-to-one ratio with garden soil in the planting bed. The planting hole should be 2 feet wide for a single plant, but if you intend it to spread, loosen the top 6 inches of soil throughout the planting bed. They spread slowly by underground roots, so lady ferns can be planted 16 inches apart and not become crowded over time.

Growing Tips
Spread a ½-inch layer of manure or compost over the bed each spring. If the summer is hot and dry, plan to water your ferns once each week, thoroughly soaking the soil around them to a depth of 6 inches.

Regional Advice and Care
The aboveground part of the plant will die back after the first frost. The stems are generally not noticeable after they turn brown, but you can remove them to tidy up a bed. Lady fern can have either red or green stalks in the same clump. Although this might appear to be a nutrient deficiency, it is a common occurrence. Slugs and snails enjoy the same habitat as lady fern, but rarely dine on its fronds.

Companion Planting and Design
Planted along the shady side of your house, lady ferns will grow just tall enough to hide the bare lower limbs of overgrown hollies. While most ferns send up fiddleheads only in spring, lady fern will, in a favorable spot, continue to produce them until late summer.

Try These
Athyrium 'Ghost', a hybrid between Japanese painted fern and Southern lady fern, has silvery gray-green foliage and a maroon midrib.

ORNAMENTAL GRASSES

FOR GEORGIA

Like Rodney Dangerfield, ornamental grasses sometimes get little respect in the landscape. Despite their tough character and attractive foliage, few gardeners go to a nursery looking for an ornamental grass. Most often it seems that ornamental grasses are bought to match the grass already in place at a newly purchased house . . . or because someone wants fluffy plumes or tan seedheads to use in flower arrangements . . . or because a landscape spot is so hot and inhospitable that only a grass can survive there. Yet, there is something to be said for the yearly senescence and renewal that ornamental grasses undergo. Perhaps perennial flowers do the same, but they are rarely as big as grasses. Most ornamental grasses in Georgia require severe winter pruning.

Tips for Success with Ornamental Grasses

Planting an ornamental grass is only slightly different from planting a shrub. The requirement to loosen soil in the planting area to three to six times the width of the rootball still applies. However, grasses are best planted in spring, not in fall as with woody plants. Exposing

Annual purple fountain grass 'Rubrum'

a container-grown ornamental grass to the vagaries of winter weather is a chancy proposition in all but the warmest parts of the state.

The rootball of a container-grown grass is very fibrous. It is likely that the roots have formed a solid mass inside the plastic pot in which it grew. Use scissors or a sharp knife to slice the rootball at four equidistant spots, working from the bottom up to the halfway point. When you plant, splay these sections out in the planting hole so that the roots are forced to grow outward. Newly planted grasses need lots of water after planting (approximately 5 gallons) in order to settle the soil and soak the rootball. Though they are drought tolerant once established, plan to give your plant 5 gallons of water per week for the first month. Irrigation will not be needed thereafter.

Depending on whether they are warm- or cool-season grasses, vigorous growth occurs from mid-spring to midsummer. In the absence of specific directions, give new plants ⅛ cup of 10-10-10 fertilizer in April and the same amount in early June and late August. Give mature clumps ½ cup of 10-10-10 in May only. Truthfully, most gardeners use the "couple of handfuls of fertilizer whenever I think of it" method to feed these plants.

More Great Choices

There was only room to include eight favorite and popular grasses in this book, but there are many more to consider. Here are several for you to investigate.

Common Name	Botanical Name	Color and Height
Black sedge	*Carex nigra*	blue foliage, black stems; 24 inches
Blue fescue	*Festuca glauca* 'Elijah Blue'	silver blue; 6 to 10 inches
Blue lyme grass	*Leymus arenarius*	blue leaves; 24 to 36 inches
Feather grass	*Nasella tenuissima*	pink to light red feathery plumes; 12 to 24 inches
Golden sedge	*Carex elata* 'Bowles Golden'	gold foliage; dark green margin; 24 to 36 inches
Oriental fountain grass	*Pennisetum orientale* 'Tall Tales'	pearl-colored plumes; 8 to 16 inches
Reed canary grass	*Phalaris arundinacea*	white-edged green leaves; 24 to 48 inches
Variegated sedge	*Carex morrowii* 'Ice Dance'	white-edged foliage; 12 to 24 inches

Time for a Little Respect

It is unfortunate that grasses are not appreciated for their own unique contributions to a landscape. Their stems bring a stronger vertical form than any other plant. Their seedheads are unlike any flower, yet they are attractive in their own right. Their foliage can range from green to purple, solid to variegated, and stiff to weeping. Try some in your garden, and help ornamental grasses "get a little respect."

Feather Reed Grass

Calamagrostis spp.

Botanical Pronunciation
ka-la-mo-GROSS-tis

Bloom Period and Seasonal Colors
June blooms in pink to light red, with color varying by species

Mature Height × Spread
4 ft. × 4 to 5 ft.

Planted as a group, the flower spikes of feather reed grass form an ocean of pinkish tan that bends and undulates with every breeze of summer. The light red, upright flower spikes emerge above the green foliage in early June. Spikes gradually dry to a golden, then buff color by autumn. Two species of feather reed grass are useful in Georgia landscapes. *Calamagrostis × acutiflora* is sun loving; it has few blooms in the shade. In southern Georgia, it is semievergreen, but from Atlanta northward, the foliage is yellow in October, then an attractive brown for the rest of the season. *C. brachytricha* blooms in late summer and tolerates considerable shade. The flowers are denser than those of *C. × acutiflora*. The foliage of both turns brown in winter.

When, Where, and How to Plant
Plant feather reed grass in spring, when days are warm and nights are cool, so that it establishes a good root system before summer. Plant *Calamagrostis × acutiflora* in full sun, preferably where it is breezy. While *C. brachytricha* can grow in shade, it will certainly do better in full sun. Both prefer loamy soil. Dig a hole 12 inches deep and three times as wide as the rootball. Spread the roots by hand before placing them in the hole. Tamp down the soil around the roots and water thoroughly.

Growing Tips
Fertilize feather reed grass late in spring, when leaves begin to grow vigorously. Give new plants ⅛ cup of 10-10-10 fertilizer in May and again in late June and late August. Give mature clumps ¼ cup of 10-10-10 in May only. Water weekly for a month after planting. Feather reed grass prefers a moist root system, even in full sun; so be ready to water if summer rains do not appear weekly.

Regional Advice and Care
Cut back to 6 inches tall in January or February. Divide established clumps in March after it has been cut back. Divide a large clump into three or four separate divisions with a shovel. As with other ornamental grasses, feather reed grass has few problems. Beetles may chew briefly on the edges of grass blades, but no control is necessary.

Companion Planting and Design
Calamagrostis brachytricha is an asset to woodland plantings and areas too shady for other grasses. Try placing it in front of a camellia or an evergreen hedge of wax myrtle. In a perennial flower bed, put *C. × acutiflora* toward the back with *Sedum* 'Autumn Joy' or fall aster, for late-season color. 'Sunny Border Blue' veronica would look nice in front.

Try These
'Karl Foerster' reed grass was named a Perennial Plant of the Year—and for good reason. 'Avalanche' has a silver streak down the center of each blade. Mexican feather grass, *Nasella tenuissima* 'Pony Tails' forms airy clumps 12 to 24 inches tall.

Fountain Grass

Pennisetum spp.

Botanical Pronunciation
pen-ih-SEE-tum

Bloom Period and Seasonal Colors
Summer to fall seedheads in tan or red, colorful foliage

Mature Height × Spread
2 to 5 ft. × 2 ft.

The purple foliage and the tan bottlebrush seedheads of purple fountain grass (*Pennisetum setaceum* 'Rubrum') give it just the right texture and height to beautify many garden spots without taking up a lot of room. The base is very narrow, and only in late summer will the blades arch outward and shade neighboring plants. It became an overnight sensation during and after the 1996 Olympics because it was the prominent center in hundreds of color bowls scattered throughout Atlanta. Unfortunately, this striking example of fountain grass is an annual in the upper three-fourths of Georgia. It is killed at temperatures below 20°F, but it is readily available at nurseries each spring. Species of perennial fountain grass, with varying characteristics, are noted here.

When, Where, and How to Plant
Plant *Pennisetum* in full sun in spring, when days are warm and nights are cool, so that it establishes before summer. Fountain grass prefers moist, well-drained soil, but it will tolerate a wide range of soil types. Dig a hole three times as wide as the root system; no need to mix in soil amendments. Tamp down the soil around the roots and water thoroughly.

Growing Tips
Fertilize late in spring, when leaves have begun to grow vigorously. Give new plants ⅛ cup of 10-10-10 fertilizer in May, again in late June, and in late August. Give mature clumps ¼ cup of 10-10-10 in May only. Watering is rarely needed, except during establishment.

Regional Advice and Care
Remove purple fountain grass (an annual) from beds in November. Shear the perennial *Pennisetum alopecuroides* to 3 inches in February. Divide mature clumps every three years in spring after the green blades have emerged. Seedlings of *P. alopecuroides* show themselves, in desired as well as undesired places by May. Pull them as weeds or transplant them to new spots.

Companion Planting and Design
Fountain grass is attractive in mass plantings or as a small clump. It is a good choice for a mixed perennial flowerbed or edging a building. Because the grass does well without watering, similarly low-maintenance plants make good companions. The purple foliage of *Pennisetum setaceum* 'Rubrum' contrasts well with yellow flowers. Plant in front of perennial sunflower (*Helianthus atrorubens*) or behind 'New Gold' lantana. Try *P. alopecuroides* as a groundcover for a slope or in a center island with a dogwood or small maple in the center.

Try These
Pennisetum 'Fireworks' has hot pink blades with a purple midvein. Black fountain grass, *Pennisetum alopecuroides* 'Moudry', has exceptionally dark seedheads. 'Hameln' grows to 2 feet tall. 'Burgundy Giant' is not hardy in the northern half of the state, but it is perennial in southern Georgia. It's very large, possibly to 10 feet tall with 3-foot seed spikes. 'Little Bunny' is the smallest of the dwarf fountain grasses. It is particularly useful in a rock garden.

Maiden Grass

Miscanthus sinensis

Botanical Pronunciation
miss-KANTH-us sy-NEN-sis

Other Name Eulalia grass

Bloom Period and Seasonal Colors
August seedheads in tan to pink

Mature Height × Spread
4 to 7 ft. × 8 ft.

Maiden grass is among the showiest of ornamental grasses. A small clump can grow to 6 feet high by late summer. The top of a clump is wider than the bottom. It may be 8 feet wide, emerging from a 24-inch diameter base. The stiff, arching leaves extend on all sides. Various cultivars have foliage variegations that contrast with the green leaf tissue. The beauty of the leaves in summer is supplanted by the magnificent pink to tan seedheads appearing in late August. Winter brings another period of beauty when leaves turn buff brown and the seedheads fade to silver. The plant surfaces seem to attract frost. Few things are more eye-catching than a frosted clump of maiden grass in front of a tall evergreen hedge.

When, Where, and How to Plant
Plant in spring so that strong roots establish before summer's heat. If planted in summer, water occasionally when temperatures are above 95°F. Dig a hole in full sun three times as wide as the container. Do not plant deeper than the surrounding soil; no need to mix in soil amendments. Tamp down the soil around the roots and water thoroughly.

Growing Tips
Give new plants ¼ cup of 10-10-10 fertilizer in May, late June, and late August. Give mature clumps ½ cup of 10-10-10 fertilizer in May. Except at establishment, watering is rarely needed.

Regional Advice and Care
By spring, the leaves and stems will be broken and tattered. Cut off all foliage to a height of 6 to 8 inches. When the center of a mature clump becomes open or dead, divide it in spring when new blades reach 12 inches tall. Dig up the whole rootball, then plunge a sharp shovel through the center. Each half can then be halved again. Plant one section in the original hole, and look for other places in your landscape or neighborhood where the grass can flourish. Never divide in fall. No pests affect maiden grass, but it may become a pest itself in northern Georgia. Pull up unwanted seedlings religiously each spring. If water stands around the clump after rain, root rot will ensue.

Companion Planting and Design
Maiden grass's texture is unlike any other plant, making it a striking accent next to tall, bold plants, such as black-eyed Susan or purple coneflower. Use it as a background for a perennial flower border, as a specimen plant in a lawn, or even as a hedge between properties.

Try These
'Zebrinus' is striking, with bands of yellow variegation that cut across the blade every 6 inches from the base to the tip. 'Strictus' is similar but has a rigid, upright habit and stiff, pointed leaf blades. 'Cabaret' and 'Morning Light' are excellent cultivars. 'Gracillimus' has a silver-colored midleaf vein. 'Little Zebra' grows only 3 to 4 feet high.

Muhly Grass

Muhlenbergia capillaris

Botanical Pronunciation
mew-len-BERG-gee-uh kap-ill-AIR-iss

Other Name Sweetgrass

Bloom Period and Seasonal Colors
Deciduous foliage; early fall seedheads in pink
to purple

Mature Height × Spread
3 ft. × 3 ft.

Observant drivers traveling along Interstate 16 between Macon and Savannah early in the fall can see ample reason to plant muhly grass. Look for pink-purple feathery plumes swaying in the breeze along the sides and in the median of the road. When massed, muhly grass is among the showiest of any ornamental grass. A rugged native, muhly grass grows naturally in the sandy soils of the southern coastal plain, but this tough little grass is hardy throughout the entire state. Like most ornamental grasses, muhly grass is drought tolerant and grows with little to no care. In the late summer, it sends up stalks (actually seedheads), which expand into a pinkish purple spray. After frost, the entire grass takes on a lovely golden appearance.

When, Where, and How to Plant
Muhly grass is a warm-season grass and is best planted in spring. New growth appears when temperatures stay reliably in the mid-60s. Full sun is important for success. Muhly grass tolerates a wide range of soil conditions. It grows slowly and compactly in drier soils and becomes lush and large in moister soils. For best growth, amend compacted areas with equal parts of native soil, coarse sand, and soil conditioner to a depth of 4 to 6 inches. Muhly grass tolerates wind and salt, which makes it a fine choice for coastal regions.

Growing Tips
Water weekly the first year. Once established, muhly grass is very drought tolerant and does not need supplemental water. Excessive fertilizer may produce lush growth and taller seedheads, which flop over later in the season. A 2- to 3-inch layer of organic mulch applied annually in spring will supply all of its nutritional needs. Plants can be divided every few years in spring to increase their number.

Regional Advice and Care
Shear to a height of 4 to 5 inches in late winter or early spring, just before the new growth begins. Muhly grass is generally free from pests and disease.

Companion Planting and Design
Muhly grass has a soft texture, making it a fine companion for late-season perennials—such as goldenrod or coneflower—in an informal or cottage-style garden. The color seems showier when plants are massed in groups of three or more. The seedheads make fine cuttings for arrangements, either when cut fresh with color in the fall or after frost when they are golden. It is also an important grass for restoration of natural areas south of the Fall Line and is outstanding along roadsides where breezes make it dance.

Try These
Lindheimer's muhly grass, *Muhlenbergia lindheimeri*, has bluish gray foliage. A clump is 2 to 4 feet wide and 1 to 2 feet tall. The 5-foot-tall flowering spikes stand well above the foliage. The seed heads of 'White Cloud' stand out against an evergreen background in the fall.

Northern Sea Oats

Chasmanthium latifolium

Botanical Pronunciation
chas-MAN-thee-um lat-ee-FOH-lee-um

Bloom Period and Seasonal Colors
Deciduous foliage; late summer
showy seedheads

Mature Height × Spread
3 ft. × 2 ft.

Northern sea oats remind some gardeners of the *Star Trek* episode "The Trouble with Tribbles." It is a wonderful, native, shade-tolerant ornamental grass with decorative oat-like seedheads. Of course, each one of the seeds is guaranteed to germinate (like Tribbles) at the base of the mother plant. If left unchecked, an original clump becomes an expanding grove. However, this grass (with apologies to *Star Trek*) will grow where no grass has grown before. Even in dense shade, it has a showy texture and habit. Frost or light snow covering seedheads is gorgeous! Most gardeners don't worry about its rabbit-like reproductive habits. They simply remove the seedheads before ripening or give the seedlings to friends along with a gentle warning about its tendency to propagate.

When, Where, and How to Plant
Northern sea oats is best planted in spring. In reality, planting can be done almost anytime if the clump is watered deeply during summer heat. It prefers a moist soil that is rich in organic matter. Do not plant the crown below soil level, to avoid root rot. Full sun is best for fuller growth and seedhead production, but it will grow almost equally well in partial to full shade.

Growing Tips
Once established, northern sea oats is drought-tolerant. Seed production will be slowed down during periods of very dry weather. Fertilizer is not needed. A 2- to 3-inch layer of mulch will provide sufficient nutrients.

Regional Advice and Care
Prune to a height of 3 to 4 inches in early spring before new growth begins. Remove seedheads in late summer before ripening to reduce the spread of this plant. Plants grow easily from seed, and some gardeners consider it invasive. Like most ornamental grasses, northern sea oats is usually free from pests and disease. Divide mature clumps in spring.

Companion Planting and Design
With a slightly coarser appearance than muhly grass, northern sea oats makes a great companion for plants with a rough or fine texture. This is one of the few ornamental grasses that will grow well in shade. Gardeners have had as much success planting it among ferns and hostas as they have among sun-loving perennials, such as lamb's ears and cannas. After frost, blades and seedheads become tan. They make lovely additions to dried flower arrangements. Left in the garden, this tan- to straw-color adds good winter interest. The stiff blades also stand up better to heavy rain, snow, or ice, which can beat down the foliage of softer ornamental grasses.

Try These
'River Mist' was discovered by our friends at ItSaul Plants. The upright green stalks produce leaves heavily striped with white. As the flower stalks expand in early summer, the variegation follows the new growth into the developing seed heads. Northern sea oats shows promise in the fight against Japanese stilt grass (*Microstegium vimineum*), an exotic invasive plant, in moist, shady areas.

Pampas Grass

Cortaderia selloana

Botanical Pronunciation
kor-tuh-DEER-ee-uh sel-lo-AH-nuh

Bloom Period and Seasonal Colors
September blooms in silvery white

Mature Height × Spread
8 to 10 ft. × 6 to 8 ft.

Pampas grass is usually the first ornamental grass gardeners try. It is ranked among the most durable landscape plants. It has few pest problems, grows well in a wide range of soils, and requires little fertilizer—making it perfect for someone who hates yard work! It can be a pest, so pull out any unwanted seedlings as they appear. It does require early spring care; without it, pampas grass will become just a big, messy haystack. This grass is hardy in all but extreme northern Georgia. The silvery white plumes look like cotton candy on a stick. There is considerable variation among plants in size and shape of plumes. If you want large ones, purchase plants when they are blooming so that you can see what you get.

When, Where, and How to Plant
Plant pampas grass in spring, when days are warm and nights are cool, so it can establish before summer. Pampas grass grows and flowers best in full sun and in loose, loamy soil. Dig a hole three times as wide as the root system of the container in which the plant is growing. Spread the roots a little by hand before placing them in the hole. Tamp down the soil around roots and water thoroughly.

Growing Tips
Fertilize a new clump with ½ cup of 10-10-10 in March, May, and September. A mature clump needs only 2 pounds of 10-10-10 fertilizer in March. In sandy soil, watering is necessary for the first year, but rarely thereafter.

Regional Advice and Care
Pampas grass requires yearly pruning in February, after you enjoy the plumes and dry foliage all winter. The grass blades are sharp, so wear leather gloves. Tie a rope very tightly around the clump about 4 feet from the ground. Use a carpenter's saw, chainsaw, or power weed trimmer to remove everything above 12 inches high. Divide old pampas grass clumps in spring after it has been sheared. A large clump can be divided into 6 or 8 separate plants with a shovel. This grass is pest and disease free.

Companion Planting and Design
Pampas grass makes an excellent screen plant at the edge of a lawn, but it should not be planted at the end of a driveway where it can obscure vision. It tolerates salt spray and is ideal for coastal landscapes. The grass blades have very coarse edges, so don't put a clump in a spot you pass frequently. Pampas grass makes a dramatic sight when the sun can shine through the foliage and plumes.

Try These
Cortaderia selloana 'Rosea' has rosy pink plumes. 'Pumila' is a dwarf form, barely reaching 5 feet. 'Silver Stripe' grows to 5 feet and has a white stripe along the edge of each blade. 'Gold Band' has—as one might imagine—a gold stripe along each blade. This cultivar does not set seed and is considered non-invasive.

Striped Sweet Flag

Acorus gramineus 'Variegatus'

Botanical Pronunciation
AK-or-us gram-IN-ee-us

Other Name Variegated sweet flag

Bloom Period and Seasonal Colors
Semievergreen, variegated foliage; summer blooms are insignficant

Mature Height × Spread
3 to 5 ft. × 2 to 3 ft.

If you have a pond, bog, or a wet landscape area, this ornamental grass is for you. Actually, sweet flag is not really a grass, but is more closely related to Jack-in-the-pulpit and calla lily. Sweet flag is cold-hardy throughout most of the United States. Its variegated foliage is a great addition to the edge of a pond, marsh, bog, or other low area, where it spreads by belowground rhizomes—and it is almost equally at home in average garden soil. This iris-mimic is a great addition to brighten up areas in need of color and vertical accents. Most ornamental grasses have showy seedheads, but not sweet flag. The insignificant flowers occur deep in the leaves, but heck, the foliage lasts a lot longer than any flower!

When, Where, and How to Plant

Plant sweet flag in spring at the edge of a pond or bog in a container with a soil mix recommended for water-loving plants. You can also plant it directly in humus-rich, moist garden soil. When grown as an aquatic plant, place in water no deeper than 9 inches. Sweet flag prefers full sun to partial shade, whether in aquatic or garden environments.

Growing Tips

Because sweet flag grows naturally in a wet environment, it makes sense to duplicate these conditions in the garden. In-ground plants may need supplemental water during dry periods. Watch for drooping leaves, and water deeply once a week during drought. Fertilize garden plants with a slow-release fertilizer in spring as new growth emerges.

Regional Advice and Care

In ponds, remove dead foliage after the first frost to prevent the buildup of a gooey muck on the pond bottom. If uncontained in a pond or bog, sweet flag can become invasive. Thin periodically to keep it in check. Divide garden plants in early spring as new foliage appears. Plants growing in a container should be repotted and divided, if necessary, every three to four years. Sweet flag occasionally suffers from fungal leaf spots and rust, but these are rarely serious.

Companion Planting and Design

Sweet flag adds a vertical accent to ponds or wet areas in gardens; it further highlights these areas with its variegated, aromatic foliage. It makes a wonderful companion plant at the water's edge next to water lilies or dwarf papyrus. Plant some next to pickerel weed, *Pontederia cordata*, to contrast with its bold foliage and bright blue flowers. In the garden, sweet flag can take up residence with calla or canna lily. It also accents the bold foliage of *Ligularia* or the bright blooms of cardinal flower.

Try These

For gardeners with dry soil wanting to have a similar plant, try the variegated iris, *Iris pallida* 'Variegata'. Those with moist soil could also try *Acorus gramineus* 'Ogon', *Carex morrowii* 'Ice Dance', or *Juncus effusus* 'Big Twister'.

Switch Grass

Panicum virgatum

Botanical Pronunciation
PAN-ih-kum vir-GA-tum

Other Name Panic grass

Bloom Period and Seasonal Colors
Deciduous foliage with showy summer and fall color; colorful fall seedheads

Mature Height × Spread
3 to 6 ft. × 3 ft.

Before the arrival of Europeans to North America, vast areas of prairie in the central United States and open areas westward from the Atlantic Ocean were home to switch grass. Along with the native bluestems, switch grass comprised a major component of prairies and savannahs. It wasn't until after we had been exposed to non-native grasses, such as maiden grass and pampas grass, that horticulturists and gardeners began to appreciate the beauty of our native grasses. As a result, this grass is becoming more widely available, with showy cultivars now on the market. New and improved cultivars will also be headed for nurseries soon. A somewhat tall clumping grass, switch grass lends itself to prairie restorations, meadows, savannahs, informal gardens, and cottage-style gardens.

When, Where, and How to Plant
Full sun is much preferred, but part sun is tolerated. Switch grass does best when planted in spring in sandy, loamy soil that is rich in organic matter. It prefers a neutral soil pH, so add a tablespoon of garden lime to the site before installing each plant. Switch grass performs poorly in heavy soils with slow drainage. Amend compacted soils with equal parts of soil conditioner and coarse sand to a depth of 12 inches. Roots grow deeply in sandy soil. Extensive stands are slow to establish because this grass has a specific relationship with particular soil fungi. This is not usually a problem in amended soil.

Growing Tips
Switch grass is drought tolerant once established and resents overwatering. Little fertilizer is needed once established, especially if old foliage is removed and allowed to decay as mulch. Excessive amounts of fertilizer will actually inhibit growth.

Regional Advice and Care
In a perfect world, areas of switch grass would be burned every three to five years. However, since most neighbors and fire departments frown upon such practices, an annual late-winter mowing or hand pruning will have to suffice. Prune no lower than 8 inches. Divide clumps in early spring. When sited properly, few pests affect it.

Companion Planting and Design
Switch grass is an essential part of a prairie restoration or wildflower meadow. However, its looks alone warrant switch grass a place in a garden capable of accommodating a tall ornamental grass. Switch grass provides great foliage color in hues of purple. Its broad, stiff seedheads of purple-green are attractive in late summer. In the fall, the foliage changes to yellow and then to light brown in winter. The leaves rustle soothingly in a gentle breeze. Plant with Joe Pye weed and swamp sunflower (*Helianthus angustifolius*).

Try These
This native plant is a nice replacement for maiden grass. 'Shenandoah' makes a neat 3-foot-tall clump with deep purple fall foliage. 'Heavy Metal' has stiff, metallic blue leaves that turn bright yellow in fall.

PERENNIALS
FOR GEORGIA

Hellebores blooming underneath a pine tree.

Unlike annuals, which must be replaced each season, most perennials will grow and bloom in the same spot year after year. With a minimum of care, perennials may outlive the gardeners who plant them. Perennials produce fleshy stems that die down each winter, but their roots stay alive and send up new growth in the spring. In some parts of Georgia, certain perennials will remain evergreen year-round. There are even perennials, such as hellebore, whose flowers brave the cold days of winter.

Another advantage of growing perennials over annuals is that many are easy to divide and transplant, providing you with additional plants in very little time. A wealth of perennials thrives in Georgia gardens, including types for sun and shade and many that have striking foliage or dramatic flowers. You're sure to find many that are just right for your garden.

When a book says that a plant is hardy from zones 4 to 8, what it often doesn't say is whether or not the plant will tolerate hot, humid summers like those we experience in Georgia. Plants like the much-loved delphiniums are perennials in the North, but they rarely survive our summers and are best treated like annuals here. In recent years, a greater variety of perennials have become available that not only tolerate, but thrive in our hot, humid weather.

The Key to Success Is the Soil

The key to growing successful perennials is having the right soil for the right plant. The best insurance for growing healthy perennials is to begin with a soil that has been amended with organic matter and that holds moisture, but is also well drained. Once established, perennials should not need to be fertilized regularly, especially if the soil is topdressed with an organic mulch in spring and fall. Drainage is important; soil that stays wet in winter will quickly lead to the demise of most perennials.

Preparing the soil for planting can be done in advance. Before you begin to work in the soil, scoop up a handful and squeeze it. If it crumbles easily, the soil is dry enough to work. Wet soils with a high percentage of clay can turn into large impervious clods. Rototill or hand dig to a depth of 12 inches, adding soil amendments as you go. The materials you add to the soil will be determined by the type of soil that you have. Heavy clay soils need lots of organic matter to improve drainage, add microbes, and improve overall soil structure. Sandy soils might need clay added as well as some organic matter. If the soil is hard clay, raised beds are an option. Fill the bed with soil you create, using a mixture of one-third organic matter, one-third coarse sand, and one-third topsoil.

Dividing Perennials

After three or four years perennial plants may get too large for their space; this is a good time to divide them. Before you begin, make sure you have all your tools ready, a source of water, and a spot picked out for the transplants. Timing is important: some perennials need to be divided in spring and others in fall.

When you divide plants, make sure the divisions are healthy, they have roots and shoots, and they don't dry out before you replant them. Trim back foliage to help compensate for root loss. Provide temporary shade to help transplants adjust more quickly to their new homes.

Staking

The best time to stake is before plants begin to flop over. Stake as soon as flower buds begin to show color. There are numerous types of stakes, including single stakes, a series of linked stakes for multistemmed plants, bamboo stakes and twiggy branches from trees. You can also plant closely so that plants support one another.

Crape myrtle, foxglove, and hosta

Arkansas Blue Star

Amsonia hubrichtii

Botanical Pronunciation
am-SOE-nee-uh HEW-brikt-ee-eye

Bloom Period and Seasonal Colors
Late spring blooms in pale sky-blue; fall foliage is golden yellow, orange

Mature Height × Spread
2½ to 3 ft. × 3 ft.

Because blooms are often here today and gone tomorrow, it is important to consider foliage when choosing perennials for our Georgia gardens. One perennial gem is the little-known Arkansas blue star, which offers delicate, star-shaped blue flowers in late spring and handsome foliage throughout the growing season. Its needle-like leaves whorl around the stem; the effect is like that of a small willow. In fall, these delicate leaves turn golden yellow, sometimes orange. A slightly acidic, moist, well-drained soil is ideal in full sun or part shade, but this *Amsonia* is a tough, carefree sort that can adapt well to a wide range of growing conditions. In just a few years, this perennial will form large clumps that grow as wide as they do high.

When, Where, and How to Plant
Plant container-grown Arkansas blue star in early spring or fall. It can also be grown from seed, divisions, or cuttings taken in spring. Site it in full sun or light shade. If planted in too much shade, the clumps will be open and floppy. Moderately fertile soil that is evenly moist is ideal, but average soil is fine. If you plant young divisions, take them in early spring or fall. Plant them as soon as you divide them and water well. If you buy a container-grown plant, dig a hole two to three times wider than its container, and plant blue star at a depth equal to what it was in the container.

Growing Tips
Water during periods of drought when there is no rain for two weeks. Soak the soil repeatedly for several minutes. Topdress once every spring and fall with organic matter; this will take the place of commercial fertilizers.

Regional Advice and Care
This perennial should not need pruning unless you want to cut it back immediately after blooming to keep the plants bushy. You can cut them back by one-half and they will recover by fall, in time for you to appreciate the golden foliage. If clumps become too large and floppy, divide them in fall or early spring. Dig up the entire clump and then divide it into sections, making sure each division has several growing points (distinctive swollen buds). Replant immediately and water well. *Amsonia* does not suffer from any serious pest or disease problems.

Companion Planting and Design
Its fine texture contrasts nicely with plants such as chrysanthemum, iris, black-eyed Susan, purple coneflower, beebalm, and coral bells. For a dramatic effect, plant this perennial in groups. Plant it in combination summer-blooming and fall-blooming perennials like asters.

Try These
If you want a plant with a more compact habit, try *Amsonia* 'Blue Ice', which grows 12 to 18 inches tall. Another species that is slightly more cold-hardy is *Amsonia tabernaemontana*, which grows to about 3 feet. The leaves are much wider, and the foliage effect is not the same.

Artemisia 'Powis Castle'

Artemisia 'Powis Castle'

Botanical Pronunciation
are-ti-MEEZ-ee-a

Other Name Wormwood

Bloom Period and Seasonal Colors
Evergreen foliage in silver-gray

Mature Height × Spread
2 to 3 ft. × 3 to 5 ft.

Long before they became popular as garden plants, the leaves and flowers of *Artemisia* (wormwood) were grown for their medicinal and healing properties. *Artemisia absinthium*, thought to be one of the parents of 'Powis Castle', was used to make the drink absinthe, which is a potent stimulant that can cause mental illness. Because of its toxic properties, wormwood is not recommended for use in home remedies! This plant may be too vigorous, sometimes taking over other plants. Placed in the right location, its finely textured, silver-gray foliage offers year-round interest. It also helps break up blocks of color in the garden. 'Powis Castle' has lacy, fragrant foliage and is one of the best cultivars for our hot, humid summers.

When, Where, and How to Plant
Plant 'Powis Castle' in spring when soil temperatures begin to warm in late April or early May, or plant it in fall when soil temperatures are still warm. Site it in a location where it will get lots of sun. Allow it some space as it grows 2 to 3 feet high and wide very quickly. Plant in well-drained soil. If necessary, add coarse sand to improve the drainage.

Growing Tips
There is no need to fertilize. This perennial may suffer during wet weather, but is quick to recover, unless the soil remains wet. Water it once every two weeks during the first growing season, and thereafter only during periods of drought (no rain for two weeks).

Regional Advice and Care
Cut the plant back in late spring if it gets leggy and open. Any cutting back should be done in early to late spring or in early summer so that plants can recover before winter. This hardy perennial becomes woody after one season of growth. If *Artemisia* get too woody after three or four years, it is probably easier to replace it altogether. It does not suffer from any pests or diseases.

Companion Planting and Design
The divided fern-like leaves, 2 to 5 inches long, have a silver cast that make this plant a good candidate for planting next to harsh colors, such as the scarlet red flowers of *Crocosmia* 'Lucifer'. Pair it with garden phlox and roses. Artemisia's height can cover the ugly knees that roses often develop. It is also a happy companion for other perennials, such as coneflower, salvia, and chrysanthemum. It looks great paired with *Verbena* 'Homestead Purple' or *Verbena bonariensis*, which has tall airy stems.

Try These
Artemisia 'Huntington Gardens' is similar to 'Powis Castle', but may be longer lived in the garden. *Artemisia lactiflora* has white flowers and grows 4 to 6 feet tall, ideal for the back of the border in late summer. *Artemisia stelleriana* 'Silver Brocade' only grows 6 to 12 inches tall and has soft gray foliage, perfect for edging in front of bigger perennials.

Aster

Aster spp. and cvs.

Botanical Pronunciation
as-TUR

Bloom Period and Seasonal Colors
Late summer through fall blooms in shades of mauve, purple, blue, red, pink, white

Mature Height × Spread
6 in. to 7 ft. (by variety) × 3 ft.

While there are types of asters that bloom in spring and summer, fall is when asters really become the stars of the garden. With tall, short, sprawling, and even climbing varieties, asters brighten the autumn landscape. Their daisy-like flowers bloom in shades of mauve, purple, blue, red, pink, and white; most with yellow centers. Some, such as *Aster tataricus*, which reaches to 6 feet high, can become invasive as they spread by underground roots. These carefree beauties like full sun or part shade and a moderately fertile soil. With some planning, you can have a sequence of bloom beginning in spring and continuing until November. *A. carolinianus*, often called climbing aster, has so many stems that it can be trained to grow up walls or over shrubs.

When, Where, and How to Plant
Plant container-grown plants in fall or in early spring after the frost-free date, which is usually around April 15. Asters will tolerate most soils, but for the best performance, plant them in a soil that has been amended with organic matter. A blend of one-third organic matter, one-third coarse sand, and one-third existing soil is fine. Site asters in a location where they will receive full sun or part shade. Water after planting.

Growing Tips
Asters will respond to fertile conditions by producing abundant blooms. Topdress plantings once every spring and fall with compost or other bagged products that contain at least 50 percent organic matter. Water garden plants once every two weeks if there is no rain. Water containers when the top ½-inch of soil is dry to the touch.

Regional Advice and Care
Asters are vigorous growers and, in fertile soils, certain varieties may need staking. Stake plants early in the season before they become leggy and flop over. To maintain vigor and delay blooms by a week or two, prune plants back by one-third in early summer. This may also reduce the amount of staking required. Divide vigorous growing types yearly in early spring or fall; divide smaller, less aggressive types once every two years. Replant young healthy shoots and discard old parts of the plant. Asters do not suffer from any serious pest or disease problems, although some varieties may be attacked by mildew. The best control is to plant mildew-resistant varieties.

Companion Planting and Design
The fall garden comes alive when you add asters to the formula. Pair them with goldenrod, ornamental grasses, fall-blooming crocus, and other asters. I like the combination of the blazing yellow autumn foliage of *Amsonia hubrichtii* with blue-flowered asters.

Try These
The diminutive white wood aster, *Aster divaricatus*, does best in part shade, making it ideal for use in the woodland garden. For late summer color, there are many selections of the native *Aster novi-belgii* with flowers in shades of violet, carmine, white, and blue.

Bearsfoot Hellebore

Helleborus foetidus

Botanical Pronunciation
Hell-e-BOR-us FE-ti-dus

Bloom Period and Seasonal Colors
Evergreen; February to April blooms in light green, almost chartreuse

Mature Height × Spread
2 ft. × 2 ft.

This hellebore, a relative to the popular Lenten rose (*Helleborus × hybridus*), offers clusters of light green flowers at the end of its branches. Blooms appear as early as February and can continue until April. An elegant, evergreen perennial for late winter and early spring bloom, bearsfoot hellebore has leaves that are divided into seven to ten leaflets. Even when it's not in bloom, this hellebore, with its palmate leaves, provides interesting texture and color in the landscape. Although it is not a native, this woodland beauty looks right at home next to native ferns and perennials. Combine it with other hellebores or ferns and hostas. Supposedly this plant emits an unpleasant odor when bruised, but I have not detected it.

When, Where, and How to Plant
Plant container-grown bearsfoot hellebore in spring or fall. In early spring, transplant clumps of young seedlings that sprout up under the mother plant. Site this hellebore in part shade; a location where it receives morning sun is fine, but protect it from hot afternoon sun. Plant it in a soil that is rich in organic matter but well drained. You can also grow it in a decorative container, provided it has good drainage. Water well after planting, soaking the area several times. Apply a ½-inch layer of an organic mulch to help conserve moisture.

Growing Tips
The first spring after planting, fertilize bearsfoot hellebore using 1 to 2 tablespoons of 10-10-10 per plant to give it a boost. Topdress once every spring and fall with ½ inch of organic matter. Water once a week during the first growing season to help establish a strong root system. As it matures, bearsfoot becomes more drought resistant. After it is established, it should require little care except for watering during periods of drought (no rain for two weeks).

Regional Advice and Care
Although this hellebore is evergreen, its leaves can sometimes look tattered after a hard winter. Prune to remove any unsightly leaves in early spring. It does not suffer from any serious pest or disease problems, and it is one of the few plants that deer do not eat. It can suffer from fungal problems in poorly drained sites. It will reseed, however.

Companion Planting and Design
Bearsfoot adds elegance to the shade garden and looks good in combination with hostas, ferns, and other hellebores. It is also attractive paired with *Carex oshimensis* 'Evergold', a variegated sedge with green leaves edged in cream that looks very much like an ornamental grass. Plant bearsfoot hellebores under dogwoods and azaleas in a woodland garden. Plant daffodils among clumps of hellebores.

Try These
Helleborus argutifolius has leathery, dark green leaves and pale green flowers from late winter to early spring. There are also many interesting selections of *H. × hybridus* with dark plum-colored blooms.

Black-Eyed Susan

Rudbeckia fulgida 'Goldsturm'

Botanical Pronunciation
rud-BEK-ee-A ful-GI-da

Other Name Orange coneflower

Bloom Period and Seasonal Colors
Summer to fall blooms in golden yellow

Mature Height × Spread
1 ½ to 3 ft. × 2 to 3 ft.

Even the most inexperienced gardener can identify black-eyed Susan. These flowers bloom for weeks in summer along roadsides and in fields throughout the southern and eastern United States. There are a number of different garden-worthy species of this native wildflower and its hybrids, including annuals, perennials, and biennials. A perennial favorite that shows up in formal landscapes and small cottage gardens, *Rudbeckia fulgida* 'Goldsturm' blooms for weeks with deep yellow daisy-like flowers with a brown center. Quick to colonize by underground roots, it is easy to control in the garden. Once established in the garden, it is a long-lived, easy-care perennial. Its cheerful flowers are welcome wherever they grow, and it's a great addition to the late-summer garden. It makes a great companion for grasses.

When, Where, and How to Plant

Plant container-grown black-eyed Susan in spring or fall. Annual types are easy to grow from seed, but perennial selections such as 'Goldsturm' will not come true from seed and must be propagated by cuttings or divisions. Plants are easy to divide and transplant in spring or fall. 'Goldsturm' prefers well-drained soil that has been amended with some organic matter. Select a site in full sun. Tilling the area first will result in better growth and will help it come into bloom more quickly. More planting tips can be found on page 86.

Growing Tips

While it is not necessary to fertilize, applying a ½-inch topdressing of organic matter once every spring and fall will provide adequate nutrients for strong, healthy plants. Water plants once a week during the first growing season and then as needed during periods of drought (no rain for two weeks).

Regional Advice and Care

Cutting flowers for bouquets when they first appear may encourage another flush of bloom later in the season. Leave the dried seedheads (coneflowers) at the end of the season to add interest to the fall and winter garden. This fast grower will probably need to be divided every few years unless you want it to take over. Black-eyed Susan does not suffer from any serious pest or disease problems. Clean up leaf litter in the fall and remove dead stalks to reduce overwintering pests.

Companion Planting and Design

Black-eyed Susan is ideal for naturalized plantings in meadows and is also wonderful in the flower garden annuals and other perennials. It looks good in combination with ornamental grasses and plants, such as *Sedum* 'Autumn Joy', *Phlox paniculata*, salvia, and spiky blazing star. Try it in combination with other types of coneflower, such as *Rudbeckia maxima*.

Try These

Rudbeckia subtomentosa 'Henry Eilers' grows 4 to 5 feet tall and has unique rolled petals (they look like they are tubes) with a brown center; it blooms late summer to early fall. *R. nitida* 'Herbstonne' grows up to 7 feet tall bearing large, single flowers; yellow petals surround green disks.

Blanket Flower

Gaillardia × *grandiflora* cvs.

Botanical Pronunciation
gay-LARD-ee-a grand-i-FLOR-a

Other Name Gaillardia

Bloom Period and Seasonal Colors
Summer to fall blooms in red, yellow, orange, and multicolored

Mature Height × Spread
2 to 3 ft. × 2 ft.

Blanket flower's colorful, daisy-like blooms offer a mix of reds and yellow. They make good cut flowers and are happy when left to mingle with other perennials and annuals in the garden. Other than deadheading (removing spent flowers), blanket flower requires no special care. It blooms from early summer until frost. In the coastal areas of Georgia where soils are sandy, plants may bloom more profusely, but they may not grow as tall as they do in a more compact soil. In heavy clay soils, blanket flower is a short-lived perennial, but it reseeds itself freely, so don't worry if your plant doesn't overwinter. The plants grown from seed produce interesting color variations. Two popular dwarf cultivars are 'Goblin' and 'Baby Cole'.

When, Where, and How to Plant

Unlike many perennials that take two or more years to develop into blooming-size plants, *Gaillardia* grown from seed will flower the first year. Seeds started indoors (refer to the packet for directions) in early spring should be ready to transplant into the garden in six to eight weeks. Plant container-grown plants in spring or fall. Divide and transplant new growth in spring that appears from the old crown. Plant blanket flower in full sun and in well-drained, moderately fertile soil. Dig a hole as large as the container and as deep. Firm the soil around the rootball, water it, and watch blanket flower grow. Apply a ½-inch layer of mulch to conserve moisture and help control weeds.

Growing Tips

No special care is needed for this tough heat lover. During periods of drought (no rain for two weeks), water once every two weeks. Soak the area around the plant, wait a few minutes, and then soak it again.

Regional Advice and Care

Blanket flower does not like wet soils in winter, which can lead to its rapid demise. Deadhead to encourage longer bloom time. Cutting plants back in late summer will encourage a second flush of growth and blooms in fall. Don't deadhead plants at the end of the season or you will eliminate the seeds that normally scatter themselves freely. If you don't want it to self-sow then cut off the seedheads. Neither bugs nor diseases bother it.

Companion Planting and Design

Blanket flower provides almost constant bloom from early summer to fall. It works well in the front or middle of the border. You can plant blanket flower on the strip between the sidewalk and the street; just let it take over. Combine it with annuals (such as lantana) and perennials (such as salvias and daylilies). It also looks good with coreopsis, with the intensely red flowers of *Crocosmia* 'Lucifer', or with the bright orange blooms of Mexican sunflower (*Tithonia*).

Try These

Sunburst™ 'Scarlet Halo' has a compact habit and is a profuse bloomer with multicolored blooms of orange and yellow.

Butterfly Weed

Asclepias tuberosa

Botanical Pronunciation
as-KLEE-pe-as tew-be-RO-sa

Bloom Period and Seasonal Colors
Midsummer blooms in shades of yellow, orange, lipstick red

Mature Height × Spread
2 to 3 ft. × 2 ft.

Butterfly weed is a familiar wildflower. It is often seen growing along the same roadside ditches and open sunny fields that later display asters and goldenrods. A native wildflower, butterfly weed also makes a good ornamental for the flower garden. The blooms, clusters of bright orange and orange-red flowers, appear on 3-foot-high stems and are especially attractive to Aphrodite and Fritillary butterflies. Mark the spot where you place this plant in the garden; it comes up late in the spring and might be mistaken for a weed by the uninformed. The name *Asclepias* comes from the Greek—Asclepius was the god of healing. There is also a selection called 'Gay Butterflies' with flowers that are yellow to red, and one called 'Hello Yellow' with bright yellow flowers.

When, Where, and How to Plant

Plant container-grown butterfly weed in fall or in spring once new growth is visible. Plant in a hot, full-sun spot where the soil is well drained. It will tolerate both clay and sandy soils, but avoid wet areas. While it is possible to propagate this native by divisions taken in fall, it is not practical. Because it has a long taproot, you must dig deeply to avoid cutting it and replant the division immediately so that it won't dry out. It is also not recommended that you dig plants from the wild unless you are part of a plant rescue. Instead, collect the seedpods once they turn brown and before they split open to disperse their seeds. Water after planting.

Growing Tips

Hot temperatures and dry soils are all this tough perennial needs to thrive in your garden, but it does require watering during periods of drought (no rain for two weeks). Soak the area around the plant, wait a few minutes, and repeat.

Regional Advice and Care

Butterfly weed requires no special grooming or pruning and is virtually free of disease. If you notice caterpillars chewing the leaves, don't spray the plants. These chewing insects will one day turn into beautiful monarch butterflies. Just plant more butterfly weed. After it flowers, leave the seedpods to ripen on the plant, and you may get seedlings nearby.

Companion Planting and Design

Butterfly weed is perfect for wildflower meadows and naturalized plantings. Combine it with other native plants, such as ironweed and Joe Pye weed. Grow it with other milkweeds and butterfly bush and you can count on having hordes of butterflies. Pair it with other perennials, including purple coneflower, lantana, coreopsis, and blazing star.

Try These

The tropical milkweed, *Asclepias curassavica*, is a good source of larval (caterpillar) food for the monarch butterfly. Swamp milkweed (*Asclepias incarnata*) grows 3 to 5 feet tall and displays clusters of pink flowers. Unlike *A. tuberosa*, swamp milkweed will tolerate wet soils. *A. incarnata* 'Ice Ballet' is a more compact selection with white flowers.

Cardinal Flower

Lobelia cardinalis

Botanical Pronunciation
lo-BEE-lia kar-di-NAH-lis

Bloom Period and Seasonal Colors
Summer blooms in bright red

Mature Height × Spread
2 to 6 ft. × 2 ft.

Cardinal flower is a welcome spot of bright color in the late summer garden when few other perennials bloom. It attracts hummingbirds and humans alike with its 2- to 4-foot spikes of inch-long, jewel-like flame-red flowers. In its native habitat, this plant grows in bogs, swamps, or along streams and river banks. It is perfect for the edge of a pond with other moisture-loving plants, such as Louisiana or Japanese iris. In the flower garden, it is happy with ferns, including royal fern, cinnamon fern, and autumn fern, as well as with hostas. The perfect site is one that gets partial shade and lots of moisture. Closely related, but not as showy, is *Lobelia siphilitica*, the blue cardinal flower, with 2- to 3-foot-tall stalks of blue flowers.

When, Where, and How to Plant

Plant container-grown cardinal flower in spring. A partially sunny spot that gets plenty of moisture—such as a bog or the edge of a pond—is ideal. The soil should be amended by mixing together one-third organic matter, one-third coarse sand, and one-third existing soil. If the soil is not amended with organic matter, plant cardinal flower in shade. If you plant it in a flower garden, make sure it gets watered regularly throughout the growing season, whenever the top inch of the soil is dry to the touch. Space plants 6 to 8 inches apart. Apply a ½-inch layer of mulch after planting.

Growing Tips

Topdress with ½ inch of organic matter once every spring and fall; this should provide adequate fertilizer. Plants that are in boggy situations will not need watering unless the bog dries out. In the garden, water regularly as needed whenever the top inch of soil is dry, at least once a week. Soak the area around the plants, wait a few minutes, and repeat several times.

Regional Advice and Care

Remove faded flower stalks at the end of the season or leave them to set seed. If you're lucky and conditions are right, you will get seedlings the following spring. Cardinal flower does not suffer from any serious pest or disease problems. Propagate by division in early spring.

Companion Planting and Design

Plant cardinal flower with hostas, royal fern, cinnamon fern, or autumn fern. In the flower garden, plant it with Joe Pye weed and black-eyed Susan. In a boggy situation, pair it up with *Ligularia*, Japanese iris, and primrose. Cannas are also a candidate for growing with cardinal flower. In the shrub border, plant it next to iris with a backdrop of native Virginia sweetspire, *Itea virginica* 'Henry's Garnet'. In its native habitat it grows on the banks of baldcypress swamps.

Try These

The hybrid *Lobelia* × *gerardii* 'Vedrariensis' has dark green leaves tinged with red and dark violet flowers. Site this lobelia in a place that is shaded from hot afternoon sun; it likes lots of moisture too.

Cheddar Pinks

Dianthus gratianopolitanus cvs.

Botanical Pronunciation
dye-AN-thus grah-tee-ah-no-po-li-TAY-nus

Other Name Dianthus

Bloom Period and Seasonal Colors
April to May blooms in soft pink, deep pink, magenta, white

Mature Height × Spread
9 to 12 in. × 12 in.

This delightful fragrant species varies depending on the cultivar. 'Bath's Pink' was discovered in Georgia by Jane Bath of Stone Mountain. It was named in her honor by the owners of Goodness Grows, a nursery in Lexington, Georgia, that specializes in perennials. In early spring, usually in April when some of the early tulips begin to open, masses of clove-scented, pink-fringed flowers create a blooming blanket atop mounds of blue-gray, needle-like foliage. The quick-spreading, handsome foliage forms a tightly woven carpet that looks good all year. Use it between steppingstones on a garden path or border edge. 'Bath's Pink' is especially heat tolerant and does not "melt" during our hot summers. There are many dianthus species and cultivars, a plant that many of our grandmothers grew.

When, Where, and How to Plant
Plant container-grown dianthus in early spring or fall. You can also plant divisions or tip cuttings taken the previous summer. Plant 'Bath's Pink' in full sun in a soil that is well drained. Plant a little high if drainage is a concern. A moderately fertile soil is fine, as long as it's well drained.

Growing Tips
No special fertilization is required. Water once a week during the first growing season. After this the plant should be established, and you should only need to water during periods of drought when there is no rain for two weeks.

Regional Advice and Care
To prolong the flowering, remove spent flowers before they set seed. After the plants have bloomed, shear them back to tidy mounds; the plants will continue to bloom on and off through the summer. After two or three years, large clumps may begin to open up, losing fullness in the center. Pull out any dead parts from the center, keeping good air circulation for the healthy parts. This is a good time to start new plants using divisions or rooted cuttings. Cuttings root easily in wet sand. For divisions, use a sharp knife or spade to cut off sections of plants with roots; replant immediately. This dianthus does not suffer from any serious pest or disease problems.

Companion Planting and Design
Ideal as an edging in front of the flower border, as a groundcover creeping over a wall, or in the rock garden alongside other small treasures, this dianthus may be the perfect perennial for Georgia gardens. 'Bath's Pink' is also a good weaver to fill in gaps between perennials such as *Phlox, Salvia, Guara,* and Stokes' aster. It makes an effective groundcover under roses or peonies. Plant it with other fragrant plants like rosemary and lavender for a garden of scents.

Try These
Dianthus 'Firewitch' has magenta flowers and holds up well in Georgia's heat and humidity. Another selection that is not bothered by the heat is *Dianthus* 'Frosty Fire', with cherry red fragrant flowers and a 15-inch mound of silvery blue foliage.

Columbine

Aquilegia spp. and cvs.

Botanical Pronunciation
ack-wi-LEE-gee-A

Bloom Period and Seasonal Colors
Spring to early summer blooms in many colors,
including red, white, yellow, blue, pink

Mature Height × Spread
10 in. to 3 ft. × 1 to 2 ft.

Most columbines are long-lived perennials, except in the hottest parts of Georgia where they may perform like an annual. *Aquilegia canadensis*, also known as wild columbine, grows 1 to 1½ feet tall and produces nodding 1½-inch red and yellow flowers. It sometimes appears to grow out of the crevices of rocks, a tribute to its toughness. Columbine's magical flowers are delicate and distinctive. Some have long spurs, and they come in a range of colors, including pastels, darker colors, and white. Columbines may bloom on and off for three to six weeks, depending on how cool the temperatures are in spring. Columbine reseeds itself freely, and a large number of hybrids occur naturally. *Aquilegia flabellata* has bluish green leaves and lilac to blue flowers.

When, Where, and How to Plant
Plant columbine in early spring or fall when the soil is warm. Plants grown from seed sown in spring may not flower the first year. Site columbine in a woodland garden where it gets plenty of light, but not full sun, all day long. Columbine prefers a rich, moist, well-drained soil. If planted in full sun, it is essential that the soil be rich and moist. Columbine plants growing in dappled shade will bloom over a longer period of time than plants growing in full sun.

Growing Tips
Water once a week during dry periods when there is no rain for two weeks. If the top ½ inch of soil is dry to the touch, it is time to water. Fertilize once every spring with a general 10-10-10.

Regional Advice and Care
When growing columbine, a gardener may encounter damage done by leafminers. Leaves riddled with lighter-colored tunnels are a sign that leafminers are present. Plants are also attacked by powdery mildew. A simple and nontoxic remedy for both problems is to cut back the foliage (to a few inches from the ground) as soon as you see damage after blooming. Plants will soon put out a flush of fresh dark green leaves that will look good until frost. After blooming, you can also cut back old stems to encourage a second crop of flowers. Divide after blooms finish in late summer or early fall. Dig up the entire clump and carefully tease apart sections with a digging fork. Make sure each division has some buds and roots. Replant, mulch, and water well.

Companion Planting and Design
Grow columbine in the flower border, rock garden, and woodland with trilliums, hostas, and Virginia bluebells and other wildflowers.

Try These
The Song Bird™ series offers striking colors, such as the brilliant red of 'Cardinal' and the blue of 'Blue Jay'. They are early bloomers with compact flowers. A good dwarf is *Aquilegia flabellata* var. *pumila*. It grows less than 12 inches tall and is good for the front of a border or in a rock garden.

Coral Bell

Heuchera spp. and cvs.

Botanical Pronunciation
HEW-ker-a

Other Name Alumroot

Bloom Period and Seasonal Colors
Colorful evergreen foliage; April to August
blooms in pink, crimson, red, green, white

Mature Height × Spread
2 to 3 ft. × 2 ft.

Coral bell was once grown for the delicate sprays of bell-shaped flowers, but today there are dozens of varieties to choose from that offer colorful evergreen foliage, in a wide range of colors including chartreuse, peach, burgundy, and dark brown. While some selections tolerate full sun, most are happiest growing in light shade and a moist, well-drained soil. The tiny flowers appear on wiry stems anywhere from April to August in shades of pink, crimson, red, green, and white. The American alumroot, *Heuchera americana*, is perfect for the woodland garden, forming a clump of mottled purple, brown, and green leaves 12 inches high, reaching 3 feet high when it blooms. Hybrids that include this native coral bell are better suited to tolerate the heat and humidity in Georgia.

When, Where, and How to Plant
Plant container-grown coral bell or rooted divisions in spring or fall. Before planting, amend the soil by mixing equal parts of organic matter, coarse sand, and the existing soil. A location that receives at least partial shade is ideal. Site to protect plants from hot afternoon sun. Water well after planting and once weekly until plants are established. Apply a ½-inch layer of mulch after planting to help conserve moisture. Keep mulch away from the crown of the plant.

Growing Tips
After planting, fertilize plants with a slow-release fertilizer. Topdress with organic matter once every fall and every spring. Established coral bells should only need watering during periods of drought, at which time once a week is adequate. Drench the soil, let it soak in, and repeat.

Regional Advice and Care
Divide clumps every three or four years in spring or fall to keep plants vigorous. Replant young, healthy divisions and discard woody sections. Remove any tattered leaves in early spring. They will quickly be replaced with new growth. Plants occasionally suffer from dieback that is the result of soil that stays too dry or too wet. If this happens do not replant in the same spot; rather, relocate plants to another area to avoid the problem. Coral bell does not suffer from any serious pest or disease problems.

Companion Planting and Design
Coral bell makes great companions for royal fern, autumn fern, and maidenhair fern. Use them in the woodland garden or perennial border to break up blocks of colors. They are also attractive when paired with hostas. Selections with variegated foliage, such as *Heuchera* 'Pewter Veil', look particularly nice next to hostas with chartreuse or blue-green leaves. Coral bell also make colorful additions to mixed container plantings and offer year-round color.

Try These
With lime green foliage *Heuchera villosa* 'Autumn Bride' grows 1 to 3 feet tall and produces delicate white flowers in August and September and, most important, is a "good doer." *Heuchera* 'Citronelle' has chartreuse foliage that brightens the woodland. 'Caramel' is reportedly more heat tolerant than others.

Daylily

Hemerocallis spp. and hybrids

Botanical Pronunciation
hem-er-o-KAL-is

Bloom Period and Seasonal Colors
Summer to fall, many different colors

Mature Height × Spread
1 ft to 6 ft. × 1 ft. to 3 ft. depending on
the selection

Daylilies have been popular in gardens for generations. They belong to the genus *Hemerocallis*, native to Asia but throughout the United States the common tawny daylily, *Hemerocallis fulva*, has escaped from gardens and is a familiar site growing in drainage ditches, meadows, and roadsides. Although individual flowers last only a day, there are numerous hybrids with multibranched plants and dozens of flower buds that open over a period of weeks or months. While the flower buds are edible, it's their amazing range of colors and sizes that make this perennial so appealing to gardeners. Many daylilies are also fragrant. From the smaller types like *H.* 'Stella D' Oro' with orange-yellow blooms to the tall types like *H.* 'Autumn Minaret', which reaches 6 feet tall, there are myriad choices.

When, Where, and How to Plant

Daylilies thrive in full sun and a soil that is moist but well drained although some will tolerate periods of excess moisture. Plant them in spring, summer, or fall. Water well after you plant and once a week while they become established. Apply a 1-inch layer of mulch to reduce weeds and help keep the soil temperatures cool in summer and warm in winter. While daylilies survive in average garden soil, they will reward you with the most blooms and healthy foliage if you amend the soil with organic matter and provide regular watering. Plant daylilies in the flower garden or in containers. Plant a variety of types to extend your season of blooms. Be sure to give them ample room to grow; check the need for the individual selections you plant.

Growing Tips

Daylilies are easy to grow provided they have a good garden soil, adequate moisture, and full sun; some selections will grow in part shade. If clumps get too large, divide them in early spring or fall. Make sure you have some roots (usually fibrous or cord-like, some look like fat sausages) with each fan of foliage. Water divisions well after you transplant. Dig a wide hole but only as deep as the length of the roots.

Regional Advice and Care

Plants on occasion can be bothered by rust disease, which looks like yellow and brown streaks on the leaves. At its worst the leaves turn yellow and dry up. Prevention is the best control— sanitation and spraying with fungicides. If spider mites or thrips attack plants, use insecticidal soap to control them. For chemical controls check with your local Extension office for specific recommendations.

Companion Planting and Design

Plant daylilies with *Phlox, Salvia,* roses, and ornamental grasses. Use them on sunny slopes to help control erosion. Combine those that grow in part sun with hellebores. This will provide you with months of color.

Try These

'Happy Returns' is a repeat bloomer with fragrant lemon yellow flowers on plants that are only 1 to 1½ feet tall and wide.

Euphorbia

Euphorbia characias subsp. wulfenii

Botanical Pronunciation
yew-FOR-bee-a ka-RA-kee-as

Other Name Mediterranean spurge

Bloom Period and Seasonal Colors
Evergreen foliage, yellow-green flowers in spring

Mature Height × Spread
2 to 4 ft. × 3 ft.

*E*uphorbia, also known as spurge, is a large genus that includes annual and perennial types with colorful foliage and interesting flowers in spring and summer, depending on the individual selection. *Euphorbia characias* subsp. *wulfenii* looks good for months. New plants display handsome evergreen (blue-green) foliage and the striking flowers (which are really colored bracts) appear atop the 3-foot-tall stems in late winter to early spring, a lime green. Described as looking like "Medusa" by one gardener, this curious perennial persists for several years and then it may die in one spot, only to show up in another. A constant supply of seedlings means you can edit and decide whether you like where it plants itself or not. Seedlings are easy to pull out.

When, Where, and How to Plant

Plant this *Euphorbia* in full sun, though some selections will grow in shade, in well-drained soil for the best results. Plant container grown plants in spring or fall. Transplant seedlings in early spring or fall.

Growing Tips

If plants are in too much shade, they will get floppy and fall over. After a few years in the same spot, plants may decline but will put up new seedlings that will mature in no time. Pull out plants if they get tall and floppy. If you amend the soil with organic matter when you plant, you shouldn't have to fertilize this perennial. Topdress with compost in the fall to give them a boost.

Regional Advice and Care

Some people have a skin reaction to the milky sap that euphorbias produce (the same family poinsettias are in). To avoid potential problems, wear gloves when pruning this plant. The sap is reported to be poisonous. Keep it away from your eyes. After the colorful bracts begin to turn brown and dry in the summer, seeds may form. Once the seeds have dropped off the plants (the bracts will look open) cut off the dead bracts. If you notice seedlings, keep them watered and you will be certain to have a new crop of plants when you need them.

Companion Planting and Design

Plant *Euhorbia c.* ssp. *wulfenii* in the flower garden with iris, lamb's ear, and blue flowers including *Veronica* 'Georgia Blue' and hardy geraniums. The blue-green foliage provides a contrast to many shades of green and the unique bracts add texture to the garden. Combine *Euphorbia* with hardy *Sedum* groundcovers and hardy succulents.

Try These

For small gardens *Euphorbia characias* 'Shorty' offers the same qualities of *wulfenii* but in a smaller, shorter version just 12 inches tall. For dry shade the evergreen *Euphorbia amygdaloides* var. *robbiae* is a good doer. If it gets regular moisture it can become an aggressive spreader. Hybrid euphorbias with colorful foliage include 'Blackbird' with dark purple foliage and 'Cherokee' with dark purple leaves, stems, and flowers.

Fringed Bleeding Heart

Dicentra eximia cvs. and hybrids

Botanical Pronunciation
dy-SEN-tra eks-EE-mee-a

Bloom Period and Seasonal Colors
Midspring to summer blooms in rose-pink, pink, white

Mature Height × Spread
1½ to 2 ft. × 2 ft.

For color in the shade garden bleeding hearts are ideal. Fringed bleeding heart is the native counterpart to common giant bleeding heart, *Dicentra spectabilis*. Although common bleeding heart is showier (with bigger flowers), fringed bleeding heart blooms longer and is more persistent in the garden. This gem has ferny, blue-gray foliage and forms neat clumps that are 1 to 1½ feet high. The deep rose pink flowers, midspring to summer, are happiest in the shade garden. 'Bountiful' tolerates a good bit of sun, blooming on and off through the summer. In the woodland garden, fringed bleeding hearts add interesting color and texture when grown with ferns, foam flower, dwarf crested iris, and hosta.

When, Where, and How to Plant
Plant container-grown fringed bleeding heart in spring or fall. Plant divisions in spring so that they will have time to develop a strong root system before winter. Site in a soil that is rich in organic matter and well drained. It will not tolerate standing water around its roots. It needs a location that receives at least part shade. A deciduous woodland is ideal. If you have mostly sun, try some of the varieties that will tolerate sun. Dig a hole that is as deep and wide as the container it is growing in. This perennial is short-lived (one to two years) in the most southern regions of the state.

Growing Tips
During the first growing season, fertilize fringed bleeding heart in spring with 1 to 2 tablespoons of 10-10-10 per plant. After this, you can topdress once every spring and fall with ½ inch of organic matter. Water plants once a week when they are actively growing.

Regional Advice and Care
Prune fringed bleeding heart back after the first flush of bloom, and you may get a second flush of flowers. This bleeding heart does not suffer from any serious pest or disease problems, but it will rot if its roots stay wet.

Companion Planting and Design
Because it doesn't get too large, place fringed bleeding heart in the middle or front of the border. Plant it under rhododendrons and azaleas, or other spring-blooming shrubs, to create a tapestry of color and texture. Combine with foam flower, coral bell, hosta, ferns, *Epimedium*, hellebore, and giant bleeding heart. You can also grow them in combination with midseason tulips or smaller types of daffodils, such as *Narcissus* 'Tete-a-Tete'. Try fringed bleeding heart paired with dwarf crested iris, *Iris cristata*.

Try These
Dicentra eximia 'Luxuriant', with its deep pink flowers, is a variety selected for its long season of bloom and its ability to tolerate drier soils and more sun than most varieties. For a long-blooming, white-flowered form, try *Dicentra eximia* 'Snowdrift'.

Garden Phlox

Phlox paniculata 'David'

Botanical Pronunciation
FLOKS pa-NIC-ew-LAH-ta

Bloom Period and Seasonal Colors
White flowers in summer

Mature Height × Spread
3 to 4 ft. × 2 ft.

Garden phlox is a favorite perennial flower for the cottage garden as well as the formal or mixed border. The species has magenta flowers but 'David' offers white blooms and the ability to thrive in hot, humid Georgia summers. Unlike many other garden phlox, 'David' is resistant to powdery mildew, and the foliage is bright green and clean, even in the heat of the summer. Plants will easily reach a height of 3 feet or taller when they are in full bloom and are a magnet for butterflies. If you stake them, use natural stakes. By removing spent flowers it's possible to get a second small flush of flowers. Garden phlox provide a nice complement for roses and 'Casa Blanca' lilies, which bloom at a similar time.

When, Where, and How to Plant

The best time to plant is in fall, but if you plant in spring, make sure to keep plants well watered, especially on hot sunny days. Plant garden phlox in full sun, in a soil that is moist and well drained. Add a shovelful of compost and mix it in with existing soil before you plant. Dig a hole that is twice as wide but only as deep as the container the plant is growing in. Water plants after you plant them and then whenever the top ½ inch of the soil is dry. Locate garden phlox in the middle or back of the border.

Growing Tips

Apply a liquid fertilizer in early spring and topdress with compost in fall. When possible locate phlox in a site with good air circulation. This will cut down on disease problemns.

Regional Advice and Care

Occasionally plants may need staking. If you want to keep a natural look, use twiggy branches from dogwoods or birch trees for stakes. By cutting plants back in early spring (after they have put out about 1 foot of growth) by about one-third you can delay the flowering by a few weeks. In a normal season, this phlox will bloom from July until September. In extreme hot weather spider mites can cause potential problems. Contact the local Extension office for the best recommendations on control. Avoid overhead watering; this will help with powdery mildew.

Companion Planting and Design

Plant garden phlox in the sunny mixed border with butterfly bush, hardy geraniums, roses, rosemary, coneflowers, Russian sage, and lilies. Plant them near water and watch the butterflies flock. 'David' looks especially lovely with soft gray lamb's ears planted in front of it. With their delicate white fragrant flowers, *Calamintha nepeta* var. *nepeta* provides a contrast to garden phlox.

Try These

'Peacock White' is shorter but reported to be disease resistant and heat tolerant. 'Purple Kiss' is a compact selection with purple flowers and resistance to powdery mildew problems. *P. paniculata* 'Bright Eyes' has pink flowers with a red center, great for cut flowers.

Gaura

Gaura lindheimeri

Botanical Pronunciation
GAW-ra lind-HI-mer-eye

Other Name Wandflower

Bloom Period and Seasonal Colors
Late spring until fall blooms in pink, dark pink, white

Mature Height × Spread
3 to 4 ft. × 3 ft.

Native to Texas and Louisiana, this tough guy is lean and mean. Gaura offers a lot and asks for little in return. Growing 3 to 4 feet high, gaura features 1½- to 3½-inch-long, stalkless leaves that attach directly to the stems. Blossoms open from late spring into fall on long, wiry stems. The pink buds become a darker rose when they open. A "see-through plant," it brings lightness to the garden. This adaptable perennial is happy in the flower border or between the sidewalk and street in hot sun and in soil that is not very fertile. It thrives with minimum water. It rarely needs dividing, and it self-seeds freely. Add it to the butterfly garden where it will be appreciated by winged visitors.

When, Where, and How to Plant

Plant container-grown *Gaura* in early spring or fall. Transplant seedlings in spring when they are still small and before they develop a large taproot. Site *Gaura* in full sun, or in a spot that receives at least six hours of sun. Do not amend the soil, but make sure it is well drained. If it is too rich, plants will not bloom well. Water thoroughly after planting, soaking the ground around the plant.

Growing Tips

Gaura does not require fertilizing. Regular watering is only needed once every two weeks to help it get established during the first growing season. After this period, it should not require supplemental watering.

Regional Advice and Care

Prune flower spikes off when they form seeds to prevent seedlings from taking over your garden. *Gaura* does not suffer from any serious pest or disease problems, but if the soil is too rich, plants will become leggy and not flower well. Do not let its roots sit in water. Too much moisture is the main enemy of this Texas native. They can also suffer from aphids in early summer. Blast them with a hose or use insecticial soap.

Companion Planting and Design

Plant *Gaura* in hot, sunny sites where it can reseed freely. It is a good candidate for the strip between the sidewalk and the street where little else will grow. Naturalized plantings that include other native plants—such as butterfly weed—are good, too. In the flower border, combine it with coreopsis, purple coneflower, *Artemisia*, lamb's ear, and hardy lantana. This perennial is also a good partner for blanket flower. A bonus is all the beneficial insects that *Gaura* attracts to the garden.

Try These

'Whirling Butterflies' has larger flowers than the species and a more compact habit. 'Sunny Butterflies' is a compact grower with variegated leaves of green edged in cream. Its flowers, on 18- to 24-inch stems, start out as crimson buds and open to rose pink with markings of darker rose. 'Pink Cloud' grows to 30 inches tall and is covered with pink flowers as late as October.

Hardy Begonia

Begonia grandis

Botanical Pronunciation
Beg-ON-ee-a GRAN-dis

Bloom Period and Seasonal Colors
Late summer to fall blooms in pink, colorful
foliage, green leaves, red on the undersides

Mature Height × Spread
1 ½ to 2 ft. × 1 to 2 ft.

The elegant hardy begonia is like Cinderella waiting to be discovered, while her gaudy stepsisters—the wax begonias—get all the attention. Wax begonias, which are annuals, are planted in huge numbers every year in Georgia gardens, while hardy begonias are often overlooked. Hardy begonia waits until late in the season to put on a show, in the woodland or the shady corner of a flower border. The waxy leaves glow when the late afternoon light hits the red undersides from behind. Airy sprays of pink flowers rise above the foliage and bloom for weeks. The seed capsules dry on the plant, providing additional ornamental interest that lasts into winter. Hardy begonia spreads by little bulbils that mature into plants of flowering size in one season.

When, Where, and How to Plant
Plant hardy begonias in spring or fall. Propagate by seed, by the bulbils that form in the leaf axils, by stem cuttings, or by divisions taken in late summer. Plant container-grown begonias in spring. Because it self-sows, look for seedlings in late spring that can be transplanted. This plant can grow in acidic or alkaline soils. The best soil is one that is reasonably fertile and well drained, but hardy begonias have been known to do well even in clay soil. Hardy begonia grows best in dappled sunlight, but tolerates full shade. If you plant it in a site with too much sun, the leaves take on a bleached-out look. Water after planting.

Growing Tips
If you amend the soil with organic matter, this will provide plenty of nutrients for this begonia. Mulch plants in fall to protect the roots over winter. Water once every two weeks during the growing season, soaking the soil around the plants.

Regional Advice and Care
Unlike many begonias, hardy begonias require no staking or pruning. Let the seeds ripen on the plant. Collect and sow them in early spring if you want flowers that same year. If plants become leggy, cut them back in late spring and they will be bushy by late summer or early fall when they begin to bloom. With the first hard frost, the tops die down—so the plants essentially prune themselves. It does not suffer from any serious pest or disease problems.

Companion Planting and Design
Plant as a groundcover under spring-blooming shrubs like hydrangeas. Combine it with other shade-loving perennials, or anywhere you want a touch of color from midsummer into early fall. It's a good idea to draw a map of where you plant this perennial because it comes up so late in the season. It grows happily in combination with variegated Solomon's seal or evergreen ferns, such as autumn fern and Christmas fern. Hardy begonia also looks good on a slope near a pond or stream.

Try These
Begonia grandis 'Alba' has white flowers instead of pink.

Hardy Geranium

Geranium spp. and cvs.

Botanical Pronunciation
jer-AYE-knee-um

Other Name Cranesbill

Bloom Period and Seasonal Colors
Flowers in spring and summer are shades of white, pink, lilac, magenta, blue, violet-blue, and dark purple

Mature Height × Spread
6 in. to 4 ft. × 1 to 2½ ft.

As a group of plants, hardy geraniums (no relation to the pelargoniums, which are the houseplant types grown as summer annuals) offer a variety of foliage and flowers for gardens of all types. Some have colorful or fragrant foliage that stays green during mild winters, while others die back completely to the ground, only to put out new leaves next spring. To recognize these perennials, look for a big rosette of mounded foliage with leaves that are typically palmate (similar to a hand with the fingers extended) flowers with five petals and beak-like fruits. They bloom for weeks and even when they finish blooming, many offer an attractive rosette of foliage that helps offset blooms of other perennials. Use them in containers with other perennials and annuals.

When, Where, and How to Plant
Depending on the selection, hardy geraniums typically prefer a moist, well-drained soil in a site that gets full sun or part shade. Plant these perennials in your garden in spring or fall. Dig a hole that is only as deep (but twice as wide) as the container the plant is growing in when you purchase it.

Growing Tips
Add a shovelful of compost to your planting hole and mix it in with the existing soil. Topdress once a year with compost and this will feed your soil and your plants. If you plant during the heat of summer, be sure to water regularly and don't be surprised if your plants just sit there. Once the weather cools off a bit, they will begin to grow again.

Regional Advice and Care
Not all hardy geraniums are created equal. Some do not like the heat and humidity that our summers are famous for. Check with gardeners in your region to see which ones they have had the best success with. After planting, apply a ½-inch layer of mulch and water plants once a week for the first few months. After they are established, you should only have to water if there are periods without rainfall. If you have big clumps after a few years, you can divide them in spring or fall and share them with friends or grow them from seed. *Geranium* 'Rozanne' is a trailer and spreader that disappears almost completely in the winter, so you may want to mark where plants are to avoid planting other plants on top of existing ones.

Companion Planting and Design
Plant hardy geraniums with *Iris sibirica*, catmint, and lamb's ear. You can also plant them under roses and with rosemary.

Try These
Geranium sanguineum, known as bloody cranesbill, tolerates heat better than some types, and in fall the leaves take on shades of crimson. *Geranium macrorrhizum*, bigroot geranium, has dark magenta flowers and aromatic foliage (crush the leaves to release the fragrance). Unlike some geraniums, in Georgia it prefers part shade.

Hardy Lantana

Lantana camara 'Miss Huff'

Botanical Pronunciation
lan-TAN-ah kam-AIR-ah

Other Name Miss Huff lantana

Bloom Period and Seasonal Colors
Summer to frost blooms in red, orange, pink

Mature Height × Spread
3 to 6 ft × 10 ft.

Lantana has long been a favorite of Southern gardeners, because it's easy to grow and because it blooms all summer and attracts hordes of butterflies and bees. Fairly drought resistant, 'Miss Huff' is reputed to be hardier than many of the other lantanas. Clusters of orange and pink flowers cover 'Miss Huff' for months, thriving in our hot, humid weather. Avoid planting it in areas where the soil will stay wet during the winter. Annual types of lantana come in many different colors and forms. Popular varieties include 'Irene' with rose and yellow flowers, 'New Gold' with gold flowers, and 'Lemon Drop' with light yellow flowers. Lantana makes a wonderful addition to a butterfly garden.

When, Where, and How to Plant
Plant container-grown lantana in spring. Plants will sometimes layer themselves (this is when a branch touches soil and takes root). Propagate from cuttings in summer. Plant lantana in full sun, the hotter the better. It needs just an average garden soil. Avoid soils that stay wet or don't drain well. Space plants at least 6 feet apart, as they will quickly cover a large area.

Growing Tips
Lantana requires no special care. If you want to give your plant a jump start, fertilize it with a liquid fertilizer such as 20-20-20 after you plant it in spring. Plants in containers will benefit from a regular fertilizer applied once a month during the growing season. Container-grown lantana should

be watered when the top ½ inch of soil is dry to the touch—this may be daily. During times of drought (no rain for two weeks), water plants in the ground once every two weeks. Soak the area, wait a few minutes, and repeat.

Regional Advice and Care
Few perennials require so little care and bloom so long. While deadheading encourages maximum flower production, even the busy gardener who does not deadhead will have plenty of flowers. It is best to mulch lantana. This practice helps the plant make it through winter. (Lantana is more accurately a tender perennial.) Wait until spring, just before new growth starts, to cut it back. Lantana does not suffer from any serious pest or disease problems. However, when the weather is wet and overcast for an extended period of time, or when plants grow in too much shade, it is subject to mildew. Do not use insecticidal soap to control pest problems.

Companion Planting and Design
Lantana is good for summer color in the garden, especially in hot and dry spots. Grow lantana in the flower garden, in containers, or in hanging baskets. Plant it in a mass on a sunny slope. Combine with other perennials like coneflowers, salvia, and phlox.

Try These
Luscious Citrus Blend™ is an annual lantana with hot colors—a blend of orange, yellow, and red.

Hibiscus

Hibiscus spp. and cvs.

Botanical Pronunciation
hi-BIS-cus

Other Name Common mallow

Bloom Period and Seasonal Colors
Spring to frost blooms in shades of red, pink, rose, white

Mature Height × Spread
5 to 10 ft. (by variety) × 3 ft.

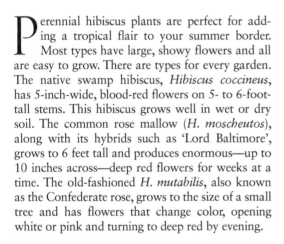

Perennial hibiscus plants are perfect for adding a tropical flair to your summer border. Most types have large, showy flowers and all are easy to grow. There are types for every garden. The native swamp hibiscus, *Hibiscus coccineus*, has 5-inch-wide, blood-red flowers on 5- to 6-foot-tall stems. This hibiscus grows well in wet or dry soil. The common rose mallow (*H. moscheutos*), along with its hybrids such as 'Lord Baltimore', grows to 6 feet tall and produces enormous—up to 10 inches across—deep red flowers for weeks at a time. The old-fashioned *H. mutabilis*, also known as the Confederate rose, grows to the size of a small tree and has flowers that change color, opening white or pink and turning to deep red by evening.

When, Where, and How to Plant

Plant container-grown hibiscus in early spring or fall. All hibiscus varieties thrive in full sun, and most will not flower well in part shade. Some—such as *Hibiscus coccineus* and *H. militaris*—tolerate swampy conditions but will also grow in average soil. *H. moscheutos* grows well in an average soil. It comes up late in spring, so keep this in mind when you place it in the garden; it also likes protection from the wind. *H. mutabilis* can grow to 10 feet tall in a single season, so site it accordingly. Space other types on 3-foot centers. Apply a ½-inch layer of an organic mulch after planting all hibiscus.

Growing Tips

For *H. moscheutos* and its hybrids such as 'Lord Baltimore', feed every six to eight weeks during the growing season. Use a 20-20-20 liquid fertilizer or a granular 10-10-10. Topdress *H. mutabilis* and *H. coccineus* once every spring and fall. Water weekly during the growing season; this applies to other hibiscus unless they are growing in swampy conditions.

Regional Advice and Care

Hibiscus should not require regular pruning. If branches or stems are dead come December, prune plants back to a few inches from the ground. These exotic flowers appeal to Japanese beetles and whiteflies in particular. To control whiteflies use an insecticidal soap. For Japanese beetles, handpick and destroy them.

Companion Planting and Design

Depending on the type of hibiscus, site it in the perennial garden, in pots, in the shrub border, or as a focal point in your landscape. Swamp hibiscus looks nice at the back of the border and makes a good companion for cannas and daylilies. For a dramatic effect, plant a small group of 'Lord Baltimore' in the middle of your flower garden with a background of ornamental grasses and butterfly bushes.

Try These

'Disco White' has huge, stunning, white flowers, up to 8 inches across, with a red center. 'Kopper King' grows 4 feet tall. Its copper-colored leaves show off the flowers—white with a tinge of pink and a red blotch in the center.

'Homestead Purple' Verbena

Verbena 'Homestead Purple'

Botanical Pronunciation
Ver-BEEN-a

Other Name Rose verbena

Bloom Period and Seasonal Colors
Summer to fall blooms in purple

Mature Height × Spread
8 in. to 1½ ft. × 3 ft.

'Homestead Purple' verbena was discovered growing in a patch of weeds on the side of a road in Georgia by Dr. Michael Dirr and Dr. Allan Armitage, two well-known plantsmen and professors at the University of Georgia. The large clusters of velvety, rich purple flowers bloom on and off from May until frost. Its mildew-resistant foliage, dark green above and gray-green below, is attractive all season. *Verbena* 'Homestead Purple' is evergreen and perennial except in the very coldest parts of the state. Even if its foliage is killed back, its roots will overwinter and put up new growth in the spring. Like 'Homestead Purple', *Verbena tenuisecta* has a habit of creeping along the ground, but its lacy foliage displays a much more graceful texture.

When, Where, and How to Plant
Plant container-grown 'Homestead Purple' in spring or early fall to allow the roots time to get established. For best blooming, plant in full sun, in a well-drained soil that has been amended to contain one-third organic matter, one-third coarse sand, and one-third existing soil. Because it is a rapid grower, it is a good idea to propagate by separating plants every few years. Dig up divisions that have taken root and transplant them to a desired spot. Space plants at 12 inches apart. Water well after planting, soaking the area several times.

Growing Tips
After planting, you can use a 20-20-20 liquid fertilizer at half-strength. Too much fertilizer, however, will result in lots of foliage and few blooms. Water only during periods of drought, once every two weeks.

Regional Advice and Care
If verbena gets leggy in late spring or early summer, prune it back for a bushier plant. Do not cut this perennial back in fall, as it seems to survive winter better if it has more leaf surface. Cover plants in late fall with a thin layer of mulch or pine straw. Once new growth has started in early spring, remove the mulch and cut plants back. Verbena is subject to mildew and spider mites. To determine if mites are active, shake verbena's leaves over a white piece of paper. If the specks that fall onto the paper move, mites are present. Control with a strong blast from the hose or an insecticidal soap. To control mildew, avoid overhead irrigation.

Companion Planting and Design
Plant 'Homestead Purple' in a rock garden or flower garden where it will get full sun and can creep around at will. This adaptable perennial is good for hanging baskets or containers, especially in combination with dark foliage plants, such as purple sweet potato vine. It is also attractive with *Artemisia*, lamb's ear, salvia, coneflower, and daisies.

Try These
Verbena bonariensis has stems 3 to 6 feet tall and purple flowers. *Verbena* 'Mabel's Maroon' has fluorescent maroon flowers and reportedly the vigor of 'Homestead Purple'.

Hosta

Hosta cvs.

Botanical Pronunciation
HOS-ta

Other Name Plantain lily

Bloom Period and Seasonal Colors
Late summer blooms in white or lavender

Mature Height × Spread
2 to 3 ft. × 3 ft.

When it comes to shade gardening, hostas are indispensable perennials. While many are heat resistant, few can tolerate full sun. One exception is *Hosta* 'Royal Standard'. This adaptable hybrid of the old-fashioned favorite *Hosta plantaginea* grows happily in shade or sun, forming large mounds of bold, yellow-green, deeply veined foliage. With large, heart-shaped leaves up to 8 inches long and 5 inches wide, even one plant makes a bold statement in the garden. Worth growing for the handsome foliage alone, this hosta also rewards us with sweetly scented, white flowers in late summer at a time when few other perennials are blooming. There are hundreds of varieties of hostas available to gardeners today, including large and small types. There is a hosta for almost every garden situation.

When, Where, and How to Plant
Plant hostas in early spring or fall. Divide and transplant clumps early in spring, just as the leaves are emerging and the crowns are visible. *Hosta* 'Royal Standard' will grow in sun or light shade. Hostas can survive in most soils, including heavy clay, but to reach their full potential, they need a rich, moist, well-drained soil. If the soil is compact or too dry, plants will be stunted and leaves discolored.

Growing Tips
After planting hostas, feed them with a fertilizer of a 10-10-10 ratio to give them a boost. After this, you can topdress them once every spring and fall with organic matter. Water when the top ½ inch of soil is dry to the touch, usually about once a week; do this while the plants become established during the first growing season and when they are actively growing. Hostas do not like dry soil.

Regional Advice and Care
Remove unsightly flower stalks as soon as hostas finish blooming and before they set seed. If the foliage becomes tattered early in the season, shear plants back to encourage a flush of new growth. Hostas are mostly free of pests and disease, but they do suffer from slugs that can turn leaves into an ugly mess of holes. Check with your county Extension office (page 225) for recommended controls. One pest that loves hosta are deer. The most effective control is a deer fence.

Companion Planting and Design
Use hostas in the shade garden in combination with ferns like the Japanese painted fern or the autumn fern. There are hostas with variegated foliage, blue foliage, and even chartreuse foliage like *Hosta* 'Sum and Substance', which will grow in full sun or part shade. This is one of the largest hostas with leaves up to 9 inches long and 20 inches wide. You can grow hostas in containers; just make sure you provide a soil that is well drained and you amend it with organic matter. There are dwarf hostas, which are less than 10 inches tall.

Try These
'Blue Angel' has beautiful textured blue leaves.

Japanese Anemone

Anemone × *hybrida* 'Honorine Jobert'

Botanical Pronunciation
a-NEM-o-nee hi-BRED-a

Other Name Hybrid anemone

Bloom Period and Seasonal Colors
Early fall blooms in white

Mature Height × Spread
3 to 4 ft. × 3 ft.

In the garden, white flowers can either soften intense hues or help show them off. Popular since before the Civil War, 'Honorine Jobert' is still a favorite selection of Georgia gardeners (except those who live in the coastal areas where the weather is too hot for it). A strong grower, it produces a large mound of foliage with leaves divided into three leaflets. As the summer progresses, its bright green, leafy mass gives no hint of what's to come in fall, when the slender sturdy stems shoot up to 3 feet or more. Loaded with buds for what seems like weeks, they finally open to beautiful white flowers that dance in the autumn breezes. The silky flowers are 2 to 3 inches across.

When, Where, and How to Plant

Plant container-grown Japanese anemone in spring or fall. Divisions should be taken in spring; root cuttings should be taken in winter when the plant is dormant. Morning sun combined with shade during the hottest part of the day is ideal. If you plant in full sun, keep the soil moist. Avoid areas where the soil does not dry out or drain well during winter, the plant's dormant period. Soggy roots in winter will lead to a quick death. Plant Japanese anemone so that it has at least 2 to 3 feet to spread and grow. Amend the soil before planting by mixing one-third organic matter, one-third coarse sand, and one-third of the existing soil, which usually has a high clay content. Water after planting. Cover with ½ inch of mulch, making sure to keep it away from the crown of the plant.

This will help keep the roots cool during the hot summer months

Growing Tips

Topdress with organic matter twice yearly, in spring and fall. Water plants once a week during summer and during periods of drought (no rain for two weeks).

Regional Advice and Care

Planting this perennial in a site that has rich, moist, well-drained soil; morning sun; and shade during the hottest part of the day will result in its rapid spread. No pruning is necessary. If you plant it in a windy area, it is best to stake the stalks before they begin to flower. Japanese anemone does not suffer from any serious pest or disease problems.

Companion Planting and Design

Plant this perennial in the middle or back of the flower border where its blooms can arch over other plants. Combine them with gray-foliaged plants, such as *Artemisia* or lamb's ears. They also contrast well with purple asters. If you can bear to cut them, Japanese anemone makes an elegant cut flower.

Try These

'September Charm' produces an abundance of rose-pink flowers. For a different look there are several selections with semidouble flowers including 'Whirlwind' with white blooms and 'Queen Charlotte' with pink flowers.

Japanese Iris

Iris ensata

Botanical Pronunciation
EYE-riss en-SAY-tuh

Bloom Period and Seasonal Colors
Spring blooms in violet, purple, pink, rose, white, streaked

Mature Height × Spread
4 ft. × 2 ft.

*I*ris ensata (formerly known as *Iris kaempferi*) produces blossoms that look good enough to eat. The flowers are made up of three inner segments—standards, which are petals—and three outer segments—falls, which are petal-like sepals. The blooms, among the biggest in the genus, range in size from 4 to 12 inches across; some are the size of a small dinner plate. The large, flat-topped flowers (beardless blooms) are elegant and come in both single and double forms. The single types have a triangular shape, while the doubles look almost circular. The upright, narrow foliage (3 to 4 feet tall) looks elegant even when plants are not blooming. Planted at the edge of a pond or steam, Japanese iris adds grace and beauty to the garden.

When, Where, and How to Plant

Plant container-grown plants in spring or fall. This is also the time to plant rhizomes (thickened underground parts from which roots and shoots initiate) 2 inches deep and 1½ feet apart. If you plant them in containers, you can plant up to three rhizomes in a 12-inch pot. Japanese iris will grow in swampy conditions or in average garden soil, but it requires lots of moisture when actively growing and blooming. It prefers an acidic to neutral soil. Amend soil with one-third organic matter and one-third coarse sand combined with one-third existing soil. Site Japanese iris where they will receive full sun or part shade. Plant them along ponds or stream banks, or even in plunge pots in a garden pool or water feature until the water is halfway to the rim. Apply a ½-inch layer of organic mulch to conserve moisture and help keep roots cool.

Growing Tips

Fertilize Japanese iris once in spring and once in fall with 20-20-20. Water them daily when they are growing and blooming. In fall, reduce watering to once every two weeks.

Regional Advice and Care

You do not need to prune Japanese iris unless the foliage becomes unsightly. Trim foliage back accordingly with scissors. Japanese iris are subject to borers. They feed on the edges of leaves and work their way down to the rhizomes, eating them and leaving only hollow shells. Piles of sawdust around the bases of plants indicate borers. Because eggs overwinter in fall debris and hatch in spring, the best control is prevention. Remove all leaf litter in fall before winter.

Companion Planting and Design

Plant Japanese iris in the flower border with other perennials, such as hardy geranium, garden phlox, and Siberian iris (*Iris sibirica*). Plant it next to a pool with cardinal flower, swamp hibiscus, and *Acorus* 'Ogon'.

Try These

Louisiana iris, also called swamp iris, is well adapted to growing in heat and heavy, wet soils. The Japanese roof iris, *Iris tectorum*, is also a good garden plant but does not grow in damp soils.

Joe Pye Weed

Eupatorium purpureum

Botanical Pronunciation
you-puh-TORE-ee-um pur-PUR-ee-um

Bloom Period and Seasonal Colors
Fall blooms in purple-pink

Mature Height × Spread
5 to 7 ft. × to 3 ft.

A classic American native, Joe Pye weed grows along roadsides, in meadows, and in fields as far north as Maine and as far south as Georgia. A perfect choice for a bold architectural statement in the perennial border, Joe Pye weed has 8- to 12-inch-long leaves that are whorled, usually with three to five leaves at each node. Strong, hollow, cane-like green stems are often marked with purple where the leaves attach. The huge, purple flower heads (up to 1½ feet in diameter) are showy for weeks beginning in early fall. A dramatic plant, Joe Pye weed can be a focal point in the fall garden, attracting butterflies and eliciting admiring comments as its large masses of flowers sway in the breeze.

When, Where, and How to Plant
Plant container-grown Joe Pye weed in spring or early fall so that it will have plenty of time to establish a good root system before winter. Divide clumps every two to three years. In its native habitat, Joe Pye weed grows in damp meadows, so keep this in mind when you select a site. Full sun and a moist soil are ideal, but Joe Pye weed will also grow in shadier gardens. A moderately fertile soil is best. Water young plants well after planting, soaking the ground several times. Apply a ½-inch layer of mulch after planting. Refer to page 86 for more planting tips.

Growing Tips
This perennial does not need fertilization. Topdress once every spring and fall with ½ inch of organic matter. If Joe Pye weed is planted in a very dry soil in full sun, it will become scorched and wilted during the heat of Georgia's summers. Keep it well watered; once a week should be adequate.

Regional Advice and Care
In early summer, prune the stalks back by one-third to one-half to achieve a more compact plant. Cut off spent flower heads once the bloom finishes to prevent this native from spreading seed. Joe Pye weed does not suffer from any serious pest or disease problems.

Companion Planting and Design
This garden giant is not for a small garden, but it does work well in a flower border as a bold background accent, or in a naturalized planting in a meadow or along a stream. Plant Joe Pye weed behind smaller and earlier flowering perennials. For naturalized plantings, combine it with ironweed, goldenrod, swamp sunflower, and black-eyed Susan. It also looks good with purple and white asters, old-fashioned single chrysanthemums, and ornamental grasses such as *Miscanthus* 'Morning Light'.

Try These
For the same effect on a somewhat smaller scale, *Eupatorium purpureum* 'Gateway' reaches only 5 feet tall and has rosy purple flowers atop purplish stems. For colorful foliage, *Eupatorium rugosum* 'Chocolate' has chocolate-colored leaves and tiny white blooms. *Eupatorium dubium* 'Little Joe' grows only 4 feet high.

Lenten Rose

Helleborus × hybridus

Botanical Pronunciation
HELL-e-BOR-us HI–bred-us

Other Name Hellebore

Bloom Period and Seasonal Colors
Evergreen; early spring blooms in white, purple, maroon, variegated

Mature Height × Spread
15 to 20 in. × 18 to 24 in.

An aristocrat of the garden, the Lenten rose bridges the gap from winter to spring. Elegantly evergreen, Lenten rose has shiny, leathery, 12- to 16-inch-wide leaves that are divided into seven to nine segments. One of the gems of the winter garden, it is attractive year-round. Its colorful, nodding flowers—ranging in color from pure white to dark maroon, and sometimes speckled or splotched with green or purple—appear as early as January or February and may produce flowers over a period of eight to ten weeks. Both the leaves and flowers on this hellebore are stemless and arise directly from the rootstock. Once it becomes established in the garden, the Lenten rose will thrive, even in a dry shade situation.

When, Where, and How to Plant
For best success, plant container-grown Lenten rose in spring or early fall. Once established in the garden (usually in two to three years), it will often produce masses of seedlings around the base of the mother plant; these can easily be dug as clumps and transplanted in spring. Plant Lenten rose in partial to full shade, in a well-drained soil that is rich in organic matter. If planted in full sun, plants will need extra water and they may loose their elegant look. You can also grow Lenten rose in a decorative container, provided it has good drainage. Water well after planting, soaking the area several times. Apply a ½-inch layer of organic mulch to help conserve moisture.

Growing Tips
Fertilize the first spring after planting, using a 10-10-10 fertilizer to give it a boost. Topdress once every spring and fall with organic matter. Water once a week during the growing season to help it establish a strong root system. Once established, it should require little care except for watering during periods of drought (no rain for two weeks).

Regional Advice and Care
If any leaves suffer from winter burn, cut them off at the base where they are attached and they will quickly be replaced by new ones. Deer (supposedly) do not eat this perennial. Lenten rose resents having its root system disturbed, and you will have a bigger and better clump if you don't divide it. Because it reseeds freely, you can transplant seedlings easily in spring or fall. It does not suffer from any serious pest or disease problems.

Companion Planting and Design
This long-lived perennial is perfect for the shade garden and grows happily alongside ferns and hostas. Plant Lenten rose with daffodils; the daffodils will flower in spring and, later in the season, the Lenten rose will help mask their ugly foliage.

Try These
Helleborus niger, the Christmas rose, offers beautiful white blooms. The hybrid 'Ivory Prince' is one of many choice selections of hellebore. Look for introductions by Pine Knot Farms, a hellebore nursery in Virginia.

Moss Phlox

Phlox subulata

Botanical Pronunciation
FLOKS sub-ew-LAH-ta

Bloom Period and Seasonal Colors
Early to midspring blooms in shades of blue,
red-purple, violet-purple, pink, white

Mature Height × Spread
3 to 6 in. × 18 in.

Moss phlox is just the plant for gardeners who want bright, bold colors. Forget about those subtle pastel flowers, and bring on the moss phlox! Quickly forming a dense mound, moss phlox is a familiar flower in many old, country gardens where it covers a steep bank or drainage ditch, or creeps over an old stone wall next to a farmhouse. Wherever it grows, moss phlox does not go unnoticed. There are numerous cultivars available, including some whose flowers come in colors softer than those of the species. *Phlox subulata* 'Oakington Blue' has sky blue flowers, and 'White Delight' has large white flowers. A good creeping phlox for shade gardens is *P. stolonifera*. It bears flowers in a range of colors, including white, pink, violet, and blue.

When, Where, and How to Plant
Plant container-grown moss phlox in spring or fall. Propagate by layering (take a nonflowering stem and cover it lightly with soil, when roots form, cut off your new plant) or division in summer or fall. Cuttings taken in fall should be overwintered in a greenhouse or cold frame. Moss phlox has a shallow root system, so cut back the foliage before transplanting divisions; this will cause the least amount of stress for new plants. Moss phlox likes full sun and a well-drained soil, especially a soil that is somewhat sandy or gritty. A slightly alkaline soil is fine too. Space plants 12 inches apart. Water well after planting.

Growing Tips
No special fertilization is required; just make sure the soil is well drained. Water only during periods of drought (no rain for two weeks).

Regional Advice and Care
To keep foliage looking its best, shear plants back after blooms finish. Spider mites may occasionally attack plants. Symptoms include yellowing leaves with tiny, light green spots. The best way to test for spider mites is to hold a piece of white paper under a leaf and shake the leaf. If the specks that fall onto the paper move, you have mites. Try to blast them off with the water hose, or use an insecticidal soap or horticultural oil.

Companion Planting and Design
Moss phlox makes an effective evergreen groundcover or edging plant. To make a bold statement, plant some of each color in a grouping. Plant moss phlox in the crevices of a rock garden, in a flower garden, or on a steep, sunny slope. Plant it as a groundcover between early blooming bulbs, such as lavender crocus or small varieties of pale-colored daffodils. For a bold combination, plant red tulips and moss phlox together.

Try These
A creeping phlox that is best suited for a woodland garden (light shade is ideal) is *Phlox divaricata*. Growing to 1 foot high, it blooms in spring with flowers ¾ to 1½ inches wide, in shades of blue and white.

Mottled Wild Ginger

Hexastylis shuttleworthii var. *harperi* 'Callaway'

Botanical Pronunciation
hex-uh-STY-lus shut-tle-WORTH-ee-eye

Bloom Period and Seasonal Colors
Evergreen; early spring blooms in purple-brown

Mature Height × Spread
4 to 6 in. × 2 ft.

Discovered at Callaway Gardens in Pine Mountain, Georgia, this vigorous selection of wild ginger has evergreen, heart-shaped, shiny green leaves with lighter cream markings. The leaves resemble those of cyclamen. Planted in a woodland, in a moist but well-drained soil, this selection of wild ginger forms evergreen clumps that look good year-round, even during the heat of Georgia summers when other plants look wilted and worn out. Children will have fun discovering the "little brown jugs," its inconspicuous flowers that are hidden under the leaves. Mottled wild ginger gets its common name from the ginger-like scent released by bruised or cut roots. It is truly an aristocrat, worth seeking out for a shade garden. *Asarum canadense*, the Canadian wild ginger, tolerates the extreme heat in lower Georgia.

When, Where, and How to Plant
Plant container-grown mottled wild ginger in spring or early fall. Take divisions in late winter or early spring. This native ginger needs a moist, well-drained, woodland site in shade or at least half shade. Plant in a soil amended with organic matter, avoiding areas where there may be competition from tree roots. If you grow it in pots, wild ginger can be moved about the garden year-round to brighten up a dark corner. Once established *Asarum* and *Hexastylis* plants are fairly drought tolerant.

Growing Tips
No special fertilization is needed; just be sure the soil is rich in organic matter. Apply ½ inch of compost in spring and fall. Composted leaves make a great mulch, and when they break down, they provide welcome organic matter. If the soil stays too dry, mottled wild ginger will look wilted and unattractive. Keep plants well watered weekly. Water container plants when the top ½ inch of soil is dry to the touch.

Regional Advice and Care
Slow to spread, mottled wild ginger can be easily propagated by dividing the underground rhizomes in late winter. Other than removing the occasional tattered leaf, this ginger does not require pruning. It does not suffer from any serious pest or disease problems.

Companion Planting and Design
Although *Hexastylis* 'Callaway' is evergreen, it is not fast spreading like ivy or vinca; it is perhaps best used as a specimen plant. A good companion for hellebores and ferns, it will brighten up any shade garden. To create a tapestry effect, plant this woodland gem in combination with more aggressive groundcovers, such as ajuga or foam flower. Wild ginger is a good companion for spring-blooming woodland phlox and small bulbs, such as dwarf iris. If you don't have the proper garden environment or space, this ginger is a good candidate for containers.

Try These
There are many different types of ginger from the Orient, including *Hexastylis splendens* with silver-variegated foliage that stands out in the garden. *Hexastylis* 'Ling Ling', called the Panda Face ginger, is also attractive. A native species found in our woodlands is *Hexastylis arifolium*.

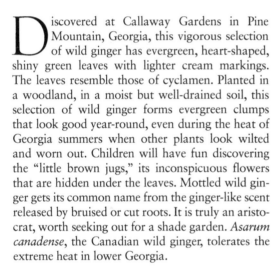

Purple Coneflower

Echinacea purpurea

Botanical Pronunciation
EK-in-AY-see-a pur-PEWR-ree-a

Other Name Coneflower

Bloom Period and Seasonal Colors
Summer blooms in purple, orange, pink, red, white

Mature Height × Spread
12 in. to 4 ft. × 2 ft.

If you've ever touched the cone of a purple coneflower, it will come as no surprise that *Echinacea* comes from the Greek *echinos*, meaning "hedgehog." Coneflower's hairy, dark green leaves that are up to 8 inches in length, its stiff branching stems, and its drooping ray petals all contribute to its coarse texture. Blooming for a long period in the summer, it resembles black-eyed Susan except for its purple petals. A perennial favorite of flower arrangers for its flowers and dried cone heads, purple coneflower is an easy-care flower that can go in the sunny border or meadow garden. *Echinacea* 'Bright Star' has bright, rose-red flowers with maroon centers that grow to 2 to 3 feet tall. White selections include 'White Lustre' and 'White Swan'.

When, Where, and How to Plant
Divide clumps and plant divisions of purple coneflower in spring. Plant container-grown plants in spring or fall. Be advised: Seeds take two or more years to flower, and cultivars will not come true from seed. Plant purple coneflower in full sun or part shade in a well-drained soil. There is no need to amend the soil. Just make sure it is well drained, adding coarse sand if necessary. Avoid soil that is overly rich in organic matter. Plant coneflower on 2-foot centers. Water well after planting.

Growing Tips
No special fertilization is needed. Water purple coneflower once a week during the first growing season, when it is becoming established in the garden. After this period, it should not require watering except during periods of drought (no rain for two weeks). Saturate the soil around the plants once every two weeks.

Regional Advice and Care
Plants benefit from being divided once every four years, but no special pruning is required. If the soil is too rich, or if there is too much shade, you may need to stake them. Coneflowers are susceptible to some leaf spot and to Japanese beetles. Check with your county Extension office for recommended controls. One of the best controls is to clean up any leaf litter every fall, eliminating the potential for overwintering disease. Make sure the soil does not stay wet in the winter, this can lead to problems with rot.

Companion Planting and Design
Plant purple coneflower in the middle or back of a border, next to finer-textured perennials and annuals to soften its coarse look. *Artemisia* 'Powis Castle' is a good, gray, soft-textured perennial to plant in combination with coneflower. Planted next to butterfly bush and coreopsis, coneflower will quickly transform your garden into a haven for butterflies. It also looks good planted in combination with the purple-leafed selections of Chinese witchhazel (*Loropetalum chinese*).

Try These
The native Tennessee coneflower (*Echinacea tennesseensis*) has greenish cones, horizontal ray flowers, and stems to 1½ feet tall. This rare beauty is available from wildflower nurseries.

Sedum 'Autumn Joy'

Sedum 'Autumn Joy'

Botanical Pronunciation
SED-um

Bloom Period and Seasonal Colors
Late summer to fall blooms in white changing to pink and then deep rose

Mature Height × Spread
1 to 2 ft. × 1 to 2 ft.

Unlike many perennials that are suited to either hot or cold climates, 'Autumn Joy' sedum performs equally well in Northern and Southern gardens. In early spring, it sends up gray-green buds. By midsummer, the 6-inch, flat-topped flower heads look like broccoli. As summer progresses, the flower buds turn from a whitish shade to a pink and then finally a deep rose color. The flowers are showy late into the fall, dry on their stems, and turn a rust color as they age. Perfect for creating interest in the winter garden, the dried flower stalks last until spring. *Sedum kamtschaticum* grows to 4 inches tall and produces masses of tiny yellow flowers in summer. A sun lover, *Sedum* 'Neon' has neon rose-colored flowers.

When, Where, and How to Plant

Divide and transplant clumps of 'Autumn Joy' in spring. Propagate by leaf cuttings in summer. Plant container-grown plants in spring or fall. This sedum may be planted in full sun or light shade in a well-drained soil. This is one perennial that does not need a rich, fertile soil. In fact, if the soil's fertility is too high, plants will become open in the center and the long flower stalks will flop over. When planting in the ground, space plants 12 inches apart. Water after planting.

Growing Tips

Nearly indestructible, all sedum needs to thrive is sun or light shade and any well-drained soil. *Sedum* does not need fertilizer or soil amendments. Water once every two weeks if there is no rain, drenching the area around the plant.

Regional Advice and Care

Sometimes—if grown in too much shade or if the soil is very fertile—'Autumn Joy' will become a big, unsightly clump that is open at the center. Dividing and transplanting clumps like this will help rejuvenate them. If they are in too much shade, cut back the flower stalks in late June to about 12 inches to keep plants bushy and full. Left undisturbed, plants will grow and bloom for years without any special care. Leave the dried flower stalks on the plants for winter interest and cut them back in early spring just as buds are swelling. 'Autumn Joy' does not suffer from any serious pest or disease problems.

Companion Planting and Design

A tough plant, 'Autumn Joy' will grow in a planting bed surrounded by pavement (it doesn't seem to be bothered by reflected heat), on a sandy slope, or in a container. Plant it in combination with ornamental grasses and other perennials, such as black-eyed Susan, to provide months of interest. It also looks good paired with other sedums, including the groundcover types *Sedum kamtschaticum* and *S. ternatum*.

Try These

Sedum makinoi 'Ogon' is a groundcover with gold leaves flushed with pink. *Sedum tetractinum* is a low-growing ground hugger with starry yellow flowers.

Variegated Solomon's Seal

Polygonatum odoratum 'Variegatum'

Botanical Pronunciation
Po-LIG-o-NAY-tum o-do-RAH-tum

Bloom Period and Seasonal Colors
Variegated green and white foliage, summer to fall, white flowers in spring

Mature Height × Spread
2 to 3 ft. × ½ to 1 ft.

This is one of the most elegant perennials for the shade. Arching stems with soft green leaves edged in creamy white light up the garden. In April, the small bell-like white flowers hang down from under the leaves and add even more interest. The foliage looks great in the garden with both evergreen and deciduous ferns, including cinnamon fern and autumn fern, as well as hostas and other shade-loving perennials. Variegated Solomon's seal also shines when it is used as a cut stem for flower arrangements. Combine it in the woodland with native groundcovers like green and gold. In autumn the leaves turn a soft yellow before they disappear for the winter. Slow to get established, but once it does, it will delight you for years.

When, Where, and How to Plant

Plant variegated Solomon's seal in the shade garden to brighten up a dark corner. It will grow in part sun or dry shade but will not increase and multiply as fast as it would in a moist, well-drained soil. Plant container-grown plants in early spring or fall. Divide plants in fall. When you plant, mix in organic matter to a depth of at least 6 inches. After you plant, apply a ½-inch layer of mulch.

Growing Tips

Water new plantings every few days for the first month while they become established. Fertilize in early spring with 20-20-20.

Regional Advice and Care

The best time to propagate this perennial is in fall. Divide clumps, making sure each division has some roots and shoots. Replant the divisions as soon as possible. To help make sure plants get off to a good start, dig out and prepare the soil where the divisions will go, ahead of time. This perennial does not seem bothered by any pest or disease problems. The soft yellow fall foliage will eventually disappear and new growth will begin again in the spring.

Companion Planting and Design

Plant this perennial under dogwoods and fringe tree, next to ferns and hellebores, and in front of evergreen shrubs. The variegated foliage will glow, adding welcome brightness to the shade. Use a mass of it to provide a transition from one group of plants to another. Variegated Solomon's seal will also help to stabilize a shady bank, and you will be able to look up to see the flowers hanging down. Combine it with other shade-loving perennials like bleeding heart and trilliums.

Try These

Polygonatum humile, dwarf Solomon's seal, only grows 5 to 9 inches tall and forms 3-foot clumps. For a bold statement, *Polygonatum commutatum*, great Solomon's seal, can reach a height of 7 feet and may form clumps that are equally as wide. Evergreen Solomon's seal, *Disporopsis*, makes a good companion for the deciduous types.

Wild Indigo

Baptisia australis

Botanical Pronunciation
Bap-TIS-ee-a ow-STRAH-lis

Other Name False blue indigo

Bloom Period and Seasonal Colors
Spring blooms in blue

Mature Height × Spread
3 to 5 ft. × 3 ft.

An adaptable native with handsome blue-green foliage and beautiful indigo blue flowers, this plant is for gardeners who claim they can't grow anything. Wild indigo is slow to establish in the garden, but after a few years it should become a large clump. Left alone, it will thrive with little or no care. Like many members of the pea family, this legume adapts to poor soils and grows in part shade or sun. The inch-long, pealike flowers bloom on 10- to 12-inch-tall stems for close to four weeks in the spring. This is an easy-to-grow plant that offers attractive foliage, beautiful flowers, and decorative seedpods. *Baptisia tinctoria* has yellow flowers and blooms in the summer. *B. alba* has white flowers in late spring.

When, Where, and How to Plant
Plant container-grown wild indigo in spring or fall. It has a taproot, and once it's established, it resents being transplanted. If you propagate it from root divisions, take them in early spring or fall. *Baptisia australis* will tolerate poor soils with low fertility, but it will thrive in full sun in soils that are moist and rich in organic matter. Wild indigo will also grow in part shade. Allow it room to grow, as a clump will eventually be 2 to 3 feet across. Water after planting, and apply a ½-inch layer of mulch.

Growing Tips
No special fertilizer is required, but you can top-dress with organic matter once every spring and fall. Water once a week in dry periods (no rain for two weeks). Soak the area where it is planted, wait a few minutes, and repeat. Make sure to give plants plenty of room as clumps spread up to 3 feet wide.

Regional Advice and Care
Stake wild indigo only if it is planted in a very shady location. No pruning is required, but removing spent flowers will encourage a second flush of blooms. Leave seedpods to dry on the plant for winter decoration, or collect them to use in dried bouquets and arrangements. Wild indigo may take several years to produce significant blooms, but once established, it will thrive for years with little or no care. It does not suffer from any insect or disease problems.

Companion Planting and Design
Site this plant at the middle or back of a flower border so that its foliage can serve as a backdrop for other perennials. This hardy ornamental makes a fine specimen plant in sunny borders or along the edge of a woodland. After the plant blooms, the foliage provides a good foil for other summer-blooming perennials. Pair it with iris, purple coneflower, and spring-blooming bulbs such as allium.

Try These
Baptisia 'Purple Smoke' has smoke-colored stems and flowers. *Baptisia* 'Carolina Moonlight' has soft yellow flowers and flowers about the same time as early roses like *Rosa* 'Zephirine Drouhin' and perennials like *Amsonia hubrichtii*.

ROSES

FOR GEORGIA

Roses have been revered by gardeners and non-gardeners alike for centuries, primarily for their perfume and as a cut flower. With the vast numbers of new selections offered each year, there are roses to suit almost every type of garden—from the very formal to the old-fashioned cottage garden.

Successful Planting and Growing

Planting

Plant your roses where they will receive a minimum of six hours of direct sun per day and no competition from tree roots for moisture. Good air circulation and generous spacing between plants (5 feet apart in most parts of Georgia except for the coast, where they should be 8 feet apart) will help minimize diseases, such as black spot and powdery mildew.

Starting with soil that is rich in organic matter and well drained is equally important. Raised beds are also an option. When you amend the soil, incorporate some all-purpose fertilizer into the hole. Check the product label for recommended amounts. Roses bloom best when the soil has a pH of 6.0 to 6.5. If possible, take a soil test (see page 12). In the absence of a soil test, mix ½ cup of lime and 2 tablespoons of triple super phosphate (0-46-0) with the soil that you pack around the roots of each rose.

For bare-root roses, it is best to plant them as soon as you receive them. However, if the canes and roots appear to have dried out, you can revive them by burying the whole plant for two days—top and roots—in moist soil, sand, or sawdust. At a minimum, soak the dry plant overnight in a bucket of water. Before planting, prune any broken canes back to a healthy bud and prune away any damaged or dead roots. Dig a hole large enough to spread out the roots, draping them over a cone of soil in the middle of the hole. Place the plant in the hole so that the graft union (a knob-like area) is just above soil level. Fill the hole, adding soil by hand. Water slowly so that the soil settles completely. Apply 1 to 1½ inches of mulch.

Fertilizing and Watering

The optimum time to fertilize is when a plant is putting on new growth and after a bloom cycle has ended. Stop feeding in late fall, about six weeks before the first frost. Both slow-release and liquid fertilizers are fine. Topdressing at least twice a year with organic matter is also a good way to provide nutrients for your roses. When the top ½ inch of soil is dry to the touch, water deeply, saturating the soil around the rootball.

Pests and Disease

The best defense against insect and disease problems is to grow varieties that are recommended for Southern gardens. Some of the common pests that attack roses include aphids, spider mites, Japanese beetles, rose midges, and thrips. For control, use insecticidal soap, horticultural oil, or contact insecticide. Diseases—such as powdery mildew, rust, and blackspot—can also cause problems. Check with your local Extension office (page 225) for controls.

Pruning

Proper pruning will contribute greatly to the overall vigor and long-term health of your roses. Remember, blooms are produced on new growth.

Clematis montana and Lady Banks
Roseal Goodnestone

- **Hybrid Teas and Grandifloras:** Prune between late February and mid-March. Remove dead, damaged, or weak growth. Make a flat cut, ½ inch below the dead or damaged portion. Remove one-third to one-half of the previous season's growth. Make cuts ¼ inch above outward-facing buds. Cut away any branch that rubs against another or crosses through the center of the plant.
- **Floribundas, Polyanthas, and Shrub Roses:** If you need to prune, don't remove more than one-fourth of the previous season's growth.
- **Climbing Roses:** Don't prune your climbers for the first two or three years after planting. With established plants, prune one-time bloomers as soon as they finish blooming (typically in May) to remove old and dead canes. Prune repeat bloomers in late February to mid-March, removing old and dead wood. Cut back lateral branches to two or three buds.

English Rose

Rosa cvs.

Botanical Pronunciation
RO-sa

Bloom Period and Seasonal Colors
Spring, summer, and fall blooms in pink, white, yellow, shades of red

Mature Height × Spread
3 to 10 ft. × 2 to 4 ft.

Rose breeder David Austin introduced a group of English roses that are the result of crossing old garden roses with modern hybrids. These roses offer the best of both types. The flowers are old-fashioned in appearance, with many petals, a delightful fragrance, and repeat blooms. These roses have a shrubby appearance. Some—such as 'Graham Thomas' with its striking yellow, cupped flowers—can easily be trained as climbers. Other favorites include 'Abraham Darby' with double blooms of apricot-yellow tones on tall, arching canes all summer long; its foliage is shiny green. 'Gertrude Jekyll', named after the famous English gardener and writer, has deep carmine pink flowers and a delicious scent reminiscent of old-fashioned Damask roses. One of the more compact selections is 'Heritage' with clear, shell-pink cupped flowers.

When, Where, and How to Plant

Plant bare-root roses as soon as you receive them. The best time to plant container-grown roses is in early spring or fall. If you plant in summer, water once a week during the first growing season. Mix one-third organic matter into the existing soil before you plant. Hand dig or rototill the area to make sure the soil is loose and crumbly. Don't plant when the soil is wet and soggy. Depending on the particular cultivar, make sure you provide ample room for your rose to spread out and grow. Site English roses in a spot where they will get plenty of sunshine, at least six hours per day. Apply a 1-inch layer of mulch after you plant.

Growing Tips

Water once a week, saturating the soil around the rose thoroughly. After the rose is established (after the first growing season), water weekly if there is no rain. Mulch twice a year with 1 to 1½ inches of a good organic matter, and then fertilize at least twice a year with a commercial product (either organic or inorganic). Roses are heavy feeders; follow the directions on the label.

Regional Advice and Care

Prune in early spring only to shape up the plant and remove long, wild shoots. Deadhead to encourage repeat blooming during the growing season. English roses tend to be pest and disease resistant, and the foliage looks good for most of the season without spraying. You may get some blackspot, but not enough to worry about.

Companion Planting and Design

Train 'Abraham Darby' as an espalier against a brick wall for a dramatic effect. 'Graham Thomas' can be trained as a climber or a large informal shrub. Incorporate 'Mary Rose' (pink blooms) into the flower border and surround it with *Verbena* 'Homestead Purple' and blue salvia. Train one of the small-flowered clematis to grow up through a shrub rose, using the rose as a trellis—a dramatic effect with two different blooms on the same plant.

Try These

'The Squire' has deep crimson blooms, up to 5 inches across, with a delicious perfume.

Floribunda Rose

Rosa cvs.

Botanical Pronunciation
RO-sa

Bloom Period and Seasonal Colors
Spring to frost blooms in white, yellow, orange, pink, red, lavender, blends

Mature Height × Spread
3 to 5 ft. × 3 to 4 ft.

Some of the best garden roses are the result of crosses between groups with very different qualities. Floribunda roses are a cross between hybrid teas and polyanthas. This group of roses with its clusters of blooms, shiny foliage, and resistance to disease holds up well in Georgia gardens. A popular floribunda is 'Sunsprite' (growing 2 to 3 feet tall) with large clusters of fragrant yellow flowers from spring until frost. The foliage looks good most of the season without regular spraying. Another choice floribunda is 'Betty Prior', a repeat bloomer with bright pink, single flowers. 'Iceberg' is a white-flowered selection that is popular trained as a standard. Use floribunda roses in containers, for informal hedges, or in the perennial garden.

When, Where, and How to Plant
Plant bare-root roses during the dormant season as soon as you receive them. Container-grown roses should be planted in early spring or in early fall. Choose a location where your rose will receive six hours or more of direct sunlight per day. The soil should be well drained and rich in organic matter. Mix at least one-third organic matter—such as compost, manure, or composted pine bark—with the existing soil. Dig a hole wider, but no deeper, than the container the rose is growing in. For a bare-root plant, dig a wide hole, deep enough to leave a mound of soil in the middle to drape the roots over. Prune off any dried-up or dead roots before planting. Prune back canes to new, healthy, green tissue. Floribundas tend to be more compact than other roses, making it easy to use them in the garden or in containers.

Growing Tips
Topdress with mulch (1 to 1½ inches) twice a year for additional organic matter and to help keep roots cool and moist. Instead of a daily surface sprinkling, water weekly during the growing season, saturating the ground around the rose. Fertilize at least three times a year—in early spring, summer, and fall—using a formula of 16-4-8 or 12-4-8.

Regional Advice and Care
Prune floribunda roses in early spring, just as buds are swelling. Prune back to five or seven buds from the base, and remove any damaged or dead wood. Prune to remove weak or wounded branches that occur below the graft union. Floribundas are not subject to any serious pest or disease problems. Good air circulation is key to prevention of disease problems.

Companion Planting and Design
Floribundas can extend the blooming season in the shrub border, offering flowers long after the traditional spring bloomers have come and gone. Plant them in combination with perennials like daisies, salvia, and iris, and ornamental grasses like *Miscanthus sinensis*.

Try These
'Charisma' is a red blend, 'Angel Face' has mauve flowers, and 'Apricot Nectar' is an apricot blend. 'Bahia' is an orange blend.

Hybrid Tea Rose

Rosa cvs.

Botanical Pronunciation
RO-sa

Bloom Period and Seasonal Colors
Spring and summer blooms in red, orange, pink, yellow, white, lavender, blends

Mature Height × Spread
2 to 10 ft. × 2 to 4 ft.

Despite the fact that hybrid tea roses grown in Georgia can require spraying every seven to ten days, along with frequent fertilizing and deadheading, growing them can be rewarding. Because of their sturdy stems, large open flowers held high above the foliage, and long blooming season, it's understandable that these high-maintenance plants are still popular, especially among beginning rose growers. 'Mr. Lincoln' represents the classic red rose. Its dark, leathery foliage and vigorous habit make it one of the better hybrid teas for Georgia, where powdery mildew and blackspot can wreak havoc. Its strong stems, urn-shaped buds, and large cupped flowers with up to thirty-five petals make it ideal for cutting and using in arrangements. Hybrid teas come in all colors, and there are even single-flowered forms.

When, Where, and How to Plant
Plant bare-root roses as soon as you receive them during the dormant season. Plant container-grown roses in early spring or early fall. Site hybrid teas in at least six hours of direct sunlight. Plant in well-drained soil that has been amended with at least one-third organic matter, such as well-composted manure or mushroom compost. For bare-root roses, dig a hole large enough to place the roots over a small mound of soil and allow the roots to spread out in all directions. Prune all damaged roots. Balance root pruning with an equal amount of top-growth pruning. Plant container-grown roses at the same depth they were growing in the pot.

Growing Tips
Topdress with 1 to 1½ inches of mulch twice yearly to provide additional organic matter and help keep roots cool and moist. Use groundcovers as living mulches. Keep hybrid teas well watered during the growing season. Consider investing in drip irrigation so you don't have to drag hoses around every week. Otherwise, saturate the area around the rose, allow the water to soak in, and repeat. Water weekly, twice weekly during drought.

Regional Advice and Care
Growing hybrid teas requires a spray program that combines fungicide and insecticide every seven to ten days during the growing season. Prune canes in early spring to a height of four to six buds from the base of the previous year's growth. Hybrid teas are susceptible to spider mites, powdery mildew, and blackspot. Contact the Atlanta Rose Society (www.atlantarose.org) for a list of the best hybrid teas for Georgia.

Companion Planting and Design
Use low-growing perennials (such as hardy geraniums) or groundcovers (such as *Ajuga reptans* 'Catlin's Giant') to hide the "ugly knees" that so many hybrid teas develop. Plant one hybrid tea in a perennial border and surround it with summer-blooming perennials, such as *Verbena bonariensis* and salvia.

Try These
'Mrs. Oakley Fisher' has single orange-yellow flowers and a "tea" scent. Others to try include 'Alabama' (pink blend), 'Cayenne' (orange blend), 'Chrysler Imperial' (dark red), and 'Matterhorn' (white).

Lady Banks Rose

Rosa banksiae 'Lutea'

Botanical Pronunciation
RO-sa BANK-see-ah

Bloom Period and Seasonal Colors
Evergreen; spring blooms in white or yellow

Mature Height × Spread
15 to 20 ft. × 5 to 10 ft.

Lady Banks rose, a vigorous evergreen climber, is outstanding among the roses that thrive in Georgia with little or no care except in the very coldest parts of the state. One of the first roses to bloom in spring, its scent has been compared to the scent of violets. When in bloom, a blanket of flowers covers the plant for three to four weeks. Chances are that if your grandmother grew this rose, it is still thriving in the same spot today. Long-lived and vigorous, large plants may threaten to pull down buildings when their trunks grow as big around as small trees! A late freeze can kill flower buds. Even without blooms, the delicate looking foliage looks good year-round and this rose is thornless!

When, Where, and How to Plant

Plant bare-root roses as soon as you receive them during the dormant season. Plant container-grown roses in early spring or early fall. Plant Lady Banks where it will receive at least four to five hours of direct sunlight per day. Roses are heavy feeders, and they benefit from a well-drained soil that is rich in organic matter. Hand dig, or use a tiller for large areas. Combine one-third coarse sand, one-third organic matter (compost, manure, or composted pine bark), and one-third clay. For a bare-root rose, dig a hole large enough to place the roots over a small mound of soil and allow them to spread out in all directions. Prune all damaged roots. Balance root pruning with an equal amount of top-growth pruning. Plant a container-grown rose at the same depth it was growing in the pot.

Growing Tips

Topdress 1 to 1½ inches of mulch twice a year for additional organic matter and keep roots cool and moist. Water deeply once a week instead of a daily surface sprinkling. Saturate the area around the plant, allow the water to sink in, and repeat several times. Many chemical and organic rose fertilizers are commercially available; regular applications of one of these during the growing season will keep plants vigorous. Follow the recommendations on the product label. Roses grown in containers need more fertilizer.

Regional Advice and Care

Prune every other year, as soon as it finishes flowering. This rose flowers on second- and third-year wood. Remove only old wood. Lady Banks does not suffer from any serious pest or disease problems.

Companion Planting and Design

Plant Lady Banks where it will have lots of room and a very substantial support. In a few years, you will be glad you did. It has the habit of producing long shoots, which makes it easy to train up a structure, up a tree, to cover a fence, or over a high wall where the foliage can cascade down. Combine it with vines like clematis.

Try These

Rosa banksiae 'Normalis' has 1-inch-wide single fragrant flowers.

Landscape Shrub Rose

Rosa cvs.

Botanical Pronunciation
RO-sa

Bloom Period and Seasonal Colors
Summer to fall blooms in yellow, orange, white, pink, red, bicolor

Mature Height × Spread
2 to 6 ft. × 2 to 4 ft.

Roses have always been popular, but some gardeners consider them a "high-maintenance" plant. Today, there is a group of roses that have been bred for hardiness, disease resistance, overall vigor, and a long bloom season. Known as landscape shrub roses, they offer beautiful blooms and ask little in return. While most repeat-bloomers require deadheading (removing spent blossoms) to keep them blooming and thriving, landscape shrub roses bloom almost continuously without deadheading. Some offer handsome foliage and colorful fruits too. Plant them as a hedge, barrier, or in the perennial border. You can also combine them with conifers and tropical plants. *Rosa* 'Carefree Beauty' is disease resistant and produces masses of semi-double coral-pink flowers all season. The colorful red-orange hips add interest to the fall and winter garden.

When, Where, and How to Plant
Plant container-grown roses anytime the ground is not frozen. Site them where they will receive at least six hours of direct sun per day. Locate them according to their growth habits. For example, many Meidiland® roses have long arching canes and make effective groundcovers, while roses in the 'Carefree' group tend to make choice shrubs in a mixed border. Amend the soil with one-third organic matter mixed into the existing soil. Dig a hole equal to or slightly larger than the container that the rose was growing in. After planting, apply 1 inch of mulch, avoiding direct contact with the main stem.

Growing Tips
It's always best to get a soil test before you plant your roses to determine how much lime you need to add, if any. Topdress with 1½ inches of mulch or organic matter twice a year. This provides another source of nutrients and helps keep roots cool and moist. Roses benefit from deep watering once a week instead of daily surface sprinkling. Saturate the area around the plant, allow the water to soak in, and repeat.

Regional Advice and Care
You don't have to prune shrub roses back in early spring. Limit pruning to reducing the size of shrubs that get too large for the spot allotted to them. As a group, landscape shrub roses don't suffer from any serious pest or disease problems.

Companion Planting and Design
Plant landscape shrub roses on steep banks where other plants won't grow. Add 'Carefree Sunshine', with its clear yellow flowers from June to October, to the perennial border. For a mass planting, try the compact bushy 'Nearly Wild', with fragrant, single, rose pink blooms. Combine landscape shrub roses with perennials, such as yarrow, salvias, and *Artemisia* and other gray-foliaged plants. 'Bonica' has a shrub-like habit and produces clusters of shell-pink blooms on upright stems to 4 feet tall.

Try These
The Knock Out™ rose known as 'Radrazz' offers florescent cherry red blooms and dark moss green foliage. There are other colors in the Knock Out™ series offered as well.

New Dawn Rose

Rosa 'New Dawn'

Botanical Pronunciation
RO-sa

Bloom Period and Seasonal Colors
Spring blooms in soft pink

Mature Height × Spread
12 to 20 ft. × 2 to 6 ft.

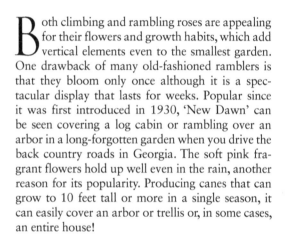

Both climbing and rambling roses are appealing for their flowers and growth habits, which add vertical elements even to the smallest garden. One drawback of many old-fashioned ramblers is that they bloom only once although it is a spectacular display that lasts for weeks. Popular since it was first introduced in 1930, 'New Dawn' can be seen covering a log cabin or rambling over an arbor in a long-forgotten garden when you drive the back country roads in Georgia. The soft pink fragrant flowers hold up well even in the rain, another reason for its popularity. Producing canes that can grow to 10 feet tall or more in a single season, it can easily cover an arbor or trellis or, in some cases, an entire house!

When, Where, and How to Plant
Plant bare-root roses during the dormant season as soon as you receive them. Container-grown roses may be planted in early spring or early fall. Like most climbers, 'New Dawn' needs a sturdy support. You will have to tie it to a fence in several spots to help it get started. Site it where it will receive at least six hours of direct sunlight daily. Dig a wide hole for bare-root roses and place the roots over a mound of soil in the middle. Plant container-grown roses at the same depth they were growing in the pot. If your rose is grafted, plant it so that the bud union is at ground level.

Growing Tips
Apply 1 to 1½ inches of mulch in spring and again in fall. During the first two years, water once a week during the growing season. After plants become established, water only during drought. Fertilize (chemicals or organic) twice a year.

Regional Advice and Care
Using twine or stretch ties that expand, train the canes to grow in a fan-like fashion. Do not use wire, as it will girdle the plant. Horizontal canes produce the most flowers. Climbing roses require less vigorous pruning than hybrid teas. In early spring, when the buds are swelling, prune old and diseased canes. Although it is disease resistant, 'New Dawn' is susceptible to blackspot, but it is usually not a severe problem. If affected by blackspot, leaves turn black and yellow and fall off. Clean up any leaf litter at the end of the season to eliminate overwintering spores. Refer to the rose chapter introduction for more details.

Companion Planting and Design
'New Dawn' is a good rose for covering an ugly chain-link fence. For a stunning effect, train a dark-flowered clematis to grow up and through a 'New Dawn' rose. Combine it on an arbor with other vines like climbing hydrangea.

Try These
'Dortmund' is a single flower, scarlet with a white eye. It is considered a climber or a pillar, growing 8 to 10 feet tall. It produces orange hips, the fruits of a rose bush.

Polyantha Rose

Rosa spp. and cvs.

Botanical Pronunciation
RO-sa

Bloom Period and Seasonal Colors
Midspring to frost blooms in pink, apricot, orange

Mature Height × Spread
1 to 4 ft. × 4 to 6 ft.

It's hard to believe that this delightful group of well-behaved roses is related to the invasive *Rosa multiflora*, considered a noxious weed in most states. Crossing them with the China roses was the secret. The result—roses with large sprays of small flowers (less than 2 inches across), a vigorous, almost ever-blooming habit, bushy form, and strong resistance to disease. Some of the polyanthas will even take part shade. Favorites in this group include 'Cecile Brunner', often called the sweetheart rose, with light pink flowers that look like hybrid teas, and 'Perle d'Or', with apricot-orange flowers and apple green foliage. These roses are easy to work into the flower border with other shrubs and perennials. Undemanding and rewarding, a great rose for beginners as well as seasoned gardeners.

When, Where, and How to Plant
Plant bare-root roses during the dormant season as soon as you receive them. Plant container-grown roses in early spring or early fall. Most roses require a minimum of six hours of direct sunlight, but polyanthas grow happily with only three to four hours of sun per day. Although they tolerate poor soil, they will thrive in a soil that is rich in organic matter. Roses are heavy feeders, and they benefit from a rich, well-drained soil. Hand dig, or use a tiller for large areas, and combine one-third coarse sand, one-third organic matter (compost, manure, or composted pine bark), and one-third clay. For bare-root roses, dig a hole large enough so that you can place the roots over a small mound of soil to allow them to spread out in all directions. Prune all damaged roots. Balance root pruning with an equal amount of top-growth pruning.

Growing Tips
A topdressing of 1 to 1½ inches of mulch applied twice a year provides additional organic matter and helps keep roots cool and moist. Water once a week, a trickling hose placed at the base of the plant and left for an hour is good. Many chemical and organic rose fertilizers are commercially available. Follow the recommendations on the product label.

Regional Advice and Care
After the first year, polyantha roses benefit from a pruning in early spring just as the buds are swelling and before they begin to leaf out. Cut back plants to about 1 to 2 feet, depending on the vigor of each plant. This will encourage lots of new growth and blooms. Good air circulation will reduce the threat of diseases, such as powdery mildew and blackspot. This group of roses does not suffer from any serious pest problems.

Companion Planting and Design
Polyantha roses provide the perfect complement to perennials and annuals, yielding maximum bloom from a minimum-sized plant.

Try These
Look for roses that have the Earth-Kind® designation for "superior pest tolerance combined with outstanding landscape performance." This list includes *Rosa* 'Perle d'Or' with its apricot buds opening to fragrant soft pink flowers.

Rugosa Rose

Rosa rugosa and cvs.

Botanical Pronunciation
RO-sa ru-GO-sah

Other Name Saltspray rose

Bloom Period and Seasonal Colors
Summer to fall flowers in white, rose, purple; red or orange hips in fall

Mature Height × Spread
4 to 6 ft. × 3to 6 ft.

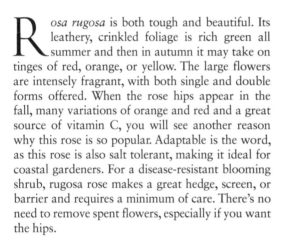

osa rugosa is both tough and beautiful. Its leathery, crinkled foliage is rich green all summer and then in autumn it may take on tinges of red, orange, or yellow. The large flowers are intensely fragrant, with both single and double forms offered. When the rose hips appear in the fall, many variations of orange and red and a great source of vitamin C, you will see another reason why this rose is so popular. Adaptable is the word, as this rose is also salt tolerant, making it ideal for coastal gardeners. For a disease-resistant blooming shrub, rugosa rose makes a great hedge, screen, or barrier and requires a minimum of care. There's no need to remove spent flowers, especially if you want the hips.

When, Where, and How to Plant

Plant container-grown *R. rugosa* in spring or fall. Make sure to give them plenty of room and provide a site that is well drained in full sun. However, this rose species is more shade tolerant than many other roses, and it will grow in part shade. Dig a hole that is only as deep, but twice as wide, as the container the rose was growing in when you purchased it. A soil that is amended with organic matter is good, but these roses tolerate sandy soils, perfect for a screen at the beach.

Growing Tips

Rosa rugosa is from China but adapts to a range of growing conditions. This rose requires only a minimum of pruning, only if there is any dieback. The best time to prune is right after they bloom but remember you may be removing potential rose hips. You should not need to spray these roses and, in fact, they may drop some of their leaves if you do. A good blast from the hose on a sunny day will take care of some insect pests. While it is not exempt from pests and diseases that attack other roses, including Japanese beetles, this rose is extremely vigorous and resilient.

Regional Advice and Care.

You can grow this rose from seed or cuttings. The best time to take softwood cuttings is in June and July. Topdress with organic matter in the early spring and fall, this will help feed your roses.

Companion Planting and Design

Plant *Rosa rugosa* as a barrier, hedge, or screen. Plant them with native grasses in coastal gardens. Combine it with summer blooming perennials including salvia, rosemary, and iris. Screen off parking lots or unsightly views. You can also grow it as a backdrop for other smaller roses.

Try These

'Blanc Double de Coubert' is a vigorous selection with semidouble white blooms. For disease resistance and beautiful fragrant blooms (silver-pink with yellow stamens), try 'Frau Dagmar Hastrup'.

SHRUBS

FOR GEORGIA

While trees help create the framework for a garden, it is shrubs that act as the middle ground between the trees and the herbaceous layer of perennials and annuals. Many add colorful flowers and berries to the riot of color that erupts each year. There are varieties for every season and every type of garden. Native, exotic, evergreen, or deciduous, shrubs come in all sizes and shapes and perform myriad functions. Some shrubs offer two seasons of interest: bottlebrush buckeye sports white flowers in summer and golden yellow leaves in autumn. Evergreen shrubs, such as anise, camellia, and holly, are effective for hedges, screening, and as solid backdrops for flowers and deciduous shrubs.

Planting Tips

Container-grown shrubs can be planted throughout the growing season, but early spring and fall are best. Follow these tips for successful planting:

1. Perform a soil test (page 13) before you plant. The results will help you determine how much lime and other nutrients to add to the soil. Cover the planting area with 4 inches of organic matter and rototill to a depth of 8 to 12 inches. Lime can be applied at this time if you need to raise the pH. A typical rate of application is 4 pounds per 100 square feet. Rototill the lime in to a depth of 4 to 6 inches.

2. Dig a hole as deep as the container in which the plant is growing and twice as wide. Remove the plant from the container and use a pair of hand pruners to make two or three cuts into the bottom of the rootball. Cut away any dead or dried out roots. If your shrub is balled and burlapped, place it in the hole, then cut away all the twine that is holding the burlap in place and remove as much of the burlap material as possible from the rootball.

3. Place the rootball in the planting hole and fill it with soil. Cover the top of the rootball slightly with soil. If the soil you are planting in has a high percentage of heavy clay, plant your shrub on a small mound so that the roots won't stand in water. Completely cover the rootball with soil.

4. Water your shrubs as soon as you plant them. A good rule of thumb is to apply 1 to 2 gallons per foot of plant height. Water once a week for the first six months, unless there is a good rain (1 inch per week). After this, water during extended periods of drought (no rain for two weeks or longer). Soak the rootball and the surrounding soil. If watering by hand, apply 5 gallons of water per 10 square

Viburnum, Heuchera, Sedum, Roses, April.

feet. This is approximately the rate of a garden hose operating for one minute at medium pressure. If you use soaker hoses, a 50-foot-long soaker hose can water 100 square feet of landscape bed in two or three hours.

Transplanting Advice

The best time to transplant most shrubs is when the demand for water is the least, in late fall or winter. Because many roots will be lost, shrubs need weeks to regenerate new ones before the hot, dry blasts of summer arrive. If moving a shrub in July is unavoidable, you can still be successful if you provide attentive watering.

Pruning

Pruning to remove dead or diseased wood on a regular basis helps to keep shrubs vigorous and can be done during any season. Pruning may also be done to maintain a shrub at the proper size or shape, to help it produce more flowers, or to rejuvenate a weary, old plant.

When you select a shrub, be sure to choose the right plant for your specific environment. Note the cultural conditions individual shrubs require—such as light, water, and soil. This book will also guide you in choosing specific types for your garden and offer suggestions for plant combinations.

Anise

Illicium spp.

Botanical Pronunciation
ih-LISS-ee-um

Bloom Period and Seasonal Colors
Evergreen; Florida anise has late spring blooms in red; small anise-tree has inconspicuous blooms in yellow or red (depends on species)

Mature Height × Spread
6 to 10 ft. × 5 to 10 ft.

Anise is an attractive, easy-to-care-for evergreen that grows well in a spot that is damp and shady or moist and well drained. Its crushed foliage has an aroma of licorice. Multi-trunked and irregularly branched, it forms an upright oval that is useful for screening. Let it grow naturally, or train it as a hedge. Two species of anise are commonly available: Florida anise (*Illicium floridanum*) with dark green leaves, and small anise-tree (*I. parviflorum*) with olive green foliage. Florida anise offers 1-inch, star-shaped, maroon blossoms that emerge at the base of the leaves in late spring. The flowers resemble deep red asters, and the blooms are followed by brown, waxy seed capsules. Small anise-tree has inconspicuous yellow flowers. It prefers part shade but will tolerate full sun.

When, Where, and How to Plant
Plant in fall while the soil is still warm (as late as November or December) or in spring after the last frost. Anise does best in spots where it can get morning sunshine and some shade during the afternoon. Small anise-tree can grow in full sun, but provide thick mulch and regular watering. The high shade of pine or poplar trees is a perfect setting. A moist soil that is high in organic matter is best. Dig a planting hole five times as wide as the rootball of your plant. Because an anise has shallow roots, the hole need not be more than 12 inches deep. If the anise is container grown, untangle the circling roots and spread them in the hole before filling it with soil.

Growing Tips
For the first two years after planting, fertilize anise three times a year (early spring, summer, and fall) with 1 tablespoon of 10-10-10 fertilizer per foot of plant height. After your anise is established, one application of fertilizer each spring will suffice. Water once a week during the first growing season, and then once every two weeks. Saturate the soil around the rootball, wait a few minutes, and then repeat this step.

Regional Advice and Care
Although anise can be sheared with hedge trimmers, the damaged leaves are not attractive. A better technique is to prune out individual branches with hand pruners, cutting back to smaller branches or buds. Pests are rare. Black vine weevils will occasionally make ¼-inch notches in the edges of leaves, but the damage is not serious.

Companion Planting and Design
Anise is useful for informal hedges, screening plants, or as evergreens under deciduous trees. Plant it in combination with Florida leucothoe, ferns, hosta, nandina, and azaleas. *Illicium parviflorum* will tolerate full sun and makes a good screening plant; just make sure to give it plenty of water.

Try These
Illicium henryi has dark, lustrous leaves and flowers that are pink on the inside and green on the outside. For some bright color in the shade try *Illicium parviflorum* 'Florida Sunshine' with yellow foliage.

Annabelle Hydrangea

Hydrangea arborescens 'Annabelle'

Botanical Pronunciation
hy-DRAIN-juh ar-bore-ESS-enz

Bloom Period and Seasonal Colors
Summer blooms in white

Mature Height × Spread
4 to 8 ft. × 4 to 8 ft.

The blooms on 'Annabelle' hydrangea are truly astounding—nearly 12 inches across! They start out white and turn light green as they age. The flowers are lacy and delicate, but this plant is tough. It blooms on current season's growth, so you can prune it back hard in early spring. This vigorous shrub holds up the big flower heads even after a rain. On closer inspection, the leaves of 'Annabelle' are much softer than those of the other hydrangeas. We call the collection of individual flowers at the end of a hydrangea branch a "bloom," but the single flowers are actually male blossoms. Look carefully inside the round flower head to find blooms with tiny petals; these are the true flowers.

When, Where, and How to Plant

Plant in spring after the last frost; a late freeze may damage new foliage. 'Annabelle' hydrangea can survive in more sunshine than most other hydrangeas, but part shade is ideal. Dig a hole five times as wide as and equal to the depth of the rootball. This hydrangea thrives in moist, well-drained soil. In a wheelbarrow, mix the soil from the hole with equal parts soil conditioner or compost. Put the plant in the hole and backfill with amended soil. Pack it down by hand, water thoroughly, and check back in an hour. If the soil has settled around the roots and exposed the top surface, add more soil to cover.

Growing Tips

'Annabelle' needs little fertilizer. The first year, apply 1 tablespoon of 10-10-10 per foot of height in March, June, and August. After the first year, fertilize in March and June with the same amount of 10-10-10. Irrigation is key to the establishment and long-term health of your hydrangea. The shrub shows its need for water with wilting leaves. Water immediately and deeply if the leaves droop. Saturate the rootball, wait a few minutes, and repeat.

Regional Advice and Care

'Annabelle' produces flowers on new growth. Cut the whole plant nearly to the ground in February or early March and vigorous regrowth will bring blooms in late June. Though flowers emerge a bright white, they gradually fade to light green and then to brown by fall. The large bloom is very sturdy and can be used in dried arrangements. Cut off flower branches when they begin to fade and hang them upside down indoors to dry. 'Annabelle' does not suffer from any serious pest or disease problems.

Companion Planting and Design

It looks best when combined with other plants that can draw attention away from it while it is not flowering. Try Virginia sweetspire (*Itea virginica*), lantana (*Lantana camara* 'Miss Huff'), or annual purple fountain grass (*Pennisetum setaceum* 'Rubrum') as sunny companions.

Try These

Hydrangea arborescens 'Grandiflora' produces 6-inch blossoms on a 4-foot plant. Invincibelle Spirit™ is a selection of *H. arborescens* with pink flowers.

Bigleaf Hydrangea

Hydrangea macrophylla

Botanical Pronunciation
hye-DRAYN-jee-uh mac-ro-FILL-a

Other Name French hydrangea

Bloom Period and Seasonal Colors
May to June blooms in shades of blue, pink, white

Mature Height × Spread
4 to 6 ft. × 2 to 8 ft. (by variety)

Bigleaf hydrangeas are commonplace in Georgia gardens. Most have blue blossoms in June. Adventurous gardeners may add lime to the soil to make the blooms turn pink. But today's common hydrangeas offer numerous options in color, foliage, and bloom time. In particular, there is great interest in the different bloom forms. Hortensia blooms are the familiar globe shapes, often called mopheads. Lacecap blooms are flat and much daintier; they can break the monotony of a hydrangea hedge. *Hydrangea macrophylla* 'Nikko Blue' is a mophead with deep blue flowers. *H. macrophylla* 'Ami Pasquier' produces pink blooms even in acidic soil. *H. macrophylla* 'Lanarth White' has white lacecap blooms. *H. macrophylla* 'Pia' is a pink dwarf. *H. serrata* 'Preziosa' has white blooms that gradually fade to maroon.

When, Where, and How to Plant

In southern Georgia, where winter is not a threat, plant common hydrangeas in fall. In Atlanta and northward, plant after April 15th to avoid a possible late frost. Hydrangeas like a moist, well-drained soil. They do best in partial shade; morning sun and afternoon shade is ideal. Dig a hole five times as wide as and equal to the depth of the rootball. In a wheelbarrow, mix the backfill soil with equal parts soil conditioner or compost. Place the plant in the hole and backfill. Pack it down by hand, then water thoroughly. Check back in an hour. If the soil has settled around the rootball and exposed its top surface, add more soil to cover.

Growing Tips

Apply 1 tablespoon of 10-10-10 fertilizer per foot of height to a newly planted shrub in March, June, and August. After the first year, fertilize with the same amount in March and June. Irrigation is important to the establishment and long-term good health of a hydrangea. Water immediately and deeply if the leaves droop. Saturate the rootball, wait a few minutes, and then repeat.

Regional Advice and Care

Do any needed pruning in late June, immediately after the flowers have faded. The pruning will stimulate new growth and might even produce more flowers in October. If you prune in winter, you will sacrifice flowers the following spring. This common hydrangea does not suffer from any serious pest or disease problems.

Companion Planting and Design

Hydrangeas do well in combination with camellia, rhododendron, azaleas, and small to medium-sized trees like dogwoods and *stewartia*. They can also provide a nice backdrop for perennials and bulbs. Underplant them with evergreens like autumn fern and the green and white *Carex* 'Evergold'. Grow them in containers underplanted with evergreen groundcovers, such as *Vinca minor*.

Try These

Hydrangea macrophylla 'Forever Pink' grows 3 feet tall and has flower heads that are 4 to 5 inches across. Endless Summer® and 'Penny Mac' are two cultivars that bloom throughout the summer.

Bottlebrush Buckeye

Aesculus parviflora

Botanical Pronunciation
ESS-kew-luss par-vih-FLORE-uh

Bloom Period and Seasonal Colors
Deciduous; June blooms in white; fall foliage in yellow; brown nuts in fall

Mature Height × Spread
8 to 10 ft. × 8 to 12 ft.

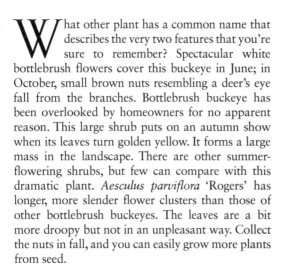

What other plant has a common name that describes the very two features that you're sure to remember? Spectacular white bottlebrush flowers cover this buckeye in June; in October, small brown nuts resembling a deer's eye fall from the branches. Bottlebrush buckeye has been overlooked by homeowners for no apparent reason. This large shrub puts on an autumn show when its leaves turn golden yellow. It forms a large mass in the landscape. There are other summer-flowering shrubs, but few can compare with this dramatic plant. *Aesculus parviflora* 'Rogers' has longer, more slender flower clusters than those of other bottlebrush buckeyes. The leaves are a bit more droopy but not in an unpleasant way. Collect the nuts in fall, and you can easily grow more plants from seed.

When, Where, and How to Plant
Plant bottlebrush buckeye in very early spring, before it has leaves, if possible. Large specimens are sold balled-and-burlapped, but it is also common to find container-grown plants for sale at nurseries. A bottlebrush buckeye will tolerate full sun, but it seems happier in dappled shade. Give this shrub plenty of room to spread. Water well after planting, saturating the area completely. Bottlebrush buckeye is a woodland native and appreciates any attempt to approximate woodland conditions.

Growing Tips
Water once every ten days during the first growing season. Add a layer of pine straw mulch or wood chips under your buckeye to conserve moisture. Do not allow the soil to dry out beneath the plant until it is well established; mulch will be your best ally in summer. Once plants are established (after two years), you should not have to water except during periods of drought when it doesn't rain for over two weeks. Bottlebrush buckeye grows well with little fertilizer. Apply 1 tablespoon of 10-10-10 fertilizer per foot of height in April and again in midsummer. After a few years, an annual reapplication of shredded leaves will be all the care that is needed.

Regional Advice and Care
Pruning is not required on a regular basis. It sends up suckers near the trunk, and if a branch touches the ground, it will usually root. Sprouts can be easily pulled and discarded if they pop up where you don't want them. No pests seem to affect bottlebrush buckeye.

Companion Planting and Design
Grow bottlebrush buckeye as a specimen shrub and underplant it with early blooming daffodils and ferns or perennials like variegated Solomon's seal. Plant it in a mixed border with other native plants, such as Virginia sweetspire, *Clethra alnifolia* and native dogwood. This will be a colorful display in autumn with red and yellow foliage.

Try These
Aesculus pavia, red buckeye (also a native), can be grown as a large shrub or small tree to 20 feet tall. Its flowers, which are deep crimson spikes, appear on upright stalks in early spring.

Boxwood

Buxus spp. and cvs.

Botanical Pronunciation
BUCKS-us

Other Name Box

Bloom Period and Seasonal Colors
Evergreen with dark foliage

Mature Height × Spread
2 to 20 ft. × 2 to 20 ft. (by variety)

Boxwoods have long been popular for use in formal gardens. Unpruned American boxwoods (*Buxus sempervirens*) can develop into large billowy masses with a distinctive character. Keep in mind, however, that this elegant evergreen may take fifty years to reach its mature size of 15 to 20 feet tall and wide. Boxwood can be used as a foundation plant or for a hedge; they even make great container plants. *B. sempervirens* 'Suffruticosa', also known as English boxwood, has a dwarf, compact habit. Because of its very slow growth rate, it is great for edging—in the vegetable garden or in a flower border. Mature examples of both the American and English boxwoods grace many an old Southern garden, where they continue to thrive next to camellias and azaleas.

When, Where, and How to Plant
Plant container-grown boxwood in early spring. Boxwood likes soil that is moist and well drained; wet feet will quickly lead to its demise. Boxwood likes full sun as long as it gets enough moisture. It will also grow in part sun or shade. However, in deep shade the growth will be spindly. Keep boxwood away from drying winds. To plant, dig a hole that is three times as wide as and equal to the depth of the rootball. Amend the soil by mixing together one-third organic matter, one-third coarse sand, and one-third existing soil. Apply 1 to 2 inches of mulch to keep roots cool, but be careful to keep the mulch away from the stems and trunk. Water well.

Growing Tips
Apply 1 tablespoon of 10-10-10 fertilizer per foot of height in spring and again in midsummer. During the first growing season, water boxwood once a week, when the top ½ inch of soil is dry to the touch. After this, water if there is no rain for two weeks.

Regional Advice and Care
Prune in early spring just as leaves begin to flush out. Even if you use electric trimmers, follow up with hand pruners to remove small sections to allow light to reach the plant's interior. If plants are overgrown and in need of renovation, prune drastically at the end of February or early March, reducing their size by one-half to one-third. Leafminers can be a problem with boxwood. The damage shows up in late summer with splotchy and yellow leaves. The best control is to spray with insecticidal soap or horticultural oil when the adults are present in April or May. Sometimes leaves will get tinges of bronze in the winter.

Companion Planting and Design
Boxwoods are great for parterres, for edging perennial gardens, or as a hedge. Plant it in combination with flowering shrubs, such as butterfly bush or hydrangea. They also make great specimens in containers.

Try These
Buxus microphylla var. *insularis* 'Winter Gem' is a hardy selection of littleleaf boxwood that keeps its dark green color through winter.

Butterfly Bush

Buddleia davidii

Botanical Pronunciation
BUD-lee-uh duh-VID-ee-eye

Other Name Summer lilac

Bloom Period and Seasonal Colors
Deciduous; summer blooms in purple, lavender, pink, yellow, white

Mature Height × Spread
5 to 15 ft. × 5 to 10 ft. (by variety)

Butterfly bush is a mainstay for the summer garden. Easy to grow, its fragrant and colorful flowers will attract butterflies and humans for months. Butterfly bush will sometimes seem to be a blur of motion as dozens of butterflies flutter from flower to flower. Give it plenty of room as this deciduous shrub can easily grow 10 to 15 feet in one season. Because it flowers on the current year's growth, cut butterfly bush back in early spring. You'll have a large plant covered with blooms by summer. Although it's not necessary for the plant's health, deadheading encourages the production of even more flowers. This sun lover blooms in purple, lavender, pink, yellow, and white. There are also dwarf types and selections with variegated foliage.

When, Where, and How to Plant
Winter is hard on a butterfly bush, so plant container-grown plants in spring to allow maximum growing time before winter. As long as the bush is watered during the first summer, establishment will proceed without problems. "More sun equals more flowers" is the motto for butterfly bush. In shade, it will grow lanky and sport few, if any, blooms. Plant in well-drained soil of any type. Water immediately after planting, then mulch under the plant. Keep the soil evenly moist for at least four weeks.

Growing Tips
If planted in sandy soil or in full sun, water to avoid drought stress for the first two summers. Unless your butterfly bush is in a hot, dry site, watering will not be needed after this. Apply 1 tablespoon of 10-10-10 fertilizer per foot of height in March (after you prune it back), June, and August.

Regional Advice and Care
Blooms appear on new spring growth. March is the time to severely prune your bush to a height of 1 to 2 feet. You'll also have more flowers for a longer period if you regularly snip off the blooms when they begin to turn brown. Spider mites can be a problem in a hot, dry site. Twisting, mottled, yellow leaves that are drying up usually mean spider mites. It is much easier to control the mites early in the season with horticultural oil or Neem insecticide than it is to wait until August, when only a miticide will help. Call your county Extension service for more advice.

Companion Planting and Design
Plant butterfly bush in the middle of the perennial border where it will be a focal point. Other tall, flowering plants that attract butterflies make good companions. These include tall verbena (*Verbena bonariensis*), Mexican sage (*Salvia leucantha*), and Joe Pye weed (*Eupatorium maculatum*).

Try These
Buddleia davidii 'Black Knight' has dark purple flowers. For a dwarf butterfly bush, try Lo and Behold™, known as 'Blue Chip', which grows 2 to 3 feet tall and pumps out fragrant lavender-blue flowers from summer until frost. 'White Ball' is another dwarf.

Camellia

Camellia spp.

Botanical Pronunciation
kuh-MEEL-yuh

Bloom Period and Seasonal Colors
Evergreen; late fall to April blooms in white, pink, red, variegated

Mature Height × Spread
6 to 20 ft. (or taller) × 4 to 8 ft.

The camellia, a mainstay in many old Southern gardens, is often grown for its large, showy blooms—both single and double—in shades of white, pink, and red, as well as variegated. An elegant evergreen that takes the heat, camellia responds well to pruning and is great for growing in containers. In the garden, camellia can grow anywhere from 6 to 15 feet high, but more mature plants may reach as tall as 25 feet. When camellia is in bloom, few plants can match its firepower. Sasanquas (*Camellia sasanqua*) begin blooming in late fall, with some varieties blooming in mid-December. Many sasanquas are fragrant, although the blooms are smaller than those of *C. japonica*. *C. japonica* flowers in late December with varieties that continue until April.

When, Where, and How to Plant
Plant in spring while it is blooming or in fall so that its roots have time to grow. Transplant or move plants in midfall. The perfect site is in part shade. The north or east side of a structure is a good location. Protect from drying winds by placing camellia in the shelter of evergreen shrubbery. Moist, well-drained soil is essential for good growth. Camellia thrives in acidic soil. Dig a planting hole five times as wide as the rootball. Because camellia is shallow-rooted, the hole need not be more than 12 inches deep. If the area is lower than the surrounding landscape, add two to three bags of compost to the backfill. The resulting mound will keep camellia's roots above standing water.

Growing Tips
For camellias to grow large, fertilize with 1 tablespoon of 10-10-10 per foot of plant height in spring, summer, and fall. Once it's grown, fertilize only in spring and summer with the same amount of fertilizer. Water weekly during the first growing season, then once every two weeks when the top ½ inch of soil is dry.

Regional Advice and Care
Prune camellia as soon as it finishes flowering. Remove dead or weak wood and thin to allow light to reach a plant's interior. For protection from severe cold (below 15°F), thoroughly cover it with a bedsheet. Petal blight is a potentially serious disease. Blooms turn an ugly brown, especially at the center. Leaf gall can also be a problem. The best control is to keep your garden clean and free of leaf litter. Remove old mulch (every spring and fall) and replace it with 3 to 4 inches of new mulch.

Companion Planting and Design
Plant camellia in dappled shade under tall pine trees, along with dogwoods and azaleas. It is beautiful in large, decorative containers.

Try These
Camellia sinensis, the tea plant, produces 1½-inch white blossoms in fall. For cold-hardy types try 'Polar Ice', 'Snow Flurry', and 'Winter's Charm'. For the Deep South, plant 'Debutante', 'Lady Clare', and 'Professor Charles S. Sargent'.

Catawba Rhododendron

Rhododendron catawbiense

Botanical Pronunciation
Rho-do-DEN-dron ca-TAW-bee-ense

Bloom Period and Seasonal Colors
Evergreen; spring blooms in white, pink, red, lavender

Mature Height × Spread
4 to 15 ft. × 4 to 15 ft. (by variety)

The Latin name for rhododendron perfectly describes its form: *rhodo* means "rose" and *dendron* means "tree." Rose-tree is the perfect name for this grand lady of the April and May landscape. What's the difference between a rhododendron and an azalea? Both are members of the genus *Rhododendron*. Catawba rhododendron flowers are bell shaped, while azalea flowers are funnel shaped. This rhododendron also has larger and more leathery leaves than azaleas. Adaptable and easy to grow, provided you site this native in the proper environment. To better understand what it needs in the garden, visit the Southern Appalachian mountains. With the right plant selection and a bit of soil preparation, some of the native rhododendrons can rival those that grow in the Pacific Northwest.

When, Where, and How to Plant
Plant rhododendrons in spring. Choose a site that gets morning sun, followed by afternoon shade. The ideal soil is moist but well drained. Dig a hole five times as wide as the rootball and no less than 4 feet across. Remove one-third of the existing soil and add to it 4 cubic feet of soil conditioner or compost. Mix everything together to make a raised mound in which to plant. Remove the plant from the pot and use a sharp knife to cut through the roots down to the bottom. Flare the roots out in the hole in all directions. Pack soil on top of the roots, then water. Spread a 2-inch layer of shredded leaves or other mulch underneath your rhododendron. To avoid stem rot, pull the mulch back from the stem 3 inches.

Growing Tips
Apply 1 tablespoon of 10-10-10 fertilizer per foot of height in spring and again in midsummer. Drip irrigation or soaker hoses are a good investment for your rhododendron's long-term health. Snake the soaker hose throughout the beds where you have planted rhododendrons and azaleas. Water once a week during the growing season.

Regional Advice and Care
If needed, prune rhododendrons in May after flowering. Sometimes the shade over a rhododendron becomes too dense, causing the plants to decline or die. Move the plant, or prune the trees overhead to let in more light. Notched leaves indicate the presence of adult root weevils. The larvae can girdle roots and kill plants. Contact your county Extension office (page 225) for recommended controls.

Companion Planting and Design
Shade-loving plants make good companions; try camellia (*Camellia japonica*), Solomon's seal (*Polygonatum commutatum*), toad lily (*Tricyrtis hirta*), and ferns.

Try These
Rhododendron degronianum ssp. *yakushimanum* is an evergreen with handsome foliage and beautiful blooms that are pink in bud, opening to white. *Rhododendron* 'Nova Zembla' grows to 8 feet tall and has large red flowers. 'Scintillation' has light pink flowers and is tolerant of Georgia heat. 'Ramapo' grows to only 2 feet tall and has violet-purple flowers.

Chaste Tree

Vitex agnus-castus

Botanical Pronunciation
VYE-tecks AG-nus KASS-tus

Bloom Period and Seasonal Colors
Midsummer blooms in light blue, white

Mature Height × Spread
15 to 20 ft. × 8 to 10 ft. (by variety)

Summer-blooming shrubs that thrive in Georgia summers are a valuable commodity. High on the list is chaste tree, which grows 15 to 20 feet tall. As its name suggests, some consider it a small tree rather than a shrub. At first glance, it will remind you of a butterfly bush. Take a closer look, and you'll see that the fragrant pale lilac or lavender flowers grow up in spikes from the leaf axils of the current season's growth. The dark gray-green leaves are divided and look almost like a hand with fingers spread apart. This is a sturdy shrub that adapts to a wide range of situations. It thrives in gardens or on banks next to highways, and doesn't seem bothered by pollution or dry conditions.

When, Where, and How to Plant

Plant chaste tree in spring in northern Georgia, and in fall in southern Georgia. Give it plenty of room to grow. Chaste tree likes full sun, but it is not particular about the soil it grows in, as long as it is well drained. Dig a hole three times as wide and to the same depth as the rootball. Thoroughly break up the soil. Gently untangle some of the larger roots and spread them in the hole before backfilling. Water immediately after planting and spread mulch under the plant. Keep the soil evenly moist for at least four weeks.

Growing Tips

For the first two years after planting, fertilize with 1 tablespoon of 10-10-10 fertilizer per foot of plant height in March, May, and July. After chaste tree is established, reduce fertilizer applications to once in April and once in June. If planted in sandy soil and full sun, drought stress may occur the first summer. Be sure to water once a week under these conditions. Saturate the rootball, wait a few minutes, and repeat.

Regional Advice and Care

Chaste tree can be damaged by a severe winter. In extreme northern Georgia, winter cold can even freeze most of the limbs off a chaste tree. It may be necessary to cut it back to 12 inches tall each spring. Because blooms emerge on new branches, cold damage does not affect the flowering. In southern Georgia, select one or two upright stems and form your shrub into a small tree. Few insects or diseases attack a healthy chaste tree. If it is grown in heavy shade, however, it may develop leaf spot.

Companion Planting and Design

Chaste tree flowers are good forage for bumblebees, so plant your shrub away from your patio if you don't care for bees. Plant chaste tree in the flower border with other butterfly-attracting plants like butterfly bush and perennials such as Joe Pye weed and *Gaura lindheimeri*, or annuals such as lantana.

Try These

Vitex agnus-castus 'Silver Spires' has white flowers and 'Colonial Blue' has blue flowers.

Crapemyrtle

Lagerstroemia indica

Botanical Pronunciation
lag-ur-STREE-mee-uh IN-dih-kuh

Bloom Period and Seasonal Colors
Deciduous; July and August blooms in white, purple, red, pink; fall foliage in yellow to red

Mature Height × Spread
3 to 20 ft. × 3 to 15 ft. (by variety)

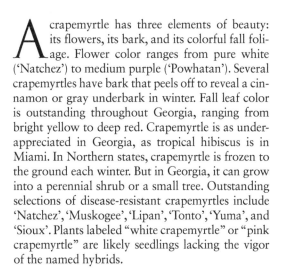

A crapemyrtle has three elements of beauty: its flowers, its bark, and its colorful fall foliage. Flower color ranges from pure white ('Natchez') to medium purple ('Powhatan'). Several crapemyrtles have bark that peels off to reveal a cinnamon or gray underbark in winter. Fall leaf color is outstanding throughout Georgia, ranging from bright yellow to deep red. Crapemyrtle is as underappreciated in Georgia, as tropical hibiscus is in Miami. In Northern states, crapemyrtle is frozen to the ground each winter. But in Georgia, it can grow into a perennial shrub or a small tree. Outstanding selections of disease-resistant crapemyrtles include 'Natchez', 'Muskogee', 'Lipan', 'Tonto', 'Yuma', and 'Sioux'. Plants labeled "white crapemyrtle" or "pink crapemyrtle" are likely seedlings lacking the vigor of the named hybrids.

When, Where, and How to Plant
Plant container-grown or balled-and-burlapped plants in spring or fall. They like full sun and a well-drained soil. Note that it may take a few years before you get blooms. Dig a hole three times as wide as the rootball and as deep as its height. Thoroughly break up the soil. Remove any burlap and twine showing after the crapemyrtle is placed in its hole. Water thoroughly, then spread 1 inch of mulch over the whole area to conserve moisture.

Growing Tips
Too much fertilizer can hinder the production of flowers. Apply 1 tablespoon of 10-10-10 per foot of plant height in April each year. Although crapemyrtle is fairly drought tolerant, water a new plant once a week during the first summer after it has been planted. After this, it should not need watering except during periods of drought (no rain for two weeks).

Regional Advice and Care
Remove small sprouts from the trunks of multi-trunked crapemyrtles each winter. Pruning is not necessary for the health of the tree, but removing seedpods may encourage more blooms the next season. Powdery mildew affects older varieties of crapemyrtle. During some summers, the foliage will be thickly covered with white powder. This does no lasting harm, but blooms will be greatly reduced. Aphids love to suck sap from crapemyrtle leaves. They secrete a sticky "honeydew" that covers lower leaves. Sooty mold turns these leaves and nearby stems black. Check with your county Extension office for controls.

Companion Planting and Design
Crapemyrtle makes a fine specimen plant, especially if a walkway is nearby so that the bark can be appreciated up close. Smaller varieties can be incorporated into a shrub or flower border. Plant it in combination with perennials, such as garden phlox, *Hydrangea paniculata* 'Limelight', black-eyed Susan, and daylilies. An alleé of 'Natchez' crapemyrtles is a sight to behold in the winter, when the bark stands out. Use dwarf types in containers with summer annuals.

Try These
Japanese crapemyrtle (*Lagerstroemia fauriei*) is a tree with striking bark that grows 20 to 30 feet high.

Daphne

Daphne odora

Botanical Pronunciation
DAFF-nee o-DOR-a

Other Name Winter daphne

Bloom Period and Seasonal Colors
Evergreen; February blooms with dark red buds opening to white

Mature Height × Spread
2 to 4 ft. (or more) × 2 to 4 ft.

aphne demands very well-drained soil, just the right amount of sun, and careful removal of diseased leaves. But oh, the aroma! On a cold February day when you are wondering if anything is still living in your perennial flower bed, a single bloom of this evergreen *Daphne* is enough to remind you that spring will come again. According to legend, the god Apollo pursued young Daphne. She did not welcome his advances, and she appealed to the other gods for help. Because they could not stop Apollo, the gods turned Daphne into a sweet-smelling shrub to escape him. This evergreen is happy in the garden or in a container. Another *Daphne* to try is *Daphne caucasica*. It has small green leaves and clusters of tiny, white, fragrant flowers.

When, Where, and How to Plant

Plant container-grown *Daphne* in early spring as soon as it's offered for sale. A spot that gets morning sun and afternoon shade is ideal. A soil with a neutral pH is best. *Daphne* requires excellent drainage for its long-term health. Dig a hole 5 feet wide and 12 inches deep. Place the top 4 inches of the soil in a wheelbarrow and discard the rest. Break up the soil and mix in one 40-pound bag of coarse builder's sand and one 50-pound bag of pea gravel. With two bags of composted pine bark nearby, shovel alternately from the wheelbarrow and from the bags of mulch until the hole is filled. Mix the contents with a shovel; then add more material until a mound is formed. Plant the *Daphne* in the center, spreading the roots slightly into the surrounding soil. Water thoroughly. Make sure the rootball does not become uncovered by rainfall after a few weeks.

Growing Tips

Apply 1 tablespoon of 10-10-10 fertilizer per foot of height in spring and again in midsummer. Mulch is vital. Apply a 2-inch layer of shredded leaves over the mound. Pull the mulch 3 inches back from the stem to prevent stem rot. Water once every ten days during the first growing season; thereafter, water once every two weeks.

Regional Advice and Care

Daphne seems to be more susceptible to disease with an excess of fertilizer. Keep the area around the plant free of leaf litter to reduce any disease problems. As soon as you notice a yellow or black leaf, remove it. Pruning is rarely needed. Planting on a slope will ensure good drainage.

Companion Planting and Design

Daphne is a great plant for a container. Its evergreen leaves and intensely sweet-smelling flowers make it a winner every time. In the garden, grow it with maidenhair fern, autumn fern, Japanese painted fern, and groundcovers, such as lungwort and 'Callaway' ginger.

Try These

Daphne odora 'Aureomarginata' has pink flowers and leaves edged with a band of yellow. *Daphne odora* 'Alba' has solid green leaves and white flowers.

Florida Leucothoe

Agarista populifolia

Botanical Pronunciation
ag-uh-RISS-tuh pop-you-lih-FOE-lee-uh

Other Name Coast leucothoe

Bloom Period and Seasonal Colors
Evergreen; May to June blooms in cream

Mature Height × Spread
8 to 12 ft. × 2 to 4 ft.

A graceful native, Florida leucothoe is a carefree evergreen that thrives in the woodland garden. Growing 8 to 12 feet tall with a fountain of glossy green leaves, this shrub makes a wonderful companion for other shade-loving shrubs, trees, and perennials. Its inconspicuous, creamy, fragrant flowers appear in May to June. In the wild, Florida leucothoe grows in damp soils in woods or in moist hummocks. Because of its tendency to send out suckers, this shrub can be used to help stabilize stream banks and control erosion. It is not as susceptible to leaf spot as is *Leucothoe fontanesiana*, drooping leucothoe. Under large pines or deciduous trees, Florida leucothoe is right at home. Its texture offers a welcome contrast to many other woodland species.

When, Where, and How to Plant
Plant container-grown Florida leucothoe in spring or fall. Select a site that is shady or at least protected from the hot afternoon sun. Although it will grow happily in damp soil, Florida leucothoe will also grow well in a moist, well-drained, acidic soil. If you plant this leucothoe in full sun, make sure to keep it well watered. Dig a hole that is three times as wide as the container the leucothoe is growing in and 12 inches deep. Do not plant it any deeper than it was originally growing in the container. Apply a 1½-inch layer of mulch after planting.

Growing Tips
During the first two growing seasons, apply 1 tablespoon of 10-10-10 fertilizer per foot of height in spring and again in midsummer. After this, topdress with organic matter once every spring and fall. Water once a week during the growing season for the first two years. After this, check plants during periods of drought (no rain for two weeks). When you water, saturate the rootball, wait a few minutes, and then repeat this step.

Regional Advice and Care
This multistemmed shrub has an open habit. Use hand pruners to remove old branches, cutting them back all the way to the ground. If your Florida leucothoe gets too large, prune it back in early spring so that it will have a chance to recover before hot weather sets in. It does not suffer from any serious pest or disease problems.

Companion Planting and Design
Plant Florida leucothoe as an evergreen backdrop for a Japanese maple like *Acer palmatum* 'Sango Kaku'. Known as the coral bark maple, its coral-colored bark stands out against the glossy green backdrop of Florida leucothoe. Florida leucothoe is also great in combination with rhododendrons, anise, azaleas, oakleaf hydrangeas, ferns, hostas, hellebores, and hardy begonias.

Try These
Although it is not related, poet's laurel (*Danae racemosa*) is an elegant evergreen with arching branches and glossy green leaves. It grows 2 to 4 feet tall and, like Florida leucothoe, it thrives in moist shade.

Fragrant Teaolive

Osmanthus fragrans

Botanical Pronunciation
oz-MAN-thus FRAY-grans

Other Name Fragrant olive

Bloom Period and Seasonal Colors
Evergreen foliage and fragrant white flowers
in fall, spring, summer

Mature Height × Spread
10 to 20 ft × 5 to 10 ft

This broadleaf evergreen would be worth growing just for its delicious perfume that fills the air, beginning in September and then continuing on and off from spring through summer. The flowers are inconspicuous but it's a rare person that doesn't comment on their fragrant qualities. Teaolive is a workhorse as a screen, hedge, or backdrop for deciduous trees and shrubs. Its lustrous dark green leaves, sometimes slightly serrated, look good year-round, and it will grow happily in sun or shade, as well as in most types of soil. It also looks good when trained as a small tree with a single trunk. This shrub is addictive, and one will never be enough. The selection 'Aurantiacus' offers striking fragrant orange flowers in the autumn.

When, Where, and How to Plant

Plant container grown plants in early spring or fall. Site them where you can appreciate their perfume when they bloom. Dig a hole that is twice as wide but only as deep as the container that the plant is growing in when you purchase it. For a screen or hedge, plant teaolive on 8- to 10-foot centers. Water plants on a regular basis during the first growing season to help them get established. Apply a 1-inch layer of mulch to help keep roots cool in summer and warm in winter.

Growing Tips

Teaolive will survive under less than ideal conditions, but if you provide it with a moist, well-drained soil, part sun to sun, and fertilize it once in early spring and once in the fall, you will be rewarded with a lush broadleaf evergreen.

Regional Advice and Care

Teaolive does not suffer from any serious pest or disease problems but severe cold (below 0°F), can cause this shrub to drop its leaves. This will slow it down, but it should recover quickly. For a dense full hedge, prune plants to shape them when they are young. Don't just prune the tips; make sure to remove a few interior branches, leaving holes where light can reach. This will result in fuller, healthier plants.

Companion Planting and Design

Plant a small group of teaolives as a backdrop for flowering shrubs or small- to medium-sized trees like dogwoods or Japanese maples. Variegated kousa dogwood, *Cornus kousa* 'Wolf Eyes', will stand out in the landscape when planted in front of the dark green of teaolive. The same is true for the corneliancherry dogwood, *Cornus mas*. In early spring, its small but bright yellow flowers on bare branches will be much more appreciated when viewed against a backdrop of teaolive.

Try These

Other species and cultivars of *Osmanthus* offer evergreen foliage and fragrant flowers. Some with extremely spiny and prickly leaves like the holly teaolive are best suited for barrier plants. Others like *O. heterophyllus* 'Goshiki' offer colorful foliage and mature at 6 feet.

Gardenia

Gardenia augusta

Botanical Pronunciation
gar-DEEN-yuh ah-GUS-ta

Other Name Cape jasmine

Bloom Period and Seasonal Colors
Evergreen; summer blooms in white

Mature Height × Spread
4 to 8 ft. × 4 to 6 ft.

For some Georgians, the aroma of gardenia flowers on a warm June afternoon is the hallmark of summer. (Indoors, a little scent goes a long way.) Though a gardenia's glossy green foliage is handsome, its flowers and their scent are what most people love about this shrub. Gardenia is marginally hardy north of Atlanta; from mid-Georgia southward, it makes a reliable specimen shrub or component of a mass planting. Because cold weather is such a threat, look for cold-hardy selections. *Gardenia augusta* 'Klein's Hardy' is cold resistant and has single flowers. *G. augusta* 'Michael' is reputed to have resistance to cold and to whiteflies. *G. jasminoides* var. *radicans* is a dwarf form, more a groundcover than a shrub, and is much less resistant to cold.

When, Where, and How to Plant
Plant container-grown or transplanted gardenia in spring when the soil is warm. Do not locate it where winter wind rushes or where the plant will be very warm in January. An eastern or northern exposure is best. Site it in full sun or part shade in a soil that is rich in organic matter but well drained. Dig a hole three times as wide as and equal to the depth of the rootball. For potbound roots, unwind the longest ones and spread them out in the hole before backfilling. Pack the earth back around the roots and saturate with water.

Growing Tips
Apply 1 tablespoon of 10-10-10 fertilizer per foot of height in spring and again in midsummer. Water occasionally for the first month, when the top 1 inch of soil is dry. Spread a layer of pine straw mulch under your gardenia to conserve moisture. After the first growing season, water when there is no rain for two weeks or longer.

Regional Advice and Care
During a severe winter, gardenia may be killed to the ground, but it will usually sprout back within a few months. If extreme cold threatens, drape a bedsheet completely over the shrub. If your gardenia grows in the shade, lower limbs may fall off. Prune the whole shrub back to 12 inches tall in late March and let it resprout. Prune (after flowering) as needed for shaping. Aphids and whiteflies are common pests that suck gardenia's sap and excrete sticky "honeydew" that covers the lower leaves. Leaves turn black when sooty mold covers the honeydew. Spray for aphids in spring. Check with your county Extension office for an effective insecticide.

Companion Planting and Design
Plant gardenia next to a patio or sidewalk, where visitors can enjoy this singular summer treat. Gardenia is a choice evergreen at the back of a perennial border or in a decorative pot.

Try These
'August Beauty' is an old variety with large, luscious flowers. 'Mystery' has double flowers, (4 to 5 inches wide), and 'Shooting Star' is known to be very hardy.

Japanese Plum Yew

Cephalotaxus harringtonia

Botanical Pronunciation
cef-a-low-TAX-us hair-ing-TONE-e-a

Bloom Period and Seasonal Colors
Evergreen

Mature Height × Spread
1½ to 10 ft. × 3 to 10 ft.

Gardeners who relocate to Georgia quickly learn that gardening in the South is different from gardening in other parts of the country. With this in mind, Japanese plum yew is the ideal choice for our climate, where in colder regions one would choose to grow yews belonging to the *Taxus* genus. While these two plants may look similar, Japanese plum yew will thrive and yews will not. There are both upright and prostrate forms of this elegant evergreen with dark, short 1- to 2-inch-long needles, with gray on their undersides. All thrive here in shade or part sun, despite heat and humidity, and some gardeners report that plum yews are also "deer resistant." Depending on the selection, they make great foundation plants or focal points.

When, Where, and How to Plant

Plant container-grown plants in early spring or fall. Choose a site in shade or part shade for the best results, with a soil that is moist but well drained. If you locate them in areas that get more sun, make sure to provide regular moisture. Plum yews do not like wet soils. Dig a hole twice as wide and equal to the depth of the container that the plant is growing in. Add a 1-inch layer of mulch after you plant. Water plants once a week while they get established during the first growing season. After that, water only during periods of drought.

Growing Tips

Fertilize plants in spring and in fall with an all-purpose fertilizer like 20-20-20. Taller growing forms may require regular pruning to shape them, but upright fastigiate types should require only occasional pruning to remove errant side shoots. This will help give them a more uniform look.

Regional Advice and Care

For low-maintenance foundation plants in the shade that don't require regular pruning to keep them in check, *Cephalotaxus harringtonia* 'Prostrata' is the near perfect plant, growing 1½ to 2 feet tall and 4 to 6 feet wide. Plum yews do not suffer from serious pest or disease problems.

Companion Planting and Design

Depending on the selection, there are plum yews for a wide range of landscape situations, including evergreen screens, backdrops, low informal hedges, vertical accents, and even container plantings. For a contrast in foliage, combine the prostrate forms with the tropical-looking *Fatsia japonica*. For a formal screen or to create a garden room, use *Cephalotaxus harringtonia* 'Fastigiata', which grows 10 feet high and 6 to 8 feet wide. Upright forms also provide a vertical focal point in the garden or in a large container.

Try These

C. harringtonia 'Duke Gardens' has a vase-shaped habit and grows 3 to 5 feet wide and high. *C. harringtonia* 'Norris Johnson' has needles that are whorled around the stems, giving it a "bottlebrush" appearance. A similar selection, Yewtopia™, grows 3 to 4 feet high and wide.

Juniper

Juniperus spp.

Botanical Pronunciation
joo-NIP-ur-us

Bloom Period and Seasonal Colors
Evergreen foliage in shades of blue,
green, yellow

Mature Height × Spread
3 to 20 ft. × 3 to 15 ft. (by variety)

Durable and versatile, junipers are evergreen shrubs and trees that get no respect. The native eastern redcedar, *Juniperus viginiana*, is a tree that will thrive in a wide range of environments, where other plants languish. Junipers can be sheared into different shapes, planted as a cover on a steep slope, and used for groundcover. Junipers are a common site on the sides of interstate highways and on the clay banks surrounding shopping malls. Inexpensive and tough, they get the landscape job done without complaint. Choose from dozens of varieties of junipers. Read the plant information tag to determine how large yours will grow. *Juniperus chinensis* 'Blue Point' is an easy-to-find, upright variety. *J. chinensis* 'Gold Coast' will brighten your garden year-round with its golden yellow foliage.

When, Where, and How to Plant

Plant juniper anytime except during the heat of summer. For best results, plant it in early spring in northern Georgia and in spring or fall in southern Georgia. The plant's ultimate width is the spacing to use when planting a group. It is a myth that a juniper can grow easily in hard, clay soil. As with any other plant, juniper grows much faster if given a good root environment. A well-drained soil that has been amended with organic matter is best. If you are planting juniper on a slope, form 18-inch terraces along its length. Dig a hole at least twice the width of and equal to the depth of the rootball. Form a slight basin around the hole to catch water.

Growing Tips

In general, junipers do not require any more care than you choose to give them. For the first two years, fertilize three times a year (spring, summer, and fall) with 1 tablespoon of 10-10-10 per foot of plant height. After it is established, ¼ cup of 10-10-10 per foot of height each spring will be enough. Water once a week during the first growing season, and then once every two weeks if there is no rain.

Regional Advice and Care

Prune when new green shoots are growing in spring, typically in early May. Spider mites can infest a weakened juniper. Call your county Extension service for control measures. Phomopsis disease reveals itself in spring when new shoots die back 6 to 10 inches; control by removing the shoots.

Companion Planting and Design

Plant junipers as part of a mixed shrub border or in drifts. A single, golden-leafed specimen will make a good focal point. Use junipers as a backdrop for flowering shrubs, such as roses and beautybush, and perennials, such as yarrow and chrysanthemum.

Try These

Juniperus chinensis 'Kiazuka', also known as Hollywood juniper, grows to 20 feet tall and 10 feet wide. The branches look like the arms of dancers. For a tough groundcover, *J. chinensis* var. *procumbens* grows 2 feet high and 10 to 12 feet wide.

Loropetalum

Loropetalum chinense

Botanical Pronunciation
lor-oh-PET-al-um chi-NEN-see

Other Name Chinese fringeflower

Bloom Period and Seasonal Colors
Evergreen; midspring blooms in white or pink
to red

Mature Height × Spread
2 to 6 ft. × 2 to 8 ft. (by variety)

The common loropetalum has deep green leaves that persist all year. The flowers are white or light cream and appear in midspring. A member of the witchhazel family, loropetalum's blooms are strap-like (spidery) and approximately 1 inch long. This carefree, drought-tolerant shrub grows rapidly, is happy in sun or shade, flowers, and is not subject to pest or disease problems. Mature specimens have showy peeling bark. What more could you ask for? It is usually hardy from Atlanta southward, but a severe winter in the northern third of Georgia will freeze many loropetalums to the ground. Fortunately, it quickly regrows the following year. The purple-leafed varieties have bright (screamingly bright!) fuchsia blooms. While the species can grow into large plants, there are dwarf types too.

When, Where, and How to Plant
In southern Georgia, plant loropetalum in fall or in spring. Because it is susceptible to cold injury when young, plant it in midspring in the northern half of the state. Loropetalum tolerates a wide range of environmental conditions. It grows faster in full sun but also does well in shade. Moist, well-drained soils are best, but loropetalum also grows well in clay or sandy soil. Dig a hole three times as wide as the rootball and as deep. Thoroughly break up the soil. Water immediately after planting and spread mulch under the plant. Keep the soil evenly moist for at least four weeks.

Growing Tips
Fertilize loropetalum twice each year—in spring and in midsummer. Use 1 tablespoon of 10-10-10 per foot of plant height. Mulch, but be careful not to pile the mulch high against the trunk. If planted in sandy soil or full sun, drought stress may occur in summer. When leaves appear dull instead of glossy, soak the area around the plants and roots. Wait a few minutes, and then repeat.

Regional Advice and Care
Pruning is usually not necessary unless a wayward shoot extends far beyond the rest of the plant. If this occurs, simply prune it off just above a lower branch or bud. Provide shelter from cold winds by choosing a site in a protected corner on the east side of a house. In winter, if temperatures below 15°F are predicted, cover the shrub completely with an old bedsheet. Loropetalum does not suffer from any serious pest or disease problems.

Companion Planting and Design
Use it as a solitary specimen or as part of a larger grouping of shrubs. It can also be trained to grow as a small tree. Use loropetalum as an informal hedge, or underplant it with ferns, hostas, and perennials.

Try These
Loropetalum chinense var. *rubrum* includes selections with dark burgundy foliage and flowers in shades of pink, hot pink, and fuschia. Purple Pixie™ is a dwarf type. Ever Red™ and Purple Diamond™ don't grow as large as most loropetalums.

Nandina

Nandina domestica

Botanical Pronunciation
nan-DEE-nuh doh-MESS-tik-a

Other Name Heavenly bamboo

Bloom Period and Seasonal Colors
Evergreen or semievergreen; fall foliage in red;
winter berries in red, yellow, white

Mature Height × Spread
1 ½ to 8 ft. × 1 ½ to 5 ft. (by variety)

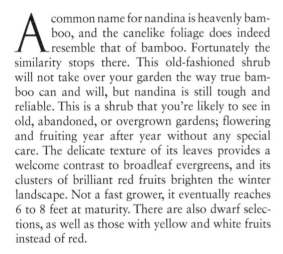

A common name for nandina is heavenly bamboo, and the canelike foliage does indeed resemble that of bamboo. Fortunately the similarity stops there. This old-fashioned shrub will not take over your garden the way true bamboo can and will, but nandina is still tough and reliable. This is a shrub that you're likely to see in old, abandoned, or overgrown gardens; flowering and fruiting year after year without any special care. The delicate texture of its leaves provides a welcome contrast to broadleaf evergreens, and its clusters of brilliant red fruits brighten the winter landscape. Not a fast grower, it eventually reaches 6 to 8 feet at maturity. There are also dwarf selections, as well as those with yellow and white fruits instead of red.

When, Where, and How to Plant
Plant in fall or spring. To transplant an old nandina to a new spot, cut back the stems to 18 inches and plant the bare root. Given some shade and a few waterings, transplanted nandina will do well. A soil rich in organic matter is best. Though shade-tolerant, common nandina grows well in full sun. The dwarf forms with red winter leaves do best in full sun. Dig a hole three times as wide as the rootball. Do not plant the main stem any deeper than it grew in the pot. Spread roots in the hole before backfilling. Pack the soil around the roots by hand, then water well. Layer mulch over the planting area to conserve moisture.

Growing Tips
Nandina will grow well with no fertilizer; however, it will produce more berries if fertilized. Apply 1 tablespoon of 10-10-10 per foot of height to a newly planted shrub in March, May, and July. After the first year, fertilize in April and June with the same amount of fertilizer. If the soil is rich in organic matter, water is needed for only a few weeks after planting. In sandy soil or a dry site, water once a week during July and August. Saturate the rootball, wait a few minutes, and repeat.

Regional Advice and Care
To reduce nandina's height, prune out the oldest stems in March. For the most attractive shape, cut one stem at 6 inches, one at 12 inches, one at 18 inches, and so on, in 6-inch increments. Nandina is remarkably free of insects and disease.

Companion Planting and Design
Nandina can be used as a foundation shrub or a screen plant. Good companions are coarse-leafed shrubs that like shade. Leatherleaf mahonia, *Mahonia bealei*, anise, *Illicium parviflorum*, and hydrangea are fine choices. Smaller, red-leafed nandinas can be used in rock gardens or containers.

Try These
Nandina domestica Gulfstream™ is a compact selection to 4 feet high. 'San Gabriel' has leaves that resemble ferns. They start out red and turn blue-green as they mature. This Japanese selection grows 3 to 4 feet high.

Oakleaf Hydrangea

Hydrangea quercifolia

Botanical Pronunciation
hye-DRAYN-jee-uh kwer-sif-FOH-lee-a

Bloom Period and Seasonal Colors
Deciduous; June blooms in white; fall foliage
in red, orange, yellow

Mature Height × Spread
4 to 6 ft. × 5 to 8 ft.

Oakleaf hydrangea is aptly named, displaying large leaves that are reminiscent of oak foliage. The tops are green, but the undersides are silvery. Other than the name, though, this shrub has no relation to oaks. A resilient native, this beauty offers large white cones of flowers in June that grace both woodlands and sunny gardens. Then in autumn, its leaf color, ranging from red to orange and yellow, adds to its charm. Left on the shrub, the dried flowers add structure to the winter garden. The cinnamon peeling bark is also attractive, especially when you site these hydrangeas in front of evergreens like hemlocks or anise. This bold shrub adds texture and color to the landscape that can be appreciated during every season.

When, Where, and How to Plant

Plant in spring after the last frost; otherwise, a late freeze may damage new foliage and potential blooms. Protect oakleaf hydrangea from hot afternoon sun. The roots prefer a moist but well-drained soil. Dig a hole five times as wide as and equal to the depth of the rootball. Mix the existing soil with equal parts of soil conditioner or compost. Place the plant in the hole and shovel the amended soil back in place. Plant, then water thoroughly. Apply a 2-inch layer of mulch, making sure to keep it away from main stems.

Growing Tips

Oakleaf hydrangea does not require much fertilizer. Apply 1 tablespoon of 10-10-10 fertilizer per foot of height to a newly planted shrub in March, June, and August. After the first year, fertilize in March and June. Irrigation is important for good establishment. Water once a week during the first growing season. After that, water as needed. The shrub shows its need for water with wilting leaves. Water immediately and deeply if the leaves get droopy. Saturate the rootball, wait a few minutes, and then repeat.

Regional Advice and Care

Oakleaf hydrangea does not need pruning unless it is outgrowing the area you've allotted it. If this is the case, prune in June after it finishes flowering. Oakleaf hydrangea does not suffer from any serious pest or disease problems. If planted in a wet spot, though, root rot will occur.

Companion Planting and Design

Plant oakleaf hydrangea in the shrub border or in a mass planting. It does best as an edge plant placed under a deciduous tree so that it gets sun in the morning and shade in the afternoon. Underplant it with evergreen groundcovers, such as autumn ferns and hardy ginger, *Hexastylis* 'Callaway'.

Try These

Hydrangea quercifolia 'Pee Wee' is a dwarf selection with a mounded habit. 'Harmony' is 6 to 8 feet tall and 6 feet wide with 12-inch cones of tightly packed flowers. 'Snow Queen' has huge, dense, white flowers that are held erect above its foliage. 'Snowflake' has double flowers, a real showstopper.

Plumleaf Azalea

Rhododendron prunifolium

Botanical Pronunciation
Ro-do-DEN-dron prew-na-FOL-ium

Bloom Period and Seasonal Colors
July and August blooms in orange-red to bright red

Mature Height × Spread
7 to 10 ft. × 6 to 8 ft.

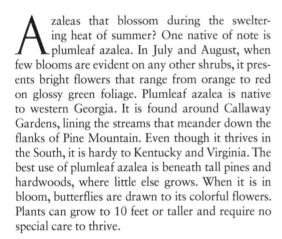

Azaleas that blossom during the sweltering heat of summer? One native of note is plumleaf azalea. In July and August, when few blooms are evident on any other shrubs, it presents bright flowers that range from orange to red on glossy green foliage. Plumleaf azalea is native to western Georgia. It is found around Callaway Gardens, lining the streams that meander down the flanks of Pine Mountain. Even though it thrives in the South, it is hardy to Kentucky and Virginia. The best use of plumleaf azalea is beneath tall pines and hardwoods, where little else grows. When it is in bloom, butterflies are drawn to its colorful flowers. Plants can grow to 10 feet or taller and require no special care to thrive.

When, Where, and How to Plant
Plant container-grown plumleaf azalea in spring or in early fall before the soil has cooled. Transplant small specimens in late November after the leaves have fallen. Instead of forming a rootball under the shrub to be moved, excavate a wide "pancake" of roots and soil around the shrub. Water after you plant, soaking the area completely. Although plumleaf azalea will tolerate full sun, a site with afternoon shade is ideal. Azaleas need a moist, well-drained, enriched soil. Dig a hole 5 feet wide and as deep as the container. Mix 4 cubic feet of soil conditioner into the backfill soil. Untangle and spread the roots before packing the amended soil around them. Mulch heavily with pine straw, being careful to pull the mulch back from the plant stem 3 inches on all sides.

Growing Tips
Provide a few light applications of fertilizer during the first year of establishment. Spread 1 tablespoon of 10-10-10 per foot of plant height in March, June, and August. Thereafter, 2 tablespoons of 10-10-10 per foot of height applied in April and June should suffice. Water once a week during the first year of establishment. After this, water during dry periods when there is no rain for two weeks. Saturate the rootball, wait a few minutes, and repeat. Even without regular applications of fertilizer, native azaleas should be good performers.

Regional Advice and Care
Buds for next year's flowers form during summer, so pruning anytime during the year reduces blooms. If you must prune to reduce the plant's size, prune immediately after it finishes flowering. Prune to remove dead wood anytime. Plumleaf azalea does not suffer from any serious pest or disease problems.

Companion Planting and Design
The eye-catching color of plumleaf azalea's blossoms is enhanced if placed in front of a dense, evergreen backdrop. For the carpet layer, add native ferns, wild ginger (*Hexastylis shuttleworthii*), and hellebores.

Try These
Sweet azalea (*Rhododendron serrulatum*) has fragrant, white blooms from July to September. For early spring, *R. canescens*, the Piedmont azalea, offers fragrant flowers of white and pink.

Prague Viburnum

Viburnum × pragense

Botanical Pronunciation
vy-BER-num pra-GEN-se

Bloom Period and Seasonal Colors
Evergreen; April blooms in pink turning to white; fall berries in red turning to black

Mature Height × Spread
8 to 12 ft. × 8 to 10 ft.

Viburnum is typically grown for either its fall fruit display or its fragrant spring flowers. Prague viburnum is considered the "best of the best" in the South. A hybrid cross between *V. rhytidophyllum*, leatherleaf viburnum, and *V. utile*, service viburnum, it is both drought tolerant and heat resistant. The fragrant flowers are pink in bud, turning white when they open in April and May. The berries, which follow the flowers, start out red and then turn to black. The shiny dark green leaves, 2 to 4 inches long, look good year-round. This evergreen shrub is easy and rewarding to grow, truly a plant for four seasons.

When, Where, and How to Plant
Plant Prague viburnum in late fall or early spring. It grows well in a wide variety of conditions and soil types, but a well-drained soil is best. Berries will be more numerous in full sun, but it can tolerate a surprising amount of shade. Dig a planting hole five times as wide as and equal to the depth of the rootball. If the soil you remove from the hole is all clay, mix in 2 cubic feet of soil conditioner or compost. Pack the earth back around the roots. Water once a week for the first month. Spread a layer of mulch (1 inch) under the viburnum to conserve moisture.

Growing Tips
This shrub will have better-looking leaves and more berries with regular fertilization. Apply 1 tablespoon of 10-10-10 fertilizer per foot of height in March, June, and August. Water weekly during the summer for the first two years. After it is established, supplemental water is only needed for sites that are hot and dry. If that is the case, water weekly when the top 1½ inches of soil are dry to the touch. Make sure to saturate the rootball.

Regional Advice and Care
Prague viburnum grows into an upright, oval form without major pruning. In very rich soil, remove the vigorous sprouts as they occur to give it a more manicured look. Prague viburnum is remarkably free of insect or disease problems. Leaf scorch can sometimes occur in winter if the site is windy. The damaged leaves will quickly be hidden in spring.

Companion Planting and Design
Use Prague viburnum as a foundation shrub at the high corner of a house. Plant it at the edge of a woodland in high shade. Its evergreen foliage also provides a good background for roses and fall blooming perennials, such as Japanese anemone, *Anemone × hybrida* 'Honorine Jobert'.

Try These
Another good choice, snowball viburnum (*V. macrocephalum*), has large, round, white flower heads in April that are similar to those found on a common hydrangea. *Viburnum setigerum*, tea viburnum, displays large clusters of orange to red, egg-shaped fruits in autumn.

Purple Beautyberry

Callicarpa dichotoma

Botanical Pronunciation
kal-ee-KAR-puh dye-KAWT-oh-ma

Bloom Period and Seasonal Colors
Deciduous; summer blooms in pink; fall berries
in purple, white, violet

Mature Height × Spread
4 to 5 ft. × 4 to 5 ft.

Purple beautyberry, a graceful arching shrub, growing 4 to 5 feet tall, branches, drops its drab yellow leaves in September to reveal "screaming purple" berries. It is eye-catching in fall, all the more so because of its nondescript nature during the rest of the year. Its tiny pink flowers are hard to see in summer, but you can't miss the individual berries that follow, ⅛ inch in diameter, appearing above the foliage in 1-inch clusters up and down the multiple gray stems. When planted in a group with *Callicarpa americana*, its native cousin (with slightly larger fruits) and American hollies with red fruits, the fall landscape glows purple, lavender, and red. It's hard to believe the intense colors are not man-made.

When, Where, and How to Plant
Plant beautyberry in fall or early spring, in full sun or part shade. Fall planting is better for the shrub's establishment, but occasionally the branch tips may be frozen by a severe winter. If this occurs and the plant was healthy at the start, don't worry—plenty of sprouts will emerge below the damage the following spring. Beautyberry can tolerate most soil types, but a moist, well-drained soil is preferred. Dig a hole three times as wide as the rootball and as deep. This shrub will do well without adding soil conditioner as long as the earth is completely broken up. Untangle the roots if necessary and spread them in the hole. Make sure the rootball is planted at the same level it was growing in the container. Pack the soil in place and water thoroughly. Add more soil if the earth

settles around the roots. Apply a ½-inch layer of mulch.

Growing Tips
Fertilize in April and midsummer with 1 tablespoon of 10-10-10 per foot of plant height. Water beautyberry weekly during the first growing season. After it is established, it will rarely need watering.

Regional Advice and Care
Beautyberry's flowers and berries grow on the current year's branches, so yearly pruning will produce more berries. Prune in early March to a height equal to half the height that you want the shrub to be by fall. Beautyberry does not suffer from any serious insect or disease problems.

Companion Planting and Design
Plant beautyberry at the back of the perennial border next to goldenrod, swamp sunflowers, and asters such as *Aster tataricus*. Evergreens—including American hollies, *Osmanthus* species, and even conifers such as hemlocks—make a good backdrop for showcasing the fruits of beautyberry.

Try These
Callicarpa dichotoma 'Albifructus' has white berries. *C. bodinieri* has willow-like leaves with violet-colored fruits. Japanese beautyberry, *C. japonica*, is somewhat larger, growing 5 to 6 feet or taller. All of these varieties of beautyberry do well in either a woodland or as a shrub border. American beautyberry will tolerate more shade than the Asian species.

Rose of Sharon

Hibiscus syriacus

Botanical Pronunciation
Hi-BIS-kus si-ri-A-kus

Other Name Shrub althea

Bloom Period and Seasonal Colors
Summer blooms in white, pink, lavender, bicolor

Mature Height × Spread
5 to 12 ft. × 8 to 12 ft.

In Georgia, rose of Sharon grows like a weed beside garden sheds and along property lines. It is one of those "passalong plants" that has been grown for generations. Today's gardeners have myriad cultivars to choose from, many of which are sterile so that this sometimes aggressive plant won't take over your garden. On those hot summer days when few shrubs are blooming, rose of Sharon pumps out blossoms that are single, double, or semidouble. In fact, rose of Sharon thrives in the heat and can even tolerate some drought. As a large shrub, it makes a welcome addition to the flower garden. With its rapid growth, rose of Sharon is easily trained as a small tree with a single trunk or as an espalier.

When, Where, and How to Plant
Plant rose of Sharon in fall, spring, or the middle of summer. It will not grow in swampy or extremely dry sites. It will grow best in full sun, part sun, or part shade in average garden soil. Dig a hole three times as wide as and equal to the depth of the rootball. There is no need to amend the soil as long as it is thoroughly broken up. Remove the shrub from its pot, gently untangle the larger roots, and spread them in the hole before filling it with earth. Water immediately after planting and mulch under the plant. Keep the soil evenly moist at least four weeks.

Growing Tips
Apply 1 tablespoon of 10-10-10 fertilizer per foot of height in spring and in midsummer. Water is rarely needed, except once a week for a month after the shrub has been planted. A plant in sandy soil or full sun may experience drought stress during the first summer if it isn't watered weekly. Water when the top inch of soil is dry to the touch.

Regional Advice and Care
Once established, rose of Sharon will grow for decades without any problems. To keep it smaller than 8 feet tall, prune it severely each winter (reducing it by half). Japanese beetles find it almost as delicious as roses, resulting in tattered leaves and blooms. Check with your county Extension office to learn about control measures.

Companion Planting and Design
To enjoy this plant without the labor of weeding its progeny, put it where it has little room to escape. If it is surrounded by turf, regular mowing will eliminate seedlings. Planted against a garage, it will hide the bare wall and provide summer beauty. Plant it with late-blooming daylilies, black-eyed Susan, and salvia.

Try These
Breeding by the National Arboretum resulted in crosses that are mostly sterile, meaning they don't produce seed. These include 'Diana' with white blooms (unlike many selections, the flowers remain open at night); 'Aphrodite', dark pink with a red eye; and 'Minerva', lavender-pink with a red eye and flowers up to 5 inches.

Smokebush

Cotinus coggygria

Botanical Pronunciation
co-TINE-us co-GIG-ree-a

Other Name Smoketree

Bloom Period and Seasonal Colors
Deciduous; June to September blooms in green to lavender-pink; fall foliage in yellow to orange-red

Mature Height × Spread
8 to 15 ft. × 8 to 12 ft.

Imagine a large shrub (or small tree) that looks as if it is surrounded by hazy smoke in the late afternoon June sunshine. That is the visual effect of smokebush. Each branch sends out fine stems that are covered with small flowers. When the flowers fall off, the flower stems, which are covered in silky hair, are left. These hairs give the shrub its distinctive, smoky look from June until September. In autumn the leaves often turn shades of orange, red, and yellow. Purple-leafed forms of smokebush are more widely available than the green-leafed varieties. Some have leaves that fade to green as the summer progresses, but a few keep their purple leaves until fall like 'Royal Purple' and 'Velvet Cloak'.

When, Where, and How to Plant

Smokebush is hardy throughout Georgia, although it may suffer from the heat in the extreme southern part of the state. Plant in fall or spring. Full sunshine stimulates both good leaf color and more flowers, but smokebush will tolerate partial shade. It needs moderately fertile, well-drained soil. Dig a hole three times as wide as the rootball. Do not plant it any deeper than the container in which it was originally growing. Spread the roots out in the hole and backfill. Pack the soil around the roots by hand, then water well. Mulch with pine straw or pine chips to conserve moisture. Refer to page 130 for more planting details.

Growing Tips

For a newly planted smokebush, apply 1 tablespoon of 10-10-10 fertilizer per foot of height in March, June, and August. After the first year, fertilize in April and June. Water weekly during the first growing season and once every two weeks after this establishment period.

Regional Advice and Care

If left to grow in an open spot, smokebush grows tall and wide by sending up a multitude of stems. If you prune, prune lightly after it blooms. If you have space, it is best to let smokebush find its own natural shape. Occasionally examine the stems and undersides of leaves for small white scale insects. Each scale covers itself with wax and does not move. The waxy covering makes them difficult to kill. If you find them, contact the county Extension office to learn about effective controls.

Companion Planting and Design

Use smokebush as specimen shrub or in a mixed shrub border. Surround it with *Artemisia*, such as 'Powis Castle'. *Artemisia*'s gray leaves contrast wonderfully with smokebush's purple leaves. Bronze fennel and Russian sage, *Perovskia atriplicifolia* also make good companions. For drama, plant red flowers in front of smokebush.

Try These

Cotinus obovatus, American smoketree, grows 20 to 30 feet tall and has outstanding fall color. *Cotinus* × 'Golden Spirit' starts out with bright yellow leaves that turn to yellow green or green, depending on the heat. *C. coggygria* 'Daydream' has dense branches, green leaves, and pink "smoke."

Southern Waxmyrtle

Myrica cerifera

Botanical Pronunciation
MER-ik-a sir-IF-er-a

Other Name Southern bayberry

Bloom Period and Seasonal Colors
Evergreen foliage

Mature Height × Spread
15 ft. × 15 ft. or larger

Southern bayberry, like its northern cousin, was popular during colonial times not as a landscape plant but for the waxy coating on the small fruits, used to scent candles after it was separated by boiling the fruits in water. Today bayberry is also appreciated for its ability to grow in almost any type of soil, including those that are wet or dry and sandy. This large native evergreen shrub or small tree has the ability to fix nitrogen from the air, which is part of the reason it thrives in a wide range of conditions. It's a great screen and, if you have females, the fruit is a source of food for wildlife. For tough spots where nothing will grow, southern bayberry may be the answer.

When, Where, and How to Plant
Plant container-grown bayberry in spring or fall for screens, in wetland areas or to help control erosion in coastal gardens. Male and female plants are separate, and if you want to ensure good fruit production, locate a male plant near females in the same area. The stoloniferous roots are ideal for stabilizing a bank. Its leaves give off a spicy pungent scent when you crush them. Water after you plant them and then only as needed when the top 1 inch of the soil dries out.

Growing Tips
This large shrub has ornamental gray bark (that looks almost bleached) and can be trained to grow as a small multistemmed tree or pruned to maintain

it as a hedge. Because it is salt tolerant, it makes a good windbreak in coastal regions.

Regional Advice and Care
Bayberry suffers from no serious pest or disease problems but may exhibit iron chlorosis in soils with high pH. It responds well to pruning, but there are dwarf selections available that may be better suited for smaller gardens.

Companion Planting and Design
For full sun gardens with sandy soils, use bayberry as an evergreen backdrop for deciduous hollies, which have colorful red berries. It also makes a good companion for *Rosa rugosa*. For the carpet layer, use the perennial Coopers hardy ice plant, *Delosperma cooperi*, and blanket flower, *Gaillardia*. In part shade, you can grow bayberry at the edge of a pine woodland with other native evergreens like *Agarista populifolia*, Florida leucothoe, or *Ilex vomitoria*, yaupon holly.

Try These
When a screen is needed that won't get as large as the species, there are dwarf cultivars, including 'Don's Dwarf', which is reported to grow only 3 feet high and wide. The variety *pumila* is also lower growing and may only reach 3 to 4 feet at maturity. *Baccharis halimifolia*, groundsel shrub, another native shrub with gray-green foliage, grows in swampy areas. In autumn the female plants display masses of white cottony fruit, a site to behold.

Spirea

Spiraea japonica cvs.

Botanical Pronunciation
Spi-REE-a ja-PON-ik-a

Bloom Period and Seasonal Colors
Deciduous; late-May to August blooms in white, pink, rose, carmine

Mature Height × Spread
1 ½ to 5 ft. × 3 to 5 ft.

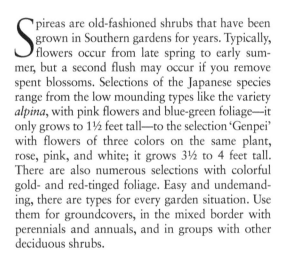

Spireas are old-fashioned shrubs that have been grown in Southern gardens for years. Typically, flowers occur from late spring to early summer, but a second flush may occur if you remove spent blossoms. Selections of the Japanese species range from the low mounding types like the variety *alpina*, with pink flowers and blue-green foliage—it only grows to 1½ feet tall—to the selection 'Genpei' with flowers of three colors on the same plant, rose, pink, and white; it grows 3½ to 4 feet tall. There are also numerous selections with colorful gold- and red-tinged foliage. Easy and undemanding, there are types for every garden situation. Use them for groundcovers, in the mixed border with perennials and annuals, and in groups with other deciduous shrubs.

When, Where, and How to Plant
Plant spirea in early spring or fall. Give your spirea full sunshine and room to spread out; it will also grow in part shade. Spirea is not particular about its soil. Dig a hole three times as wide as the rootball and as deep. Break up the soil thoroughly. Gently untangle some of the larger roots and spread them in the hole before filling it with earth. Water immediately after planting, and spread mulch under the plant. Keep the soil evenly moist for at least four weeks.

Growing Tips
Apply 1 tablespoon of 10-10-10 per foot of height to a newly planted spirea in March, June, and August.

After the first year, fertilize in March and June using the same amount. Once spirea is established, it will be able to withstand considerable drought. If the plant is in sandy soil and in full sun, water weekly during the summer to avoid drought stress. No matter what the soil type, you will get the best blooms if you water weekly during the growing season.

Regional Advice and Care
After the first flowers have begun to fade, use hedge clippers to trim 6 inches of foliage off the entire plant. The new growth that appears will give you a second flush of flowers in July. Prune in winter or very early spring. Spirea is not bothered by any serious pest or disease problems.

Companion Planting and Design
Use spirea in a mixed shrub border or as part of a perennial garden. Plant it in combination with conifers, daylilies, and black-eyed Susan for a contrast. A group of 'Goldmound', with its chartreuse foliage, provides a colorful focal point in the flower garden. 'Limemound' is similar, but the foliage turns orange-red in the fall. Plant it in combination with red-berried shrubs.

Try These
Spiraea 'Ogon' has chartreuse new growth, and it produces masses of tiny white flowers in spring. For a dwarf selection that thrives despite the heat and humidity of Georgia summers, try Little Bonnie™ with lavender-pink blooms and blue-green foliage.

Spring-Flowering Azalea

Rhododendron spp.

Botanical Pronunciation
rho-do-DEN-dron

Bloom Period and Seasonal Colors
Deciduous or evergreen (by variety);
spring blooms in red, white, pink, lavender,
orange, yellow

Mature Height × Spread
2 to 8 ft. × 4 to 10 ft. (by variety)

Hundreds of years of hybridization, not to mention the springtime availability of azaleas, means that a distinctive azalea is within reach of everyone. There are both evergreen and deciduous azaleas, as well as small-leafed and large-leafed types. In general, large-leafed azaleas are more likely to be damaged by extreme cold than are small-leafed ones. The deciduous azaleas tend to have a more open form than do most of the evergreen azaleas. Different hybrid groups are named for their original hybridizers. Glenn Dale, Robin Hill, and Girard hybrids are a few of the many. Southern Indica hybrids are evergreen with large flowers. In Japanese, *satsuke* means "fifth month," so as one might suspect the Satsuki hybrids flower in May, weeks later than most other azaleas.

When, Where, and How to Plant
Plant container-grown azaleas in spring or fall. A site with afternoon shade is ideal. Space plants according to their mature size. Azaleas need an enriched, moist soil that is well drained. Dig a hole five feet wide and mix in 4 cubic feet of soil conditioner. Plant azaleas at the same depth as they were grown. If the plant is potbound, untangle and spread the roots in the hole before packing the soil around them. Mulch heavily with pine straw, being sure to pull the mulch back 3 inches from the stem on all sides. For a month after planting, inspect weekly to make sure the rootball has not become exposed and dry.

Growing Tips
Azaleas require only moderate fertilizer the first year. Spread 1 tablespoon of 10-10-10 per each foot of plant height in March, June, and August. Thereafter, 2 tablespoons of 10-10-10 per foot of height applied in April and June should suffice. Water weekly during the growing season. Saturate the rootball, wait a few minutes, and repeat.

Regional Advice and Care
Buds for the following year's flowers form during summer, so pruning after July reduces blooms the following spring. Prune in May or June. To avoid pest and disease problems, do not plant in full sun or damp soils. Lace bugs can be a problem in warm weather, sucking the juices out of leaves and leaving them spotty and bleached. Use insecticidal soap, horticultural oil, or a systemic insecticide to control them. Petal blight can turn blossoms brown and mushy. Because spores overwinter in dead flowers, clear your garden of all debris. Azalea leaf gall is unsightly but does no permanent damage. Pick off the swollen leaves as you notice them.

Companion Planting and Design
Evergreen azaleas can be used as foundation plants. Combine with other evergreens to avoid the monotony of a single-leaf texture. Underplant with ferns, hostas, and early spring bulbs to complement azalea's flowers.

Try These
The Encore™ hybrids bloom in spring and fall, growing 1 to 3 feet high and 3 feet wide.

Summersweet

Clethra alnifolia

Botanical Pronunciation
KLETH-rah all-nih-FOE-lee-ah

Bloom Period and Seasonal Colors
Deciduous; July blooms in white; fall foliage
in yellow

Mature Height × Spread
4 to 8 ft. × 4 to 6 ft.

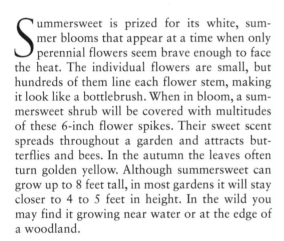

Summersweet is prized for its white, summer blooms that appear at a time when only perennial flowers seem brave enough to face the heat. The individual flowers are small, but hundreds of them line each flower stem, making it look like a bottlebrush. When in bloom, a summersweet shrub will be covered with multitudes of these 6-inch flower spikes. Their sweet scent spreads throughout a garden and attracts butterflies and bees. In the autumn the leaves often turn golden yellow. Although summersweet can grow up to 8 feet tall, in most gardens it will stay closer to 4 to 5 feet in height. In the wild you may find it growing near water or at the edge of a woodland.

When, Where, and How to Plant

Plant container-grown or balled-and-burlapped plants in fall. Spring planting can succeed, but regular summer watering is important. Summersweet produces a tremendous number of flowers if planted in full sun, but remember to keep the soil moist. Soil that is one-third coarse sand, one-third organic matter, and one-third clay is ideal. Summersweet thrives in deep shade and moist soils but produces fewer blooms. To plant, dig a hole three times as wide as the rootball; mix at least 1 cubic foot of soil conditioner with the existing soil. Cover the top of the rootball with soil so that moisture will be constant. Mulch heavily with pine straw, being sure to pull the mulch back from the stem 3 inches on all sides.

Growing Tips

Fertilize lightly for one year after planting with 1 tablespoon of 10-10-10 per foot of shrub height in March and August. After the first year, apply the same amount of fertilizer every April. Watering will be a regular chore the first year; a soaker hose laid under your summersweet and adjacent shrubs makes the job easier. Summersweet thrives in swamps and on stream banks but will tolerate well-drained soils.

Regional Advice and Care

Pruning is usually not necessary except when an older shrub has grown too large. Then, lightly clip it back for several years, each time in early spring. Summersweet does not suffer from any serious pest or disease problems.

Companion Planting and Design

Summersweet is perfect for that spot in the garden that never dries out. Combine it with Virginia sweetspire, which will grow in wet or dry soils. In shade, combine summersweet with evergreen azaleas. To attract more pollinating insects, plant perennial lantana, *Lantana camara* 'Miss Huff', and Mexican heather, *Cuphea hyssopifolia*, nearby.

Try These

Clethra acuminata, cinnamon clethra, is a native with showy cinnamon-colored bark and fragrant white flowers. It grows 8 to 12 feet tall. *Clethra alnifolia* 'Compacta' grows 2½ to 3½ feet tall. *C. alnifolia* 'Rosea' has pink flowers and matures at 4 to 5 feet tall by 4 feet wide.

Sweetshrub

Calycanthus floridus

Botanical Pronunciation
caly-CAN-thus FLOR-i-dus

Bloom Period and Seasonal Colors
Deciduous; April and May blooms in reddish maroon; fall foliage in yellow

Mature Height × Spread
6 to 10 ft. × 4 to 5 ft.

This native shrub is found from Virginia to Florida. Sweetshrub is universally easy to grow and transplant. It grows well in all but the sandiest, driest parts of Georgia. Sweetshrub's 2-inch-wide, reddish maroon flowers appear from April to May and then sporadically again throughout the summer. Their scent is variously described as "pleasantly fruity" and "a combination of banana, strawberry, and pineapple." One flower can perfume an entire room. Not only are the flowers fragrant, but the stems, leaves, and seedpods are also aromatic. The intensity of the scent varies greatly between plants. For this reason, it is a good idea to purchase sweetshrub while it is in bloom. In autumn, the leaves turn to shades of yellow, adding to this plant's appeal.

When, Where, and How to Plant

Plant or transplant in late spring while sweetshrub is flowering. This way you'll know if you have a "smeller" or not. Sweetshrub tolerates sun or shade and most types of soil. Give it a moist, organic soil, and it will thrive. Sweetshrub sprouts can simply be yanked out of the ground and handed to any friend who wants one. Even with minimal roots, sweetshrub withstands transplanting. Planting a container-grown sweetshrub is especially easy. Dig a hole three times as wide as and equal to the depth of the rootball. No soil conditioner is necessary as long as the earth is broken up. Water thoroughly after planting.

Growing Tips

Little fertilizer is needed unless you want the plant to spread rapidly. If this is the case, apply 1 tablespoon of 10-10-10 per foot of height in spring and again in midsummer. Water once a week during the first growing season. Drench the area around the main trunk, wait a few minutes, and repeat. Water in the heat of summer if the leaves become droopy.

Regional Advice and Care

For a full shrub, prune sweetshrub after it flowers. Tip branches back and prune out any crossing branches. Don't overdo it; a light touch is best. Sweetshrub has no major pests. Occasionally beetles or caterpillars chew on the leaves, but the damage is never major. Handpick the beetles and caterpillars; be sure to wear a good pair of gloves. If you have a good smelling sweetshrub you want to propagate, look for suckers at the base of the plant. They should be easy to root, and you will know you are getting a good selection.

Companion Planting and Design

Sweetshrub is mainly planted for its fragrance, so put one near your driveway or patio for an early summer treat. Plant it in combination with other old-fashioned shrubs, such as glossy abelia, native azalea, camellia, and fringe tree. Underplant with ferns, like Japanese painted fern, and early spring bulbs, such as snowdrops and dwarf iris.

Try These

Calycanthus floridus 'Athens' has yellow, sweetly scented flowers.

Tardiva Hydrangea

Hydrangea paniculata 'Tardiva'

Botanical Pronunciation
hy-DRAIN-juh pan-ik-u-LATA tar-DIVA

Bloom Period and Seasonal Colors
Deciduous; late-summer blooms in white

Mature Height × Spread
4 to 8 ft. × 4 to 6 ft.

What a delight to discover a shrub that not only looks good in August, but also produces fantastic flowers. 'Tardiva' hydrangea is just such a plant. When other plants look tired and worn during the dog days of summer, it is covered with large white cones of blooms. The mix of sterile and fertile flowers adds to the appeal of its blooms. While many hydrangeas wilt and languish in the full sun, 'Tardiva' thrives. Another reason this plant is a winner is that the blooms happen on current season's growth, so late spring freezes won't affect the flower production. Its bright green foliage looks good all spring and summer. Give this hydrangea plenty of room and watch it grow to 6 feet or higher in one season.

When, Where, and How to Plant
Plant container-grown 'Tardiva' in spring or fall. Give it plenty space to grow so that you can appreciate its big blooms. Site it in a moist, well-drained soil in full sun or part shade. Dig a hole three times as wide as and the same depth as the container it is growing in. After planting, apply 2 inches of mulch to keep the soil evenly moist. In soggy soils, 'Tardiva' will languish.

Growing Tips
Fertilize once every spring and fall using 1 tablespoon of 10-10-10 per foot of height. Water once a week during the growing season. Saturate the rootball, wait a few minutes, and repeat.

Regional Advice and Care
Because 'Tardiva' blooms on the current year's growth, the best time to prune is in early spring just before new growth emerges. Cut stems back to a height of 6 to 12 inches, and in no time you will have a large shrub covered in blooms. At the end of the growing season, you can reduce the plant by half to keep it from whipping in the winter wind, or you can enjoy the flowers as they dry on the shrub. Over a period of several years, this hydrangea can be trained as a standard with one trunk and a large head of flowers. This requires patience and lots of pruning. 'Tardiva' does not suffer from any serious pest or disease problems.

Companion Planting and Design
'Tardiva' in the middle of the flower garden looks like a big, white fountain of bloom in late summer or early fall. Plant it with other spring-blooming hydrangeas for a sequence of bloom. It is wonderful planted in combination with roses and other late-summer blooming annuals and perennials, such as salvia, ornamental grasses, and *Phlox paniculata* 'David'.

Try These
Hydrangea paniculata 'Grandiflora' is known as peegee hydrangea; its flower clusters can reach 12 to 18 inches long and 6 to 12 inches across at the base. *Hydrangea paniculata* Limelight™ has lime green flowers that turn to white as they age, growing 8 to 10 feet tall.

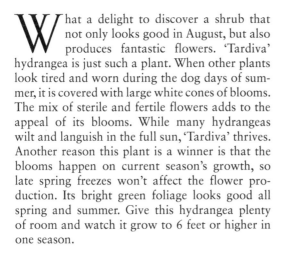

Virginia Sweetspire

Itea virginica 'Henry's Garnet'

Botanical Pronunciation
eye-te-AH vir-JIN-ik-a

Bloom Period and Seasonal Colors
Deciduous; spring blooms in white; fall foliage in garnet red

Mature Height × Spread
3 to 6 ft. × 3 to 6 ft.

The native Virginia sweetspire is an easy-to-grow deciduous shrub that offers beautiful, white, fragrant flowers in spring, bright green foliage all summer, and handsome, garnet-colored foliage in fall. In autumn, it stands out as a bright red spot growing in swamps in the same area as the russet-colored baldcypress. In the garden, Virginia sweetspire grows in full sun and makes a handsome arching shrub. 'Henry's Garnet' was first collected by Mary Henry in 1954 on a plant exploration trip to Coweta County, Georgia. Its deep red autumn foliage caught her eye, and she took the plant back to Gladwyne, Pennsylvania, where she ran the Henry Foundation. The plant was eventually named by the Scott Arboretum after it was observed growing in their collections.

When, Where, and How to Plant
Plant container-grown Virginia sweetspire in spring or fall. It will be happy in full sun and moist soil but will also grow happily in drier, shadier sites. Sweetspire will even grow in swampy or boggy areas. However, if planted in dense shade, it will not be vigorous and will not display colorful fall foliage. This plant spreads by underground suckers and is easy to propagate. Just cut off a rooted section and transplant it to a desired spot. For container-grown plants, dig a hole three times as wide as and the same depth as the container it is growing in. Give sweetspire plenty of room to grow. See page 130 for more planting tips.

Growing Tips
Fertilize Virginia sweetspire with 1 tablespoon per foot of height in the spring and summer of the first growing season after it is planted. After that, topdress with 2 inches of organic matter twice a year. Water once a week during the growing season unless plants are growing in wet soil. Saturate the rootball, wait a few minutes, and repeat.

Regional Advice and Care
Virginia sweetspire is easy to maintain and requires no special care. If you're looking for something to do, prune off the dead flowers, but this is not necessary for the vigor of the plant. Every few years remove old wood from the base of the plant. This shrub looks best if it is not cut back. *Itea virginica* does not suffer from any serious pest or disease problems.

Companion Planting and Design
Plant Virginia sweetspire in a mixed border with perennials, annuals, and other shrubs. Ornamental grasses, such as switchgrass or maiden grass, will contrast nicely with sweetspire's garnet autumn leaves. Plant it with other natives, such as *Illicium parviflorum*, cardinal flower, baldcypress, and iris.

Try These
Hollyleaf sweetspire, *Itea ilicifolia*, is a graceful evergreen for mid- to southern Georgia. An arching shrub, it grows 6 to 10 feet tall with spiny leaves that start out red and mature to dark grey. *I. virginica* Little Henry™ is a more compact selection.

Winterberry

Ilex verticillata

Botanical Pronunciation
EYE-lex vir-TIS-il-ate-a

Other Name Deciduous holly

Bloom Period and Seasonal Colors
Deciduous; winter berries in red

Mature Height × Spread
6 to 10 ft. × 6 to 8 ft.

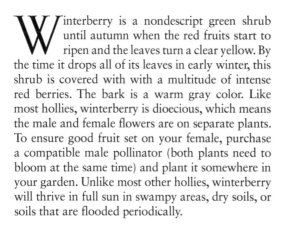

Winterberry is a nondescript green shrub until autumn when the red fruits start to ripen and the leaves turn a clear yellow. By the time it drops all of its leaves in early winter, this shrub is covered with with a multitude of intense red berries. The bark is a warm gray color. Like most hollies, winterberry is dioecious, which means the male and female flowers are on separate plants. To ensure good fruit set on your female, purchase a compatible male pollinator (both plants need to bloom at the same time) and plant it somewhere in your garden. Unlike most other hollies, winterberry will thrive in full sun in swampy areas, dry soils, or soils that are flooded periodically.

When, Where, and How to Plant
As is true of most hollies, winterberry is easy to plant or transplant in spring or fall. This adaptable shrub tolerates wet or dry soils without complaint. Plant winterberry in full sun or part shade. Low spots in the landscape, where rainwater accumulates frequently, are excellent for winterberry. Dig a hole three times as wide and equal to the depth of the rootball. Spread the roots in the hole before putting the soil back in place. Make sure the holly's main stem is not buried any deeper than it grew in the pot. Pack the soil around the roots by hand, then water well. Mulch under the newly installed plant with pine straw or bark chips to conserve moisture.

Growing Tips
Once a winterberry is established in the right spot, it will grow easily without problems. Apply 1 tablespoon 10-10-10 fertilizer per foot of height in spring and in midsummer. Water once a month after planting, and then only if needed during periods of drought (no rain for two weeks). For every five female shrubs, plant at least one male winterberry nearby for pollination and berry production.

Regional Advice and Care
Pruning is almost never needed, except when you wish to change a mature shrub into a tree form. Winterberry does not suffer from any serious pest or disease problems.

Companion Planting and Design
An evergreen background will make the brightly colored fruits of winterberry stand out in the landscape. Plant winterberry in combination with evergreen holly, anise, or *Osmanthus*. Plant it in a wet spot with other perennials that don't mind wet feet, such as yellow flag iris or cardinal flower. Winterberry spreads to form clumps by sending up suckers, which makes it a good choice for planting on slopes.

Try These
'Red Sprite' is a dwarf with large red berries. 'Afterglow' is a compact selection with orange to orange-red berries. 'Winter Red' has dark green leaves and a profusion of berries. 'Sparkleberry' is another outstanding red-berried deciduous holly. 'Apollo' is usually available in nurseries as a male pollinator for female hollies.

Witchhazel

Hamamelis × intermedia

Botanical Pronunciation
Ham-a-ME-lis in-ter-MEED-ee-a

Bloom Period and Seasonal Colors
Deciduous; February blooms in yellow, orange, red; fall foliage in yellow, orange, red

Mature Height × Spread
10 to 20 ft. × 4 to 8 ft.

For architectural interest and fragrant blooms in winter, witchhazel is at the top of the list. The hybrid *H. × intermedia* and its many selections fill the air in late winter to early spring with fragrance and color—shades of yellow, red, and orange. A large shrub, its spidery looking flowers—four narrow twisting petals, approximately 1-inch long—occur in clusters up and down the branches. The effect is dramatic if the flowers occur on bare branches, although some varieties hang on to last years' foliage and hide the flowers (but not the perfume). Some gardeners go to the trouble of removing the old leaves. In summer the handsome foliage provides welcome shade for woodland perennials and then in autumn leaves may turn yellow, red, and orange.

When, Where, and How to Plant

Plant witchhazel in early spring or fall so that you can enjoy its flowers the following February. Site plants in full sun or part shade in well-drained soil. Amend the soil with equal parts of organic matter, coarse sand, and clay, being sure to break up all the soil particles. Dig a hole three times as wide as and equal to the depth of the rootball. Untangle the roots if necessary and spread them in the hole before filling it with soil. Pack the soil in place and water thoroughly. Apply a 1-inch layer of mulch.

Growing Tips

Fertilize witchhazel lightly each year with 1 tablespoon of 10-10-10 per foot of height in March and August. A good layer of slowly decaying mulch will provide most of the nutrients needed. Water once every ten days during the first growing season. After this, you should only need to water during periods of drought when there is no rain for two weeks or longer.

Regional Advice and Care

Left to grow as Mother Nature dictates, witchhazel will have a wide, vase-shaped form. Prune to shape it by removing the top third of its central stems in late March. Remove any suckers and cut branches to bring indoors. Witchhazel attracts virtually no pests, but cone-shaped leaf galls may appear in July. You can easily cut them off.

Companion Planting and Design

Witchhazel looks good in front of large evergreen shrubs, such as American holly or cherrylaurel. The sunny edge of a shady spot that stays dark in winter is also a good spot. Underplant witchhazels with early spring bulbs, such as crocus and small daffodils.

Try These

Look for hybrids of Chinese witchhazel (*Hamamelis mollis*) and Japanese witchhazel (*H. japonica*) *Hamamelis × intermedia*. *H. × intermedia* 'Diane' is the best red-flowering variety, while *H. × intermedia* 'Primavera' has bright yellow flowers. Native witchhazel, *Hamamelis virginiana*, perfumes the air with its flowers from October to December. While not as showy as the hybrids, this species is perfect for the naturalistic garden.

Yaupon Holly

Ilex vomitoria

Botanical Pronunciation
EYE-leks vom-ih-TOR-ee-uh

Other Name Yaupon

Bloom Period and Seasonal Colors
Evergreen; winter berries in red

Mature Height × Spread
8 to 15 ft. × 6 to 10 ft. (by variety)

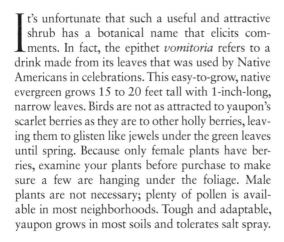

It's unfortunate that such a useful and attractive shrub has a botanical name that elicits comments. In fact, the epithet *vomitoria* refers to a drink made from its leaves that was used by Native Americans in celebrations. This easy-to-grow, native evergreen grows 15 to 20 feet tall with 1-inch-long, narrow leaves. Birds are not as attracted to yaupon's scarlet berries as they are to other holly berries, leaving them to glisten like jewels under the green leaves until spring. Because only female plants have berries, examine your plants before purchase to make sure a few are hanging under the foliage. Male plants are not necessary; plenty of pollen is available in most neighborhoods. Tough and adaptable, yaupon grows in most soils and tolerates salt spray.

When, Where, and How to Plant

Plant yaupon holly in fall or spring. It grows well in windy coastal sites, even next to the ocean. It grows densely in full sun but can survive—though with slower growth—in shade. A wet or dry problem site is a good place to try yaupon holly. Spread the roots in the hole before backfilling. Do not bury the main stem any deeper than it was growing in the pot. Transplanted yaupon hollies seem to thrive immediately as long as they are cut back by half before digging.

Growing Tips

Apply 1 tablespoon of 10-10-10 fertilizer per foot of height to a newly planted shrub in March, June, and September. After the first year, use the same amount and fertilize in April and June. Water once a week for the first month after planting. After this, water only during periods of drought. Saturate the soil around the base of the trunk, wait a few minutes, and repeat.

Regional Advice and Care

Perform light pruning anytime, but if you want to make the plant more dense, prune in March. Do drastic pruning in February. Regrowth is rapid if the original plant was healthy. Cut back new sprouts by half after they reach 12 inches in length. Occasionally black vine weevils will chew round notches in leaf edges. If damage is severe, contact your county Extension office (page 225) for control measures.

Companion Planting and Design

Yaupon holly makes a great hedge, screen, or backdrop for deciduous shrubs and perennials. It is also great in containers. Combine it in the garden with other hollies, conifers, and ornamental grasses. Because it takes well to shearing, yaupon makes a good topiary.

Try These

Dwarf yaupon, *Ilex vomitoria* 'Nana', only grows to 3 to 5 feet tall and twice as wide, great for a low hedge. 'Schilling's Dwarf' is commonly used as a foundation shrub. Because of its distinctive shape, weeping yaupon holly (*I. vomitoria* 'Pendula') is a mainstay of commercial landscapers. *Ilex vomitoria* 'Hoskin Shadow' has larger leaves and fruits. Bordeaux™ has dark green leaves that turn rich, burgundy-red in winter.

TREES
FOR GEORGIA

The home you bought several years ago has probably been redecorated more than once on the inside. Curtains have been hung and re-hung. Rooms have been painted and repainted. Furniture has been bought, used, and given to charity. All these changes may have gone on inside a home while the outside landscape looks much the same as it did a decade ago.

Step back from your landscape for a moment and think of it as an outdoor room. The trunks of tall trees form the contours of the walls, while their limbs and leaves contribute a green, light-filled ceiling. The smaller flowering trees supply the paintings that hang on the walls. A healthy tree enhances your outdoor room, while an unhealthy one degrades it. Follow our guidelines for growing healthy trees.

How to Plant a Tree
No Amendments

Scientists have tested whether or not organic matter added to the planting hole makes any difference in the health of the tree. Their research has determined that it actually makes little difference. Roots will move into soil that contains lots of oxygen, so the best recommendation is to dig a hole wide rather than deep, pulverizing the soil thoroughly.

Digging the "Hole"

Although most illustrations show a "hole" for tree planting, you may not need a "hole" at all! First, determine where you want to plant your tree. Use your shovel to "scoop and chop" the soil 4 feet in all directions around that spot. In the center, dig a hole as deep, and twice as wide, as the rootball of the tree you're planting.

Loosening the Roots

If the tree is in a pot, loosen and untangle the roots, removing any dead ones, and spread them apart as you drop the rootball into the planting hole. Pack soil in the hole around the roots with your hands. If you choose to use your foot to compact the soil, do so gently. Make a soil doughnut (a berm) around the tree, keeping the raised edges about 18 inches away from the trunk of the tree. The berm will direct water to the rootball. Destroy the berm after twelve months.

Remove String and Burlap

If your tree is "balled and burlapped," remove all strings from around the trunk and as much burlap and wire cage as you possibly can.

Live oak trees provide shade for both people and plants.

Mulch

Trees and turf engage in "root wars" under the soil. Grass roots are very aggressive, but a 2-inch layer of mulch spread under the branches of the tree will minimize competition from grass and weeds, keep the soil cool, and conserve moisture. Pine straw, bark chips, and shredded wood fiber all make good mulch materials.

Staking

One or two stakes are sufficient for trees less than 8 feet tall. Drive the stakes into the ground 12 inches from the trunk. Loosely tie the trunk to the stake using cloth or a wide nylon band. Do not use rope or wire. Remove after one year.

Pruning New Trees

The branch tips on a small tree produce plant hormones that direct the growth of roots. If you prune a tree to compensate for lost roots, the tip buds cannot tell the roots to begin growing. Don't prune a new tree for a year after planting except to remove damaged limbs or to correct its shape.

Watering New Trees

Water the tree deeply after planting, using at least 10 gallons of water. Thereafter, apply 20 to 30 gallons once each week when the soil is dry in the absence of rainfall. Water hoses deliver about 5 to 10 gallons per minute. Check your delivery volume by measuring the time it takes to fill a 5 gallon bucket.

Frequently check on evergreen trees—such as magnolia, hemlock, or pine—during times of drought for one year after planting. Roots grow only a few inches in their first year in your garden; be sure to direct your water no further than 24 inches from the trunk.

Arborvitae

Thuja spp.

Botanical Pronunciation
THOO-yuh

Bloom Period and Seasonal Colors
Evergreen

Mature Height × Spread
5 to 40 ft. × 2 to 10 ft. depending on cultivar

There are several species of arborvitae, but the most common are *Thuja occidentalis*, *Thuja orientalis*, and *Thuja plicata*. The name *arborvitae* means "tree of life" in Latin, given due to its supposed medicinal properties. Tea made from its bark and leaves was reputed to ease coughs and fever. Folklore aside, arborvitae can be good medicine for your landscape! Their flat evergreen sprays of foliage give them a distinctive look. Be sure to study the plant label: some forms are columnar, some are broadly pyramidal, and some are globular. Smaller forms are typically used for a solid background to a colorful flower bed, but the larger forms can make an excellent screen plant. Despite the fragrant foliage, deer prefer arborvitae to many other shrubs in spring.

When, Where, and How to Plant
Plant arborvitae in full sun. Growth will be open and very slow in shade. The best time to plant is in late fall. Spring planting is possible, but regular watering is required. If the plant has been in a pot for a while, the rootball will be severely potbound. Loosen and untangle the roots before planting. Spread the roots in the hole before backfilling. Make sure the main stem of the plant is not buried any deeper in the earth than it grew in the pot. Spread mulch under the plant to help conserve moisture.

Growing Tips
Once an arborvitae is established in the right spot, it will grow for decades without problems. Apply 1 tablespoon of 10-10-10 fertilizer per foot of height in spring and again in midsummer.

Regional Advice and Care
Choose arborvitae based on its eventual mature size. Light pruning can be done, but never clip foliage back to a brown stem; be sure to leave greenery behind each cut. Arborvitae tends to develop multiple trunks. If noticed when a plant is a foot or so tall, side shoots can be removed. If the plant is more than 3 feet tall, removing a vertical trunk will leave a brown area that's slow to fill with greenery. Spider mites can be a problem, but they usually infest only plants weakened by drought. Numerous 3-inch-long silken bags covered in brown needles signify an invasion of foliage-eating bagworms. Pick them off immediately.

Companion Planting and Design
Arborvitae is typically used for screening but can also be used at the corner of a building to soften the look. It is rarely the right size to be planted by a doorstep.

Try These
There are plenty of alternatives to arborvitae. Arizona cypress, *Cupressus arizonica* var. *glabra* 'Carolina Sapphire', grows to 30 feet with a distinct gray-green color. Due to its drought and heat tolerance, use it instead of Green Giant™ in southern Georgia. *T. orientalis* 'Blue Cone' has sky-blue cones that contrast nicely with green foliage. *T. orientalis* 'Rheingold' has deep golden foliage.

Baldcypress

Taxodium distichum

Botanical Pronunciation
taks-OH-dee-um DIS-tik-um

Bloom Period and Seasonal Colors
Feathery-looking green foliage turns russet in fall

Mature Height × Spread
30 ft. × 50 to 100 ft.

Baldcypress isn't an appropriate tree for every landscape, but in the right spot it grows to an imposing height and lends a majesty that few trees attain. Folklore has it that baldcypress gets its name because the top is often hit by lightning, leading to a "broken" appearance. More likely, the tree is so tall that normal wind, rain, and ice do damage to the upper limbs. Another explanation for the name is that the tree is deciduous: it drops its needles and becomes "bald" each fall. Baldcypress is similar in appearance to dawn redwood. You can tell the two apart by their branches: baldcypress has alternate branches, while dawn redwood has opposite branches.

When, Where, and How to Plant
Full sun is best. For more extensive planting tips, see the notes on page 130.

Growing Tips
Baldcypress is often said to be slow growing, but growth can be rapid if it is fertilized regularly for the first five years and if the soil is kept moist. Dry soil equals slow growth.

Regional Advice and Care
Baldcypress rust mites are occasionally a problem. They rasp the needles in summer, causing them to be yellow or red. You'll easily notice the hundreds of tiny white shed skins on a needle clump. Consult your local university Extension office for pesticides

labeled for mite control on baldcypress. Cypress gall midges make dime-sized gray, waxy galls at branch tips. They can be pruned away. Although not a particularly messy tree, be aware that you'll have to rake the fallen needles each year. Small branches often fall as well. Birds love the brown needles for spring nest building, so leave a few for them around the trunk.

Companion Planting and Design
After several years, the tree trunk will form attractive "buttresses." Baldcypress commonly produces aboveground roots called "knees." They emerge in both wet and dry situations. Plan ahead for these and do not plant within 25 feet of a lawn area. You can cover the ground around the base of the tree with mulch, allowing the knees to be seen, or you can hide the knees with groundcover plants. Do not chop them off. When driving through southern Georgia, notice the ghostly baldcypress growing in roadside swamps, where they are draped with gray Spanish moss.

Try These
'Falling Water' has a beautiful weeping form. Heritage™ baldcypress is reputed to be rust mite resistant. Shawnee Brave™ has a much narrower form than the species tree. 'Monarch of Illinois' has a very wide-spreading form. The branches on 'Pendens' droop attractively at the tips, forming a graceful canopy.

Black Gum

Nyssa sylvatica

Botanical Pronunciation
NY-suh sil-VAT-ee-kuh

Bloom Period and Seasonal Colors
Deciduous; stunning yellow fall foliage turns to scarlet and then purple; insignificant blooms in summer

Mature Height × Spread
50 to 70 ft. × 30 ft.

The scarlet fall foliage of this native tree can cause car wrecks! More intense than any maple, the autumn leaves start out yellow, quickly change to scarlet, and finally adopt a deep red-purple hue. During the growing season, the leaves, which can be 6 inches long and 3 inches wide, have a lustrous, dark green appearance. This is a wonderful shade tree for medium to large gardens. It is not commonly found in nurseries, as it has a fussy nature about its root system. Most lake or woodland property has a couple of black gum trees from which young seedlings can be transplanted as described below (get permission!). Growth rate is about 1 foot per year, but it can be accelerated with regular irrigation and fertilization.

When, Where, and How to Plant

Transplant black gum in fall. Because it is so touchy about its root system, smaller trees are easier to establish successfully. Trees not planted in fall require extra care (watering) through the first growing season. Black gum prefers a soil that is moist but well drained, rich in organic matter, and slightly acidic to neutral in pH. In the wild, it is sometimes found growing on dry upland slopes. Not tolerant of excessive pollution, it is best planted away from streets or congested areas. Plant in full sun to achieve the brightest fall color. Transplanting from the wild can be difficult unless you start with a small (3- to 4-foot) tree. Seeds sprout readily, though. If you find a mature black gum, there will be dozens of sprouts nearby. See page 130 for other planting tips.

Growing Tips

Black gum is drought tolerant once established, and supplemental water is usually not required. If located near fertilized turf areas or in a natural setting that retains leaves dropped in the fall, additional fertilizer is not necessary. In common landscape situations, maintain a 2- to 3-inch layer of mulch to retain moisture and deter weeds.

Regional Advice and Care

When planted in an open area as a shade tree or in a natural setting, pruning is not normally required. Remove dead, damaged, or diseased wood anytime. Prune large limbs in late winter or early spring. Black gum may suffer occasionally from leaf spot, canker, rust, scale, and tupelo leaf miner. Although these problems may detract from its appearance, they are rarely lethal. Rake diseased leaves in fall to remove leaf-spot fungi.

Companion Planting and Design

Black gum forms a dense canopy, so it can shelter shade-tolerant shrubs and perennials, including azaleas, rhododendrons, ferns, and hostas. Planting it as a specimen or as a group will draw attention in fall. Plant trees with bright yellow fall foliage nearby to complement black gum.

Try These

'Miss Scarlet' and Forum™ are available in the landscape trade. 'Wildfire' has spectacular orange-red spring foliage. Red Rage™ has great fall color and high leaf-spot resistance.

Canadian Hemlock

Tsuga canadensis

Botanical Pronunciation
SOO-guh ka-na-DEN-sis

Bloom Period and Seasonal Colors
Evergreen foliage

Mature Height × Spread
40 to 70 ft. × 25 to 40 ft.

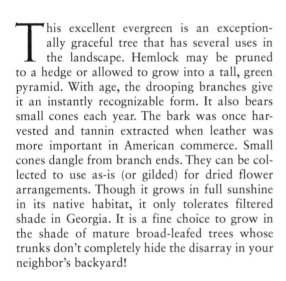

This excellent evergreen is an exceptionally graceful tree that has several uses in the landscape. Hemlock may be pruned to a hedge or allowed to grow into a tall, green pyramid. With age, the drooping branches give it an instantly recognizable form. It also bears small cones each year. The bark was once harvested and tannin extracted when leather was more important in American commerce. Small cones dangle from branch ends. They can be collected to use as-is (or gilded) for dried flower arrangements. Though it grows in full sunshine in its native habitat, it only tolerates filtered shade in Georgia. It is a fine choice to grow in the shade of mature broad-leafed trees whose trunks don't completely hide the disarray in your neighbor's backyard!

When, Where, and How to Plant
Plant balled-and-burlapped hemlock in mid-autumn or early spring. Morning sun is fine, but avoid a site that allows summer's baking glare after noon. Hemlock's growth is slower in shadier conditions, so purchase the largest tree you can afford. For a screen, stagger the trees 10 feet apart. As they grow larger, a few may need to be removed. The soil should be rich in organic matter, moist but with excellent porosity. Do not plant it where water runs or stands after a rain. Hemlock will not prosper in unamended clay soil. Mix soil conditioner, gritty sand, and native soil in a 1:1:1 ratio in the entire planting area. Excellent drainage, as well as attention to watering during summer, is important.

Growing Tips
Water young trees each week during summer drought and heat. Do not overwater. Irrigate during winter dry spells for two years after planting. See page 130 for more planting directions and fertilizing tips.

Regional Advice and Care
Prune lightly anytime. Remove big limbs in January. Pruning single trees is usually not necessary, but a hemlock hedge should be pruned in late winter or early spring, before new growth begins. Hemlock adelgid is a serious pest. Look for small, white, cottony creatures on branch tips. Uncontrolled, these sap-sucking insects can kill a tree in just a few years. Use a systemic insecticide yearly, following label directions. Contact your local Extension office (page 225) for more control options.

Companion Planting and Design
Plant in the shade of hardwoods or tall pines. The needled texture blends well with rhododendrons, azaleas, leucothoe, and Carolina cherrylaurel. Balled-and-burlapped hemlock is often sold as a living Christmas tree, to be enjoyed for the holidays and then planted outdoors afterward. Do not allow the tree to be indoors more than seven days, or it will be harmed by the cold when it is eventually planted.

Try These
Tsuga canadensis 'Sargentii' is a smaller, weeping form, 10 feet high and 20 feet wide. Carolina hemlock (*Tsuga caroliniana*) may be hardier in Georgia landscapes. It is reputed to be more tolerant of shade.

Carolina Silverbell

Halesia carolina

Botanical Pronunciation
hay-LEEZ-ee-uh kair-oh-LY-nuh

Other Name Halesia

Bloom Period and Seasonal Colors
White, bell-shaped flowers in midspring

Mature Height × Spread
30 to 40 ft. × 20 to 35 ft.

Carolina silverbell is a wonderful native tree that simply does not get the respect it deserves. When asked for a spring-flowering tree, most gardeners think immediately of native dogwood, redbud, and perhaps serviceberry. In early spring, before or with new emerging leaves, *Halesia* is covered with clusters of white ½- to 1-inch-long bells that dance in the breeze. Then, in September to October, it develops curious four-sided winged fruits that persist into winter and beyond. The bark, which is brown and peeling on young branches, becomes scaly and dark (a mixture of gray, brown, and black) as it matures, adding to the unique character of this native. An understory tree, silverbell is typically found growing near stream banks under oaks, hickory, and tulip poplar.

When, Where, and How to Plant
Plant silverbell in sun or shade as an understory tree in combination with dogwoods or other natives. Container-grown plants may be easier to establish in the garden. Plant in early spring or midautumn in moist, acidic, well-drained soil. Morning sun with afternoon shade is best. Site in the shade of larger trees or a house to shelter it from hot afternoon sun. However, silverbell will tolerate full sunshine if given deep mulch and attention to watering in dry times. If possible, plant where it is higher than passers-by, so the downward pointing flowers can be better seen. Silverbell often develops several trunks, so if you are training it to have a single trunk, you may need to stake it for the first six months after planting.

Growing Tips
Once the tree matures, particularly if growing in or near a lawn, little fertilizer is needed. If summer temperatures rise above 95°F, water heavily every two weeks. Because flowers appear on the previous year's branches, prune silverbell after spring flowering.

Regional Advice and Care
Silverbell is not tolerant of difficult sites. Plant it correctly, with attention to spading and softening a wide area around the spot where it will be planted. Spread mulch under the entire branch width to deter grass from competing with the tree's shallow roots.

Companion Planting and Design
Many native shrubs like the same woodsy environment as Carolina silverbell. Try sweetshrub, Virginia sweetspire, witchhazel, or native azaleas as companions. Site Carolina silverbell against a backdrop of conifers and it will stand out in the landscape. Underplant it with spring wildflowers like dwarf crested iris and creeping phlox.

Try These
The variety *Halesia carolina* 'Rosea' offers pink flowers, but the color may be affected by spring temperatures; cooler temperatures often lead to pinker flowers. Two-winged silverbell, *Halesia diptera* var. *magniflora*, has larger flowers and is more prolific than the species.

Cherrylaurel

Prunus caroliniana

Botanical Pronunciation
PROO-nus kair-oh-lin-ee-AN-uh

Other Name Carolina cherrylaurel

Bloom Period and Seasonal Colors
Evergreen foliage; April blooms in white

Mature Height × Spread
20 to 30 ft. × 15 to 20 ft.

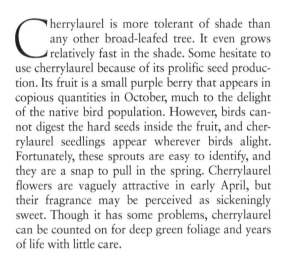

Cherrylaurel is more tolerant of shade than any other broad-leafed tree. It even grows relatively fast in the shade. Some hesitate to use cherrylaurel because of its prolific seed production. Its fruit is a small purple berry that appears in copious quantities in October, much to the delight of the native bird population. However, birds cannot digest the hard seeds inside the fruit, and cherrylaurel seedlings appear wherever birds alight. Fortunately, these sprouts are easy to identify, and they are a snap to pull in the spring. Cherrylaurel flowers are vaguely attractive in early April, but their fragrance may be perceived as sickeningly sweet. Though it has some problems, cherrylaurel can be counted on for deep green foliage and years of life with little care.

When, Where, and How to Plant
Plant balled-and-burlapped plants in midautumn or early spring. Small (4- to 6-foot) container-grown trees can be planted anytime if water is provided in summer. For screening, plant 6 to 10 feet apart. Be sure you leave some room to maneuver underneath the trees so that seedlings can be pulled each year. In the mountainous part of Georgia, cherrylaurel may lose its leaves in winter or it may even be frozen to the ground. Provide protection from strong winds in the extreme northern part of the state. Carolina cherrylaurel is tolerant of a wide range of sun conditions, from full sun to nearly full shade. The more shade cherrylaurel receives, the more open its form will be. Cherrylaurel is one of the few choices for a tall evergreen screen in shady conditions. If that is your situation, make doubly sure to follow the initial soil preparation tips on page 130. Grow in moderately fertile, evenly moist, but well-drained soil.

Growing Tips
Read page 130 for fertilizing and watering tips. Prolonged drought on a tree growing in full sun will severely weaken it.

Regional Advice and Care
Prune cherrylaurel to a tree shape or to a thick, rounded hedge. To keep the foliage growing densely in a shady spot, prune off branch tips every March. Cherrylaurel attracts few insects or diseases. Hundreds of tiny holes in the leaves are a sign of shothole disease. Fungicides offer little help in controlling this problem. The best prevention is to keep the foliage dry by watering during early morning hours or using soaker hose irrigation.

Companion Planting and Design
Cherrylaurel can form a thick screen, hedge, or windbreak for your landscape. It makes a nice native alternative to Japanese ligustrum. In shady areas, it can be underplanted with azalea, rhododendron, and shade-tolerant perennials. Anise and leucothoe are also good companions. This tree is a must for the avid bird watcher who wants to attract birds to their landscape.

Try These
Bright 'N Tight™ and Cherry Ruffles™ are two good selections that offer dense foliage and wavy leaf margins, respectively.

Chinese Elm

Ulmus parvifolia

Botanical Pronunciation
ULM-us par-vee-FOH-lee-uh

Other Name Lacebark elm

Bloom Period and Seasonal Colors
Deciduous; muted yellow fall foliage,
colorful bark

Mature Height × Spread
40 to 50 ft. × 40 to 50 ft.

One of the best disease-resistant elms is the Chinese elm (not to be confused with the markedly inferior Siberian elm, *Ulmus pumila*). Though smaller than the American elm, Chinese elm has similar ascending branches and is uniformly resistant to pests. Insignificant reddish-green flowers appear in late summer. Its bark is noticeably different from its American relative. Small patches of bark drop off to reveal a beautiful, mottled combination of gray, green, and brown. The pattern is like a jigsaw puzzle with a random but pleasing combination of colors. The superior selections noted here were chosen by Dr. Michael Dirr at the University of Georgia, who recognized that certain trees growing on the college campus had characteristics that set them apart from the typical Chinese elm.

When, Where, and How to Plant
Plant balled-and-burlapped trees in midautumn or in early spring. Even trees planted in midsummer can withstand the heat stress and establish themselves successfully if they are watered occasionally. Chinese elm tolerates a wide variety of soil types and environmental conditions, but for best results prepare a planting area that has evenly moist soil. Chinese elm should be grown in full sun and spaced at least 50 feet from other trees or buildings so that its form can be appreciated. When deciding where to plant, remember that this elm grows rapidly and casts a dense shade.

Growing Tips
See page 130 for other planting, fertilizing, and watering tips.

Regional Advice and Care
Perform light pruning anytime. Remove major limbs in January. Chinese elm is resistant to Dutch elm disease and other pests. Make sure the tree you have decided to buy is a true Chinese elm. The weak-wooded Siberian elm, *Ulmus pumila*, is sometimes mistakenly called Chinese elm.

Companion Planting and Design
Chinese elm can be evergreen in southern Georgia. Try planting cast iron plant, *Aspidistra elatior*, or Japanese azaleas underneath. It makes a fine shade tree for medium-sized and residential landscapes because of its dense, dark green foliage, lack of messiness, and smaller size. It also makes a superb small shade tree. The deep green leaves provide a nice contrast to the bricks when the tree is planted in front of a large brick home. It is also a superior small tree for street and urban plantings because of its tolerance to pollution.

Try These
Athena™ is a Georgia Gold Medal Plant. It has a broad and rounded crown. Allee™ has an upright, arching crown similar to the American elm. 'Burgundy' displays purple fall foliage. Though lacebark elm is similar, it is not identical to the American elm, *Ulmus americana*, which once graced city avenues across the country. If you insist on having a true American elm, several selections are reputed to be disease resistant including 'Liberty', 'Valley Forge', 'Princeton', and 'Jackson'.

Dawn Redwood

Metasequoia glyptostroboides

Botanical Pronunciation
met-uh-see-KWOY-uh glip-toh-stroh-BOY-deez

Bloom Period and Seasonal Colors
Deciduous; golden to orange fall foliage

Mature Height × Spread
70 to 100 ft. × 15 to 25 ft.

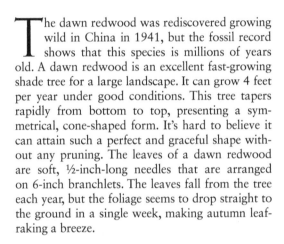

The dawn redwood was rediscovered growing wild in China in 1941, but the fossil record shows that this species is millions of years old. A dawn redwood is an excellent fast-growing shade tree for a large landscape. It can grow 4 feet per year under good conditions. This tree tapers rapidly from bottom to top, presenting a symmetrical, cone-shaped form. It's hard to believe it can attain such a perfect and graceful shape without any pruning. The leaves of a dawn redwood are soft, ½-inch-long needles that are arranged on 6-inch branchlets. The leaves fall from the tree each year, but the foliage seems to drop straight to the ground in a single week, making autumn leaf-raking a breeze.

When, Where, and How to Plant
Plant balled-and-burlapped dawn redwood in mid-autumn or in early spring. Trees will attain maximum growth rate and have the best fall color when planted in full sun. The soil should be humus-rich and moist but well drained. Turn to page 130 for additional planting advice.

Growing Tips
If planted near a maintained lawn, no fertilizer is needed. If the summer following planting is dry, water young trees with five gallons per week.

Regional Advice and Care
Prune lightly anytime. If you need to remove major limbs, do so in January. If the tree needs support, a stake located 18 inches from either side of the trunk will keep it upright. Stake so that it is allowed to sway slightly. Pests and diseases are infrequent.

Companion Planting and Design
Due to its narrow, upright shape, dawn redwood fits into a medium-sized landscape, but think carefully about its eventual size. After thirty years, only the lower tree trunk will be visible without craning your head skyward. Quick growth makes it popular as a tree that can be used for shade but still not hinder the warmth of the winter sun. Because it is one of only a few deciduous conifers with fall color and is of ancient descent, it makes a nifty conversation piece. Dawn redwood tolerates urban conditions and can be used as a street tree. It looks good planted in small groups if landscape size permits. It is a good substitute for baldcypress in situations where the "knees" of baldcypress would be objectionable.

Try These
'Ogon' has striking yellow needles that emerge in spring. If you like the look of this tree but don't have the space for it, look hard for 'Sheridan Spire' or 'National'; both are more narrowly upright. Dawn redwood is sometimes confused with the baldcypress, *Taxodium distichum*. The best way to distinguish them is to remember "A-B-C." The baldcypress has alternate leaves along a stem (**Alternate** = **Baldcypress**), while dawn redwood has leaves that are opposite each other along the stems.

Deciduous Magnolia

Magnolia spp.

Botanical Pronunciation
mag-NO-lee-a

Bloom Period and Seasonal Colors
Deciduous foliage; early spring blooms in deep purple, light pink, white

Mature Height × Spread
Saucer magnolia: 20 to 30 ft. × 15 to 25 ft.
Star magnolia: 10 to 20 ft. × 10 to 15 ft.

Saucer magnolia (*Magnolia × soulangeana*) and star magnolia (*Magnolia stellata*) flowers appear very early in the spring. If gardeners are lucky, the flowers can be enjoyed for several days. Temperatures below 32°F, though, can turn the flowers to gelatinous brown mush overnight. Saucer magnolia has large, 3- to 4-inch flowers that are typically a light pinkish white inside and a darker pink or purple color on the outside. Star magnolia is normally a large shrub, but it can be pruned into a small tree. The 3-inch blooms are usually pure white. Either plant is a conversation piece in February or early March, when no other large plant blooms. In years when Mother Nature is cold and cruel, gardeners loudly lament the untimely passing of deciduous magnolia flowers.

When, Where, and How to Plant
Deciduous magnolias will bloom when they are young and are commonly purchased while blooming in a nursery. Keep your tree in a protected spot for a few weeks until frozen blooms are not likely, then plant it. To avoid damage when temperatures are just above freezing on a windy February night, plant in a spot that is sheltered from early spring gusts. Magnolia roots are thick and tough; unwind them carefully before spreading them in the planting hole. Site in full sun for best flowering. The soil should be high in organic material, evenly moist but well drained. See page 130 for additional planting advice.

Growing Tips
Once the plant becomes mature, little fertilizer or irrigation is needed. Though it's drought tolerant when established, if summer temperatures rise above 95°F, water young trees heavily each week.

Regional Advice and Care
Perform light pruning anytime after flowering. Major limbs can be removed in January. In June or July, prune to remove any dead wood or any small, spindly branches along the trunk. Leave only the most vigorous and well-placed new branches. As with other magnolias, deciduous magnolias can suffer from plant-hoppers, scale, and powdery mildew. These are rarely serious problems.

Companion Planting and Design
Deciduous magnolias can be used as solitary specimens or planted with others in a row to line a street. They blend well with other very early blooming plants, such as creeping phlox, flowering quince, forsythia, and witchhazel. Star magnolia, with its wonderful fragrance, should be planted near areas where its aroma can be enjoyed.

Try These
'Brozzonii' and 'Lennei' are excellent examples of saucer magnolia. 'Jon Jon' flowers two weeks later than other saucer magnolias, leading to fewer frozen blooms. Magnolia 'Ann' and 'Jane' have the flower form of saucer magnolia but a more shrub-like habit. 'Royal Star' is a fine star magnolia, but also look for 'Waterlily' because it blooms later and is less likely to suffer cold damage. Don't forget the native "bigleaf magnolias," such as cucumber tree (*M. acuminate*), bigleaf magnolia (*M. macrophylla*), and Ashe magnolia (*M. ashei*).

Downy Serviceberry

Amelanchier arborea

Botanical Pronunciation
am-uh-LAN-kee-er ar-BOR-ee-uh

Bloom Period and Seasonal Colors
Deciduous; yellow-red fall foliage; spring
blooms in white; red-purple berries in summer

Mature Height × Spread
15 to 25 ft. × 20 to 30 ft.

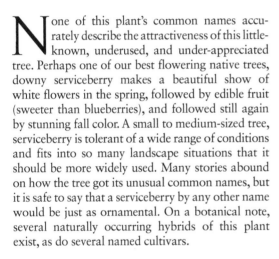

None of this plant's common names accurately describe the attractiveness of this little-known, underused, and under-appreciated tree. Perhaps one of our best flowering native trees, downy serviceberry makes a beautiful show of white flowers in the spring, followed by edible fruit (sweeter than blueberries), and followed still again by stunning fall color. A small to medium-sized tree, serviceberry is tolerant of a wide range of conditions and fits into so many landscape situations that it should be more widely used. Many stories abound on how the tree got its unusual common names, but it is safe to say that a serviceberry by any other name would be just as ornamental. On a botanical note, several naturally occurring hybrids of this plant exist, as do several named cultivars.

When, Where, and How to Plant
Planting is best done in fall. Trees planted in spring need extra care through the first growing season. Downy serviceberry prefers a soil that is moist, humus rich, and acidic. In sandy or clay soils, mix 2 cubic feet of soil conditioner per 10 square feet. Small (3- to 5-foot-tall) plants can be transplanted from their native habitat if you own the property or have friends with a stream bank or woodland hillside (their common habitat). Flowering is best when the tree is planted in full sun, but it will tolerate light shade. For planting directions, fertilizing, and watering tips, see page 130.

Growing Tips
Once established, downy serviceberry is fairly drought tolerant. Severe drought may diminish flowering and fruit. To prevent leaf spot, avoid getting the foliage wet during the daytime hours. Maintain a 3- to 5-inch layer of mulch to moderate soil temperature and moisture.

Regional Advice and Care
Prune to remove suckers from the base as they occur. Blooms occur on last year's growth, so prune right after flowering if necessary. Unfortunately, this will be done at the expense of this season's fruit. Likewise, do not remove faded flowers or the fruit will be eliminated. Harvest fruit when it's red to purple in color. You may need to cover the tree with netting to keep the birds at bay. Like most members of the rose family, serviceberry can be susceptible to fungal leaf spots, rust, fireblight, and powdery mildew. With proper irrigation, trees sited in full sun will suffer less from these problems.

Companion Planting and Design
Serviceberry is well adapted to planting beneath power lines due to its size. Plant as a specimen in smaller landscapes or group at the edges of woodlands. For an all-white landscape, plant with white-flowering azaleas and fothergilla.

Try These
Apple serviceberry, *Amelanchier × grandiflora*, is a hybrid between *Amelanchier canadensis* and *Amelanchier laevis*. According to Dr. Michael Dirr, 'Autumn Brilliance', 'Ballerina', and 'Princess Diana' have performed very well in plant trials at the University of Georgia. 'Forest Prince' foliage turns a beautiful orange-red in fall.

Eastern Redbud

Cercis canadensis

Botanical Pronunciation
SER-sis ka-na-DEN-sis

Bloom Period and Seasonal Colors
Deciduous; fall foliage in yellow; spring blooms in pink-purple

Mature Height × Spread
20 to 30 ft. × 25 to 35 ft.

A redbud, with its heart-shaped leaves and zigzag branches, stands out beautifully in a landscape. The bright pink-purple blooms emerge on bare twigs before almost any other flowering tree. Often used as a street tree, it can also provide shade for patios and make a colorful spring accent. As the summer progresses, the tree develops another interesting feature: reddish brown, pea-like seedpods. Redbud is a legume, the same plant family that contains soybeans, peanuts, and kudzu. Like these plants, a redbud collects nitrogen from the atmosphere and turns it into a small amount of fertilizer around its roots. Redbud is an understory tree. It generally prefers growing on the edge of a woodsy area, where, in February twilight, it will shimmer in pink incandescence.

When, Where, and How to Plant
Purchase a container-grown or a balled-and-burlapped specimen. Plant in midautumn or in early spring. In full sun, the limbs will grow together densely; when grown in part shade, the tree's form is loose and open. Redbud seems to do best when planted near the eastern sides of taller trees. The resulting afternoon shade protects leaves from the mid-August "droops." Redbud does not do well in poorly drained soil. Because of its ability to gather nitrogen from the air, it tolerates being planted in soil that is low in nutrients.

Growing Tips
See page 130 for additional planting guidelines and for fertilizing and watering tips. Avoid overwatering because redbuds do not like having wet roots.

Regional Advice and Care
A redbud will usually grow into a well-shaped tree with little pruning. It does not grow to a great height, so it is desirable when multiple trunks appear. Two or three strong, upright limbs growing out in different directions from the main trunk will branch and rebranch as directed by nature. Redbuds are susceptible to *Verticillium* wilt, but this disease is not common in Georgia. Leafcutter bees occasionally incise beautiful, semicircular notches in leaf edges. The result is a leaf shape that almost deserves to be gilded and made into jewelry. No controls are necessary.

Companion Planting and Design
The redbud's pods are messy when they fall. Do not plant a redbud close to a driveway, sidewalk, or patio. On the other hand, it is tough enough to be used as a street tree when planted in the "hell-strip" between sidewalk and street. Its size makes the tree good for small areas or for a focal point in the landscape.

Try These
Cercis canadensis 'Alba' displays white blooms. 'Forest Pansy' has intensely purple leaves in spring that fade to dark green in summer. 'Silver Cloud' displays irregular variegations on its leaves. It grows much better in shade than in full sun. Weeping forms, such as Lavender Twist® and 'Traveller', are also available.

Florida Maple

Acer saccharum ssp. *floridanum*

Botanical Pronunciation
AY-ser SAK-har-um

Other Name Southern sugar maple

Bloom Period and Seasonal Colors
Deciduous; fall foliage in yellow

Mature Height × Spread
20 to 30 ft. × 20 to 30 ft.

Many gardeners are not familiar with Florida maple, but it is an excellent tree to recognize. It is similar to *Acer saccharum*, the sugar maple, but it is smaller and grows much better in sweltering Georgia heat. While sugar maples growing south of Macon down to the Florida state line will suffer during the summer, a Florida maple thrives on mountainsides and in sweltering swamps from Virginia to north Florida. The fall color of a Florida maple varies from yellow to orange-red. When grown in the open in northern Georgia, a Florida maple's trunk will be short and its limbs will naturally form a graceful oval above it. In southern Georgia, the tree looks best when given a bit of afternoon shade.

When, Where, and How to Plant
Plant in midautumn, as the days begin to cool, or in early spring, in full sun or very light shade. Be sure to plant this, or any maple, where the roots can spread out in all directions without obstruction. Florida maple prefers a soil rich in organic matter; mix soil conditioner thoroughly into the planting area in sandy soils.

Growing Tips
See page 130 for other planting advice and for fertilizing and watering tips.

Regional Advice and Care
During the first two years, remove any branches that turn and race upward, parallel to the main trunk. This "codominant trunk" can result in drastic limb failure during ice storms and windstorms due to the weak trunk attachment. Perform light pruning anytime. Japanese beetles sometimes chew on Florida maple leaves. Their damage is not noticeable except on young trees. Call your county Extension office (page 225) to find out about appropriate controls. Leaf scorch or sunscald may affect young trees if they are not regularly watered the first year. Yellow-bellied sapsucker (a type of woodpecker) pecks small holes in the bark of maples in order to lick the sap that oozes out. The holes are ¼ inch in diameter and occur in rings around the trunk. Control is nearly impossible; fortunately, trees seem unaffected.

Companion Planting and Design
Florida maple is sometimes affected by air pollution, so do not plant it near a busy street. It is an excellent substitute for the less heat-tolerant sugar maple. The fall yellow to salmon leaf color mixes nicely with trees and shrubs that develop intense red foliage, including Virginia sweetspire, red maple, and black gum.

Try These
True sugar maple, *Acer saccharum*, can be used in the northern third of Georgia but suffers from the heat elsewhere. If you are determined to have a superior sugar maple, try Legacy™ or Commemoration™. Trident maple, *Acer buergerianum*, has a similar form to Florida maple. Silver maple, *Acer saccharinum*, and boxelder maple, *Acer negundo*, are considered trashy and weak wooded; they should not be planted in landscapes.

Flowering Cherry

Prunus spp.

Botanical Pronunciation
PROO-nus

Bloom Period and Seasonal Colors
April blooms in white or pink

Mature Height × Spread
15 to 20 ft. × 15 to 25 ft.

The flowering cherry is regarded with reverence in its native Japan. This tree has been important in Japanese landscapes for centuries, and it has become a symbol of friendship between the Japanese and other cultures. Citizens of Japan are drawn to the pale pink, white, and blood-red cherry blossoms that fill the air and blanket the country's green mountains and city parks for only a few days each spring, setting off a frenzy of *hanami*, or "flower viewing," parties. Closer to home, the cities of Macon and Conyers host cherry blossom festivals each year in mid-March. The late William A. Fickling Sr., a local realtor, initiated an effort that led to the planting of more than 250,000 'Yoshino' cherry trees in Bibb County.

When, Where, and How to Plant

Flowering cherry does best in full sunshine. Plant balled-and-burlapped trees in midautumn. Plant container-grown trees in midautumn or in early spring. Avoid locating flowering cherry in low spots that might flood in the spring, as soggy soil that lasts just a few days in April can cause severe root damage. Make sure not to plant too deeply. The first thick root should be level with the surrounding soil. In addition to good drainage, a rich organic soil is preferred. Flowering cherries detest acidic soil and an application every two years of 1 pound of pelletized lime per inch of trunk thickness measured four feet from the ground will help maintain a proper soil pH.

Growing Tips

See page 130 for other planting guidelines and for fertilizing and watering tips.

Regional Advice and Care

Perform light pruning anytime. Remove major limbs in January. Bacterial canker and bot canker are common diseases that appear as oozing areas on the trunk. Increase the soil pH as described below to fight these diseases. Japanese beetles prefer cherry leaves above all others. Leaves will be skeletonized if a large population of beetles hatches at one time. Cherry trees may also be attacked by Asian ambrosia beetles, causing characteristic "toothpick" projections on the trunk. Death will result quickly thereafter. Contact your county Extension office (page 225) for control recommendations.

Companion Planting and Design

Flowering cherries blend well with azaleas, rhododendrons, and nearby dogwood trees to make a wonderful color combination. Keep in mind the reddish brown bark, covered with corky lenticels, is ornamental in its own right after cherry flowers have faded.

Try These

'Kwanzan' cherry is certainly the best known of this family of flowering cherries. It is celebrated for its masses of double-ruffled, pink flowers that appear in April. 'Yoshino' cherry has abundant light pink to nearly white flowers covering the ends of the branches in early April. *Prunus subhirtella* 'Autumnalis' flowers lightly in autumn through winter with a heavy blossoming in spring. *Prunus* 'Hally Jolivette' and 'Okame' blossoms open over several weeks in spring. *P. incisa* Little Twist™ has distinctive zig-zag branches.

Flowering Crabapple

Malus cultivars

Botanical Pronunciation
MAY-lus

Bloom Period and Seasonal Colors
Deciduous; mid-April to June blooms in white, pink, red; fall fruit

Mature Height × Spread
10 to 20 ft. × 15 to 25 ft.

A flowering crabapple can be attractive during all four seasons of the year. On some varieties, flowers begin appearing in mid-April, while others reserve their blooms until early June. The foliage of various crabapples can range from light to dark green in summer. In fall, masses of red fruit remind us that the blossoms are only one colorful reason to plant this tree. A weeping crabapple's bare limbs will ornament the fourth season, but the gnarly limbs of a common crabapple silhouetted against the winter sky are also quite attractive. You might wonder about the difference between an apple and a crabapple. Basically, it involves only the fruit size: crabapples have fruit less than 2 inches in diameter and are usually most admired for their flowers.

When, Where, and How to Plant
Plant balled-and-burlapped crabapples in mid-autumn or early spring. Trees grow best in full sun and rich soil that is evenly moist but well drained. Keep in mind the fruiting habit of the selection you buy. Heavy fruiting may be a boon to wildlife, but it can be messy in the wrong place—or the wrong hands. Crabapple fruit makes tempting ammunition for bored little boys!

Growing Tips
See page 130 for complete planting guidelines and for fertilizing and watering advice.

Regional Advice and Care
Prune crabapple to maintain a spreading, rounded form. Remove pencil-sized water sprouts every spring. Do not prune heavily after early June or you'll remove next year's flowers! After your tree has been in the ground for at least a year, examine its form in January. Look for sprouts that grow parallel to the central trunk. Remove these potential "codominant trunks" without delay. Apple scab and fireblight are diseases that can literally plague these trees to death. Only buy disease-resistant cultivars. Trees labeled simply "Pink Crabapple" will inevitably lead to disappointment. Japanese beetles can almost defoliate a tree. Contact your county Extension office (page 225) for control information. Yellow-bellied sapsuckers (a woodpecker) frequently peck small holes in the bark in spring. Though numerous, these holes are not harmful.

Companion Planting and Design
Select a spot that will remain sunny for several years. Look for neighboring trees that might over-shade your crabapple in time and plant it far enough away so that shade and root competition won't become a problem. Crabapples make wonderful specimens in smaller areas but should be placed where the fruit won't be a problem. If possible, group several trees together for a spring show of flowers and fall display of fruit.

Try These
Malus 'Callaway' was selected as a markedly superior tree by experts at Callaway Gardens. *Malus* 'Donald Wyman' and *Malus* 'Dolgo' are almost as disease resistant as 'Callaway'. 'Louisa' has pink flowers and a weeping form plus dark green, glossy foliage. 'Hopi' (also known as 'Hopa') is inferior and should not be planted in Georgia.

Flowering Dogwood

Cornus florida

Botanical Pronunciation
KOR-nus FLOR-id-uh

Bloom Period and Seasonal Colors
Deciduous; fall foliage in red; April blooms in white; ornamental red berries in early fall

Mature Height × Spread
20 to 40 ft. × 20 to 30 ft.

Is there any tree more strongly associated with spring than dogwood? Dogwoods grow wild in every part of Georgia, usually as understory trees, beneath towering pines and hardwoods. They are also typically associated with landscape azaleas. The part we call a flower is actually four modified leaves more properly identified as bracts. These white bracts glow in the April twilight along the highways from the mountains to the coast. The bright red berries that follow are quite attractive in September. Despite the best horticultural efforts, dogwoods have a typical lifespan of twenty to thirty years. Any life after that is icing on your landscape cake. Agnes Scott College in Decatur, Georgia, has documented a dogwood growing on campus that survived for nearly a century!

When, Where, and How to Plant

A dogwood is usually purchased as a balled-and-burlapped plant, but it can sometimes be found in large pots. Plant in midautumn or early spring. Morning sun with afternoon shade is best. Site in the shade of larger trees or a house to shelter it from hot afternoon sun. Dogwoods will suffer if planted in full sun without deep mulch and attention to watering in dry times. The soil should be humus rich, moist but well drained, and neutral to slightly acidic. Plan to stake the young tree after planting.

Growing Tips

More planting, fertilizing, and watering tips are on page 130. Once the tree matures, particularly if growing in or near a lawn, little fertilizer is needed.

If summer temperatures rise above 95°F, water heavily every two weeks.

Regional Advice and Care

Perform light pruning anytime. Remove major limbs in January. Dogwood borers cause swollen, "crusty" bark on the lower portions of the trunk. Spot anthracnose causes small purple spots on the leaves and flowers in April. The best way to prevent disease is to keep the tree well watered in summer. "Lawnmower blight" is a common problem caused by lawnmowers or string trimmers coming into contact with a dogwood's trunk. Keep a wide band of mulch around each tree to keep soil cool, to conserve moisture, and to keep power tools at bay; however, do not pile mulch against the trunk.

Companion Planting and Design

Hybrid azaleas are commonly planted near dogwoods, but also try fothergilla, witchhazel, or native azaleas as companions.

Try These

Although a small dogwood can be transplanted out of the woods, it may never equal the beauty of a superior selection. Similarly, nursery trees simply labeled "White Dogwood" are usually inferior. *C. florida* 'Cloud 9' flowers profusely when young. 'Green Glow' has green leaves splotched with lighter green. 'Cherokee Chief' has deep red flower bracts. 'Firebird' has spectacular multicolored, variegated foliage that mixes whites and greens. Young leaves come in shades of red to burgundy.

Fringetree

Chionanthus virginicus

Botanical Pronunciation
kye-oh-NAN-thus vir-JIN-ih-kus

Bloom Period and Seasonal Colors
Deciduous; fall foliage in yellow; May blooms in white

Mature Height × Spread
15 to 20 ft. × 8 to 10 ft.

Fringetree's white flowers are held in masses just beyond its leaves; the thin, elongated flower petals hang from tiny, threadlike stems. The contrast of the white flowers against the new, vibrant green leaves is striking. Because they bloom in May, fringetree flowers are a good follow-up to the dogwood blooms of early spring. When a slight breeze appears, the whole tree will shimmer, looking almost like a disco mirror ball in your spring landscape. The flowers are slightly fragrant, with some plants seeming to give off more perfume than others. Fringetree grows in the wild from New Jersey to Florida. It was listed in the catalog of America's earliest nurseryman, John Bartram, and was cultivated at Thomas Jefferson's home, Monticello.

When, Where, and How to Plant

Fringetree is usually purchased as a balled-and-burlapped plant. Plant in midautumn or early spring, just before the earth becomes warm. It will flower and fruit best in full sun, although light shade is tolerated. Grow in soil that is high in organic matter and is loose and moist but also well drained. Fringetree does not grow well in compacted soil. If a trowel slips 4 to 6 inches into the soil easily or with moderate effort, then the soil is adequately loose. Jackhammer effort needed to penetrate the soil indicates hard earth. Loosen the soil around the tree in spring with a spading fork.

Growing Tips

See page 130 for initial planting, fertilizing, and watering tips. Once the tree is mature, little fertilizer is needed. If summer temperatures rise above 95°F, water heavily every two weeks.

Regional Advice and Care

Perform light pruning anytime. Fringetree can be a large bush or a small tree; decide early which form you want and prune accordingly. Pests and diseases are infrequent. Repair cold damage by removing dead branches in May.

Companion Planting and Design

Fringetree has an almost "fuzzy" appearance when in bloom. Flowers on both male and female trees are fragrant, so locate it near sitting areas or walkways. It makes a fine focal point in a smaller garden. Female trees produce a bluish fruit of ornamental quality beloved by birds and therefore seldom messy. Because of its small stature, fringetree is best planted with smaller shrubs and groundcovers that won't overpower it. Dark evergreens behind will contrast with fringetree's white flowers. It is late to leaf out and should be planted among early-blooming plants to hide its early-season nakedness. Good companions include Virginia sweetspire, native azaleas, anise, and redbud.

Try These

Chinese fringetree, *Chionanthus retusus*, grows larger than the native fringetree and has more glossy foliage, though it is more likely to be cold-damaged in severe winters.

Ginkgo

Ginkgo biloba

Botanical Pronunciation
GING-ko bi-LOW-buh

Other Name Maidenhair tree

Bloom Period and Seasonal Colors
Deciduous; fall foliage in yellow

Mature Height × Spread
40 to 70 ft. × 30 to 50 ft.

A view of the bright yellow carpet of fall leaves under a ginkgo tree is a memory that can last a lifetime. The central trunk grows vigorously for 20 years, producing small branches that emerge on all sides. This produces a narrow conical shape initially, but older trees spread out into a wide triangle. Ginkgo is one of our oldest trees. We know from fossils that it was native to North America 150 million years ago. Climate changes caused it to die out; it was reintroduced from China in 1784. There are both male and female trees but plant only male trees; female trees produce smelly, plum-sized fruit. The malodorous fruit can be cleaned, however, producing a white nut that is roasted and eaten in Asia.

When, Where, and How to Plant

A ginkgo can be purchased as a bare-root whip, but it is more often found as a balled-and-burlapped specimen. Plant in midautumn or in early spring. Ginkgo tolerates pollution and moderately salty air; it's often used as a street tree. Keep in mind how large the tree will grow over time. Always buy from a trusted nursery; if you transplant a seedling that has sprouted under an existing tree, you won't know if it is a male or female for many years. Full sun produces the best growth and fall color. The soil should be fertile and moist but very well drained. Ginkgo is slow growing for the first five years but achieves a moderate rate afterward if planted in full sun and good soil.

Growing Tips

Once the tree becomes mature, little fertilizer is needed. If summer temperatures rise above 95°F, water heavily every two weeks. See page 130 for other planting, fertilizing, and watering tips.

Regional Advice and Care

Perform light pruning anytime. If a young tree is damaged and sends up two competing trunks, choose the straightest trunk and remove the other one in January. Ginkgos are sometimes bothered by mealybugs, fungal leaf spots, and root rot, but any tree that has survived for eons obviously has few enemies.

Companion Planting and Design

The shade cast by a ginkgo is not very dense, so groundcovers and bulbs grow well beneath the tree. If you plant upright shrubs or perennials under the branches, these plants will ruin the autumn carpet of gold. Eventually becoming quite large, ginkgos are best left as specimen trees in a landscape able to accommodate their size. Their bright yellow fall color can be offset by the crimson foliage of red maples and black gums planted nearby. The bi-lobed fan-shaped leaves are unique and can be dried and pressed to be used in craft items.

Try These

'Autumn Gold' is a symmetrical tree with excellent, clear yellow fall color. 'Princeton Sentry' is narrowly conical.

Goldenraintree

Koelreuteria spp.

Botanical Pronunciation
keel-roo-TER-ee-uh

Other Name Chinese flame tree

Bloom Period and Seasonal Colors
Deciduous; bright yellow fall foliage;
June blooms in yellow

Mature Height × Spread
20 to 40 ft. × 20 to 30 ft.

The yellow blooms that cover goldenraintree in June are quite unusual, as are the clusters of papery, lantern-like seedpods that follow the flowers. Goldenraintree is the perfect size for a suburban landscape: it grows relatively fast, but it is not so large that it overpowers a house. Because it is very attractive, place it in a spot near a flow of pedestrian or automobile traffic. Collect short branches with seed capsules on the end to use in flower arrangements. The rosy seed capsules of bougainvillea goldenraintree (*Koelreuteria bipinnata*) retain enough color to form a swath of pink on the sidewalk and pavement when they fall in September. Seeds sprout easily, so do not let this tree become an invasive pest in your neighborhood.

When, Where, and How to Plant
Plant balled-and-burlapped trees in midautumn or early spring. Trees will only flower well when planted in full sun but will tolerate part sunshine. Goldenraintree tolerates a wide variety of soil types. Dig seedlings in December to share with friends. For general planting directions and more tips on fertilizing and watering, see page 130.

Growing Tips
If summer temperatures rise above 95°F, water young trees heavily every two weeks. Established trees are drought tolerant and are often used along Georgia Interstate highways.

Regional Advice and Care
Goldenraintree has a fairly open form. On young trees, remove branch tips each March to force more buds to sprout and form a denser crown. Stop this type of pruning after the third year. For attractive dried arrangements, harvest the pink seed capsules of bougainvillea goldenraintree when they are at their peak. To dry, hang a spray of the pods in a large plastic bag containing 1 pound of silica gel. This quick drying action keeps the color fresh. Removing seedpods before ripening also reduces the tree's spread, which can be weedlike in warmer climates. Goldenraintree is attacked by no known pests, but box elder bugs can appear by the thousands to feed on the seeds when they drop. Known by their red bodies and black wings, box elder bugs do not bite humans or animals. Control them with any garden insecticide.

Companion Planting and Design
Good planting companions include ornamental grasses, such as maiden grass or fountain grass. The tree has dark red bark in winter, contrasting with its pinkish-red young foliage, which appears later than other trees. Autumn leaves turn bright yellow and drop early.

Try These
Golden Candle™ is narrowly columnar. Common goldenraintree, *Koelreuteria paniculata*, has brown seedpods after flowering. The pink seedpods of bougainvillea goldenraintree, *K. bipinnata*, persist on the tree for several weeks. Both trees, especially *K. paniculata*, are listed as exotic pest trees in Florida and parts of southern Georgia. They have not proven problematic in northern Georgia.

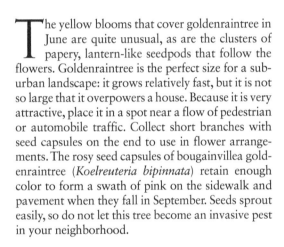

Hornbeam

Carpinus caroliniana

Botanical Pronunciation
kar-PINE-us kair-oh-lin-ee-AN-uh

Other Name Ironwood

Bloom Period and Seasonal Colors
Yellow-orange fall foliage

Mature Height × Spread
35 to 40 ft. × 20 to 25 ft.

Befitting one of its other common names, musclewood, hornbeam is a strong tree! The wood has historically been used for wagon wheels, bowls, and tool handles because it is so dense and tough. The trunk and branches are smooth and, with age, develop a rippled, sinuous appearance. It has an oval to rounded form. The dark green leaves and bushy growth habit make it a great choice for screening. The bushiness and medium size also make it attractive as an allée tree. When planted in a line, ten feet apart, hornbeam trees make a solid green wall in summer and an impenetrable vertical mass in winter. Regular pruning is required to have the effect, but when you do it right—yowsa!

When, Where, and How to Plant

Plant in full to part sun. It excels as a specimen or street tree. Musclewood is commonly found along creekbanks in the wild, so be sure to water in summer heat. Fifteen to thirty gallons per week, depending on tree size, should suffice. The best time to plant is late fall to early winter, giving the tree plenty of time to establish a strong root system before the next summer. Flowers appear in spring in separate loosely arranged male and female catkins. Clusters of winged nutlets appear in fall.

Growing Tips

This tree has a medium growth rate. This can be accelerated by making sure to provide a wide area of loosened soil before you plant, for the root to explore after planting. Minimal pruning and care are needed.

Regional Advice and Care

Hornbeam is reportedly difficult to transplant from the wild but easy to plant from a container. Perform light pruning anytime. Remove major limbs in January. Pests and diseases are infrequent. Bobwhite quail, turkey, wood duck, and squirrels eat the fruits. Deer and rabbits munch on leaves and twigs, and beaver eat the bark. Swallowtail butterflies use hornbeam as a host plant for their caterpillars.

Companion Planting and Design

Hornbeam favors the same environment as flowering dogwood, serviceberry, sweetbay magnolia, winterberry holly, and southern bayberry. As the tree grows tall, beautyberry, witchhazel, and Virginia sweetspire would look good planted beneath it. The fall color is faintly orange to yellow and stands out in the fall. Brown leaves occasionally hang on the tree in the winter.

Try These

Ball O' Fire™ is a compact form. 'J.N. Strain' is larger and has brilliant fall color in orange and yellow. European hornbeam, *Carpinus betulus*, grows in several distinct shapes. Look for columnar ('Fastigiata'), weeping ('Pendula'), and rounded ('Globosa') forms. *C. betulus* Emerald Avenue™ has butter yellow fall foliage.

Korean Dogwood

Cornus kousa

Botanical Pronunciation
KOR-nus KOO-sa

Other Name Kousa dogwood

Bloom Period and Seasonal Colors
Deciduous; fall foliage in yellow, scarlet;
May blooms in white

Mature Height × Spread
20 to 30 ft. × 30 ft.

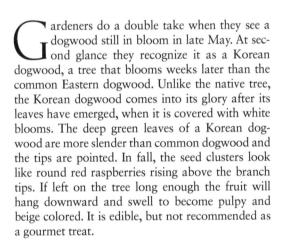

Gardeners do a double take when they see a dogwood still in bloom in late May. At second glance they recognize it as a Korean dogwood, a tree that blooms weeks later than the common Eastern dogwood. Unlike the native tree, the Korean dogwood comes into its glory after its leaves have emerged, when it is covered with white blooms. The deep green leaves of a Korean dogwood are more slender than common dogwood and the tips are pointed. In fall, the seed clusters look like round red raspberries rising above the branch tips. If left on the tree long enough the fruit will hang downward and swell to become pulpy and beige colored. It is edible, but not recommended as a gourmet treat.

When, Where, and How to Plant

Plant balled-and-burlapped trees in midautumn or early spring. Container-grown plants can be planted anytime except midsummer. Korean dogwood prefers the edge of a tree-shaded area. With mulch and occasional summer irrigation it can tolerate full sunshine. With afternoon shade, the tree's form will be open and upright. The soil should be high in organic matter, evenly moist but well drained, and a neutral to slightly acidic pH.

Growing Tips

See page 130 for other planting, fertilizing, and watering tips. Adequate irrigation is important to prevent disease. Water heavily at two-week intervals during times of heat and extreme drought. In a newly installed landscape, it is common to see a small tree surrounded by turfgrass. Aggressive grass

roots are a significant competitor for water. Do not permit grass to grow any closer than 3 feet from the trunk of a dogwood. As the tree grows, enlarge the mulched, grass-free area to match the drip line of the tree.

Regional Advice and Care

Prune lightly anytime. Remove any major limbs in January. Korean dogwood resists the dogwood blight, *Discula destructive*, which has killed many flowering dogwoods along the East Coast, and it seems to resist dogwood borer as well. It is no match, though, for "lawnmower disease"! Keep a wide band of mulch around the trunk so mowers and string trimmers will not come too close to the trunk.

Companion Planting and Design

As the tree ages and becomes more rounded, you'll appreciate its contribution to a mixed shrub border. Blooming later than native dogwoods, plant Kousa dogwoods with other dogwoods to extend the blooming season. They also tolerate a bit more sun than native dogwoods and blend well with viburnum, later-blooming native azalea, and oakleaf hydrangea.

Try These

Cornus kousa var. *chinensis* 'Milky Way' has numerous flowers and a bushy form that is nice for smaller landscapes. 'Moonbeam' has flower bracts up to 8 inches wide! 'Constellation' is a cross between *C. florida* and *C. kousa*; it is much more upright than either of its parents. 'Wolf Eyes' has distinctive variegated leaves.

Japanese Cryptomeria

Cryptomeria japonica

Botanical Pronunciation
krip-toh-MER-ee-uh juh-PON-ih-kuh

Other Name Japanese cedar

Bloom Period and Seasonal Colors
Evergreen; needles may turn bronze in winter

Mature Height × Spread
50 to 60 ft. × 10 to 25 ft.

Cryptomeria has been with us for eons. It—along with dawn redwood, giant sequoia, and baldcypress—was present when dinosaurs roamed the earth. It is surprising that Japanese cryptomeria is not more widely planted in Georgia. The tree is tall, evergreen, and symmetrical, making it a fine screen or an impressive specimen tree. When the lower limbs are removed, the reddish brown bark on the trunk is very attractive. But even with all of these good traits, *Cryptomeria* is rarely part of typical landscapes. Some landscape professionals suspect that the reason is just its name: *Cryptomeria* sounds like a tree involved somehow in code breaking. More gardeners should break the code and plant this very adaptable tree! It is widely available at garden centers.

When, Where, and How to Plant
Plant balled-and-burlapped trees in midautumn or in early spring. Remember that the tree grows quite large, from 50 to 60 feet high. If planted in the spring, do not put *Cryptomeria* in a windy spot where the foliage will scorch from summer drought. Without full sun, *Cryptomeria* will become leggy and susceptible to disease. Almost any soil is tolerable, but good drainage is essential.

Growing Tips
See page 130 for other planting, fertilizing, and watering tips. Once the tree is mature, little fertilizer is needed. If summer temperatures rise above 95°F, give the tree a heavy watering each week. Water new trees during winter dry periods after fall planting; 15 gallons should suffice. It is common for Japanese

cedar to turn slightly bronze in winter, especially in windy, exposed locations. Foliage turns green as the weather warms. Few pests attack *Cryptomeria*.

Regional Advice and Care
Provide light pruning anytime. To achieve dense foliage, shear off half the length of the new green branch tips in May. Remove lower limbs in January. Bagworms can affect all needled evergreens, and Japanese cryptomeria is no exception. Look for 3-inch-long bags of needles hanging from branch tips in August. Pick them off and destroy them. Other problems include nematodes, branch dieback, and root rot in poorly draining soil. Remove dead branches as they occur.

Companion Planting and Design
Use *Cryptomeria* in spots where a Leyland cypress would be too tall or where you want relief from the dark green needles of a ubiquitous row of Leyland cypress. They can also be used as specimen plants in a landscape that's capable of accommodating their size.

Try These
One of the best cultivars for Georgia is *Cryptomeria japonica* 'Yoshino'. It is fast growing, has blue-green summer foliage, and will grow strongly in a wide variety of situations. 'Globosa Nana' grows in a dense but fluffy sphere, up to 4 feet across, and is best used as a single specimen plant. Chapel View™ grows to 10 feet tall, with attractive blue-green needles. 'Black Dragon' is pyramidal, 7 feet tall and 4 feet wide.

Japanese Maple

Acer palmatum

Botanical Pronunciation
AY-ser pahl-MAY-tum

Bloom Period and Seasonal Colors
Deciduous; fall foliage in scarlet, orange, yellow

Mature Height × Spread
2 to 20 ft. × 4 to 20 ft.

Thousands of years of cultivation and selection have resulted in hundreds of attractive Japanese maple cultivars. Leaf color ranges from bright red-purple to deep green. Leaves can have broad, rounded lobes or finely divided, almost fern-like foliage. Japanese maples produce wonderful fall leaf color, but colors may not be as bright in the warmer parts of Georgia as in colder climates. There is a Japanese maple for every landscape. They are often used beside a landscape water feature. The most popular selections seem to be the small-statured, mounding types. It takes several years to produce an attractive retail specimen, so they are expensive to purchase. Study and follow the planting instructions provided here to make sure your maple lives up to your investment.

When, Where, and How to Plant

Plant large, balled-and-burlapped trees in fall. Container-grown specimens can be planted in spring. Find a spot that receives direct morning sun but has afternoon shade. Do not plant in the middle of a lawn without any shelter from the wind. The east or north side of a home is usually ideal. Japanese maples prefer a soil that is rich in organic matter and moist but well drained. However, they will tolerate soils that are sandy or mildly heavy with clay. Varieties in the 'Dissectum' group have very fine foliage and often tolerate and even prefer more shade.

Growing Tips

See page 130 for general watering and fertilizing guidelines. Regular watering in summer is a must. Mulch to conserve moisture and to keep the roots cool. The most common Japanese maple problem is scorched leaves in midsummer. This is a sign that not enough water is getting to the leaves. Determine whether the problem is lack of water in the ground or compaction around the plant and correct the condition.

Regional Advice and Care

Japanese maples usually grow gracefully without much pruning. Long, vigorous sprouts should be removed or shortened back to side branches in January. Perform minor pruning anytime. Many of the weeping Japanese maples are grafted onto a straight-limbed rootstock. If vertical limbs emerge from below the knob-like graft union, remove them where they originate.

Companion Planting and Design

Any of the dissected-leaf varieties makes a nice texture variation in the landscape. Japanese maple is attractive when grown in a container in a patio corner or an entranceway. The taller Japanese maples are excellent specimen trees. Use smaller varieties, such as 'Crimson Queen' or 'Fireball', near a home's foundation.

Try These

The "Atropurpureum" group of maples contains many named varieties; the red color usually fades to dark green in summer. 'Osakazuki' is famous for its intense red fall color, similar to burning bush euonymus. 'Bloodgood' has a crimson spring color that darkens to deep red in summer. 'Beni hime' has miniature leaves and a twiggy branch structure. *Acer palmatum* 'Sango Kaku', coralbark maple, can tolerate full sunshine.

Japanese Stewartia

Stewartia pseudocamellia

Botanical Pronunciation
stew-ART-ee-uh soo-doh-kuh-MEE-lee-uh

Other Name Summer camellia

Bloom Period and Seasonal Colors
Deciduous; orange and red fall foliage; early summer blooms in white

Mature Height × Spread
20 to 40 ft. × 20 to 40 ft.

A cousin of our native stewartia, the Japanese stewartia is a beautiful tree with year-round interest. The showy flowers in June resemble those of white camellias, which bloom months earlier. Indeed, it is a member of the same plant family as camellias: *Theaceae*. This is probably one of the loveliest small to medium trees for the landscape, yet it is underappreciated. With a backdrop of lustrous dark green leaves that off-set the summertime flowers, this tree should be placed in a location of high visibility for all to enjoy. As the tree ages, a mosaic of red, brown, gray, and pink develops on the trunk, which peels away to lend winter interest. In the fall, the dark green foliage changes to bright shades of orange and red.

When, Where, and How to Plant

As with most trees and shrubs, planting should be done in fall. Container-grown trees planted in the spring will need extra care through the first growing season. Japanese stewartia prefers a soil that is moist, rich in organic matter, and a slightly acidic to neutral pH. Be sure to follow the planting regimen described on page 130 to encourage a vigorous root system. For best flowering, full sun (with ample water) is preferred, but the tree will tolerate light shade. Protection from wind is important. Once established, stewartia does not transplant well.

Growing Tips

Japanese stewartia is not very tolerant of drought, and in times of dry weather, it should be watered deeply once a week. Fertilizer is not usually needed. A mulch layer 3 to 5 inches thick around the tree will help maintain soil moisture levels.

Regional Advice and Care

Pruning should only be done to maintain its shape. Wayward branches can be removed during the winter, when it's easier to see the silhouette of the tree. Japanese stewartia is usually free of pests and diseases. Removing dead flowers (deadheading) is not necessary.

Companion Planting and Design

This is one tree that definitely deserves specimen status. Groupings can be done in larger areas. Because of its smaller size, Japanese stewartia makes a great choice for the ever-shrinking landscapes of newer style homes. Although blooming is during early summer, this is a nice replacement for the ubiquitous flowering pear. In areas of full sun, companion plants such as roses make a nice splash of color in the summer.

Try These

Given a choice, native plant enthusiasts prefer the mountain stewartia (*Stewartia ovata*), which is a smaller tree with larger flowers. On the other hand, tall stewartia (*S. monadelpha*), which is also not native but sports beautiful cinnamon bark, seems to tolerate the heat of southern Georgia better than Japanese stewartia.

Oak

Quercus spp.

Botanical Pronunciation
KWER-kus

Bloom Period and Seasonal Colors
Deciduous; some with fall foliage in red

Mature Height × Spread
40 to 80 ft. × 50 to 90 ft.

Dozens of oak species grow beautifully in Georgia. You should consider several that grow well in most landscapes. Willow oak (*Quercus phellos*), about 50 feet tall, is one of the smaller oaks. It is a good choice for a street tree or a fast-growing shade tree. Shumard oak (*Q. shumardii*) and scarlet oak (*Q. coccinea*) are two of the best oaks for red fall leaf color. Red oak (*Q. rubra*) is easy to transplant and grows rapidly into a large tree. Live oak (*Q. virginiana*) is the state tree. Its limbs spread out horizontally from the trunk. Often seen as a mature tree in Savannah, it can appear to cover acres. Live oak grows with difficulty, due to winter cold, in the northern third of Georgia.

When, Where, and How to Plant

Plant balled-and-burlapped oaks in midautumn or early spring. Check on all sides for sun-loving plants that might eventually become shaded by the oak and check overhead for telephone and electrical lines. Do not plant within 50 feet of homes, driveways, or sidewalks. Site in full sun, in fertile and moist but well-drained, soil. Some species tolerate wet soils.

Growing Tips

Oaks are severely affected by extended drought. Mulching them is critical. Their roots, which occur within 12 inches of the soil surface, disappear when the soil is dry. Drought damage is slow to make itself seen. By the time the tree is in decline, little can be done to revive it. See page 130 for additional planting advice and fertilizing and watering tips.

Regional Advice and Care

Perform light pruning anytime. Remove large limbs in January. A major cause of death for mature oaks is construction damage. Install a fence under the branch ends of the tree and prohibit machinery there. If 12 inches of soil are removed from around a tree, vital feeder roots will be eliminated. Oaks can be bothered by cankers, leaf galls, and scale. Orange-striped oak worm is a dark caterpillar with light orange stripes down its back. They may be numerous enough to strip a branch or two in August, but the damage is not serious. Slime flux causes beery-smelling ooze from the trunk. Wash it off to prevent bark deterioration.

Companion Planting and Design

Avoid planting turfgrass under an oak. Instead, choose shade-tolerant groundcovers (see page 61). Planting an oak is a generous gift to future generations. Site it correctly so that your children and grandchildren can admire it.

Try These

Water oak (*Quercus nigra*) grows in a wide variety of soil types and tolerates wet or dry sites. Sawtooth oak (*Q. acutissima*) is popular but can be invasive in some parts of the state. White oak, *Quercus alba*, is considered by some the most stately of the oaks. Kindred Spirit™ is a non-native columnar evergreen that grows 35 feet tall with only 6 feet of spread after thirty years.

Red Maple

Acer rubrum

Botanical Pronunciation
AY-ser ROO-brum

Other Name Scarlet maple

Bloom Period and Seasonal Colors
Deciduous; fall foliage in red

Mature Height × Spread
40 to 60 ft. × 30 to 50 ft.

Red maple marks the beginning of spring with its blooms. Red flowers emerge in clusters along the branches in mid-February before the leaves appear. Red maple also marks the end of the growing season with fiery red leaves that stand out beautifully against the yellow leaves of tulip poplars and the green needles of evergreen trees. October drives along the Richard Russell Highway between Helen and Blairsville would be consummately boring without red maples. A red maple is an excellent choice for a landscape specimen shade tree. It grows fast, but it does not have brittle wood or a weak limb structure. This makes it useful for saving energy, as well—the tree shades your home in summer but allows warm sunshine into windows in winter.

When, Where, and How to Plant
Plant in fall or early spring. Allow plenty of room for the roots to grow. Maple roots may grow on the surface of your soil if planted in heavy clay soil. Do not chop the roots off; this will lead to root rot. Cover the roots with a thick layer of pine chips or pine straw instead. If your tree must be planted near a walk or driveway, bury 18-inch-wide aluminum flashing edgewise along the pavement to prevent roots from growing underneath. Red maples will grow faster and develop better fall color in full sun. They prefer moist soil that is acidic and high in organic matter; however, they will tolerate wet, poorly drained soils and also moderately dry spots.

Growing Tips
Turn to page 130 for more planting tips and fertilizing and watering advice.

Regional Advice and Care
Perform any needed corrective pruning at planting time. Remove or prune back limbs that "head for the sky." A desirable form offers three or four main limbs evenly spaced around the trunk initially, each one 3 to 5 feet from the ground. Do not cut the growing tip of the main trunk, as weak limbs will sprout from that point. Purple eye leaf spot disease makes groups of purple "eyes" on leaves in spring. Leaf galls caused by insects may cause thousands of warty bumps on leaf surfaces. Neither problem can be prevented, but neither causes a decline in tree health.

Companion Planting and Design
Because they do not grow as tall as pines, oaks, or poplars, red maples are excellent shade trees. Plant with other natives, such as chokeberry, summersweet, or beautyberry. If the roots buckle a sidewalk or driveway, consult an arborist for methods of protecting the hardscape while preserving your tree.

Try These
For beautiful fall color, choose Red Sunset™. October Glory™ is well formed with excellent fall color also. Autumn Blaze™ is a superior hybrid between red and silver maples. Unnamed common red maples do not always have pretty red leaves.

River Birch

Betula nigra

Botanical Pronunciation
BET-yoo-luh NY-gruh

Other Name Red birch

Bloom Period and Seasonal Colors
Deciduous; fall foliage in yellow

Mature Height × Spread
40 to 60 ft. × 30 to 50 ft.

River birch is an excellent specimen tree when planted in the center of a landscape. It is small in comparison to oak and pine trees. River birch will tolerate areas that do not drain well, but after a few years of growth, it can also stand considerable dryness. River birch is less formal than a dogwood or maple. Its grayish white bark peels away from the trunk in paper-thin layers. The brown bark revealed underneath adds to the tree's attractiveness in the winter. The branches are vigorous but do not arise symmetrically from the trunk. River birch is the only birch that can easily stand the heat of Georgia summers; Northern white birch will not prosper. River birch is commonly found in swamps and along streams.

When, Where, and How to Plant

River birch is best planted in fall in full sun. Birches prefer soil that is high in organic matter and evenly moist year-round. It can handle areas prone to flooding and therefore makes a good choice for minor erosion control. Once established, it can withstand dry soil. Do not repeat the mistake many home-builders make by planting river birch within 15 feet of a home. After just a few years, the branches will tear at gutters and scratch window screens.

Growing Tips

See page 130 for initial planting tips and more fertilizing and watering guidelines. If the roots do not have room to expand to find all available moisture, a dry summer month will cause substantial leaf drop. This is not a major problem. If you are unable to irrigate, a layer of mulch spread widely underneath the tree will help conserve moisture.

Regional Advice and Care

Pruning is not needed after the first few years. To expose its peeling white bark, remove the tree's lower limbs when it grows tall. Leaf spot disease or hot weather can cause multitudes of leaves to drop from common river birches in midsummer. Birch sawfly larvae resemble tiny green caterpillars that consume large numbers of leaves in a few days. Normal caterpillar poisons will not kill them. Contact your county Extension office (page 225) for controls.

Companion Planting and Design

As far as birch trees go, river birch is the best choice for Georgia. White birch and silver birch cannot survive in our heat and are suited for Northern climates. Three single-trunk birches planted in a group make a better statement than one birch planted by itself. For a small lot, though, you may prefer a multi-stemmed single plant. River birch tolerates wet spots and is perfect for shading a gazebo overlooking a koi pond.

Try These

Betula nigra Heritage™ is an excellent selection that is resistant to leaf spot. The bark is whiter than regular river birches, and the leaves are dark green. Dura-Heat™ has a very dense leaf habit.

Southern Magnolia

Magnolia grandiflora

Botanical Pronunciation
mag-NO-lee-a gran-dih-FLOR-uh

Other Name Bull bay

Bloom Period and Seasonal Colors
Evergreen foliage; June blooms in white

Mature Height × Spread
40 to 70 ft. × 20 to 40 ft.

Only the flowering dogwood may be more strongly associated with the South than this magnolia. Its huge, lemon-scented, white flowers appear in June and then sporadically for the rest of the summer. From the 1930s to the 1960s, no high school prom in Georgia was complete without magnolia flower centerpieces on the tables. Harris County, surrounding Callaway Gardens, is home to thousands of Southern magnolias that were given away by the Callaway family. Children appreciate some of the less-celebrated properties. The drooping branches make wonderful rooms for sharing secrets, and the branches are spaced perfectly for climbing. Biltmore Estates in Asheville, North Carolina, has a fine collection of evergreen and deciduous magnolias, which can be examined during a leisurely trip to the mountains.

When, Where, and How to Plant
Plant balled-and-burlapped Southern magnolia in midautumn or in early spring, just before the earth becomes warm. Be aware of its eventual size. In almost all situations, a magnolia should be planted at the edge of a landscape, not in the middle. Full sun is best. Southern magnolia grows best in fertile and moist but well-drained soil. It tolerates dry areas. A tree transplanted from the woods may fail to produce many flowers. It is much better to purchase one of the nursery specimens suggested here. Depending on the environment, it is typical to wait five years for the first flowers to appear.

Growing Tips
Water only for the first two years. Once the tree becomes mature, little water or fertilizer is needed.

Regional Advice and Care
Some people like to remove lower limbs, but leaving them on the tree gives a place to hide the mess of each year's fallen leaves. The leathery leaves and tough seed cones are difficult for a lawnmower to shred, and they decompose so slowly that they should not be added to a compost pile. Trees can suffer from planthoppers, weevils, scale, and powdery mildew when young, but they will grow out of these problems if maintained properly.

Companion Planting and Design
The glossy green leaves are a good backdrop for summer-flowering shrubs, such as chaste tree or smokebush. Plant magnolias well away from your house. A 15-foot specimen will eventually become an overpowering monster. Planted in groups, they can be used for screening, albeit a very large barrier. The seed-studded cone can be used in dried flower arrangements, and the green leaves are excellent for making winter holiday wreathes.

Try These
There are several excellent cultivars. 'Claudia Wannamaker' is commonly available. 'Bracken's Brown Beauty' displays rather small leaves, with brown backsides, that grow densely. One compact magnolia is 'Little Gem'. It flowers the first year and only grows 10 to 20 feet tall. Teddy Bear ™ is similar to 'Little Gem' but has distinctive brown fuzz under the leaves.

Styrax

Styrax japonicus

Botanical Pronunciation
STY-raks juh-PON-ih-kus

Bloom Period and Seasonal Colors
Deciduous foliage; late spring or early summer blooms in white; yellow fall foliage

Mature Height × Spread
30 ft. × 20 ft.

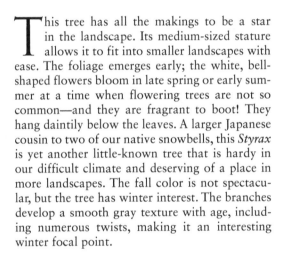

This tree has all the makings to be a star in the landscape. Its medium-sized stature allows it to fit into smaller landscapes with ease. The foliage emerges early; the white, bell-shaped flowers bloom in late spring or early summer at a time when flowering trees are not so common—and they are fragrant to boot! They hang daintily below the leaves. A larger Japanese cousin to two of our native snowbells, this *Styrax* is yet another little-known tree that is hardy in our difficult climate and deserving of a place in more landscapes. The fall color is not spectacular, but the tree has winter interest. The branches develop a smooth gray texture with age, including numerous twists, making it an interesting winter focal point.

When, Where, and How to Plant

For best results, *Styrax* should be planted in fall. Either container-grown or balled-and-burlapped trees will establish themselves easily. Trees planted in spring need extra attention to watering through the summer of the first growing season. *Styrax* prefers a soil that is moist but well drained, rich in organic matter, and slightly acidic to neutral in pH. Flowering will be better in full sun, but the tree will tolerate partial shade as long as the exposure provides it with some direct sun. Protection from wind is important.

Growing Tips

Styrax is moderately tolerant of drought conditions. In the first year after planting, weekly watering may be necessary during dry weather. A 3- to 5-inch layer of mulch will help retain moisture and shelter the roots from extreme temperatures. Light fertilizer in spring for the first three years will promote healthy growth and flowering.

Regional Advice and Care

Little pruning is necessary. Remove wayward or crossing shoots to maintain an aesthetic appearance. *Styrax* blooms on growth from the previous year, so pruning should be done after flowering. Removing dead flowers is not necessary. *Styrax* is generally free of pests and diseases, but a late frost can freeze the leaves. The tree recovers from cold damage quickly; simply prune away obviously dead branches in June.

Companion Planting and Design

Sporting fragrant flowers, *Styrax* should be planted near outdoor sitting areas. To avoid a fragrance overload, do not mix this plant with other fragrant summer-bloomers, such as gardenia. With its bold foliage, the tree also makes a fine specimen or focal point in smaller gardens, especially when grouped with plants of finer texture, such as *Cryptomeria* or Japanese plum yew.

Try These

'Pink Chimes' has pink flowers. If you are partial to native trees, plant either the American snowbell (*Styrax americanus*) or the bigleaf snowbell (*Styrax grandifolius*), both of which are also fragrant but smaller in stature. *Styrax obassia* has larger leaves and fragrant flowers equal to Japanese snowbell.

Sweetbay Magnolia

Magnolia virginiana

Botanical Pronunciation
mag-NO-lee-a vir-jin-ee-AN-uh

Bloom Period and Seasonal Colors
Evergreen to semievergreen foliage; summer blooms in white

Mature Height × Spread
25 to 30 ft. × 20 ft.

If our magnificent Southern magnolia is considered to be a garden heavyweight, then the sweetbay magnolia is its soft-spoken, smaller sibling. Dainty and more open, this native evergreen magnolia is perfect for smaller gardens. Flowering at the same time as its big brother, this tree offers a refined appearance. Flowers have a lemon fragrance that is not overpowering. Unlike other magnolias, the sweetbay grows in gardens with wet or damp soils. Try it near a pond or stream. It is also more shade tolerant than other magnolias. The leaves are light green, and in a gentle breeze they display their silvery undersides. When crushed, the leaves give off a spicy aroma. This tree is perfect for in-town gardens where quiet elegance is the prevailing decor.

When, Where, and How to Plant

In the best interests of success, plant sweetbay magnolia in fall. Plant either balled-and-burlapped or container-grown trees. Trees planted in the spring need extra love and attention through the first growing season. Sweetbay magnolia prefers a soil that is moist, rich in organic matter, and slightly acidic, but it will grow fine in regular garden soil. It tolerates sites that are occasionally flooded. Flowering is best in full sun, but the tree can handle moderate shade. In the wild, it is often seen growing under large hardwoods near streams and lakes.

Growing Tips

Once established, sweetbay magnolia is fairly drought tolerant, but watch for droopy leaves.

Water heavily if they are seen. Plants growing in full sun may require more water than those in partial shade.

Regional Advice and Care

Sweetbay magnolia rarely requires pruning; its natural shape is quite appealing. Blooms develop on the current season's growth, so if pruning is necessary, do it in late winter or early spring before new growth begins. Removing dead flowers is not necessary. Plants are susceptible to the occasional fungal leaf spot or miner, but this is usually not serious. English ivy, though, can rapidly climb a tree and shade out lower branches. In addition, the ivy collects more ice, wind, and rainfall than a tree limb would naturally; the additional weight may damage the tree. Make a habit of removing ivy from all landscape trees and clearing an area 6 feet from the tree trunk in all directions.

Companion Planting and Design

In a moist, shady garden, the sweetbay magnolia can be the main specimen tree. Underplanted with ferns and hostas with moss as a groundcover, it gives the feeling of being in a tropical rain forest. In a more open garden, trees can be massed to provide a gentle screening effect.

Try These

Several selections of the species are available and all are acceptable. 'Henry Hicks' is more columnar than most. *Magnolia virginiana* var. *australis* is more evergreen than the species.

Yellowwood

Cladrastis kentukea

Botanical Pronunciation
kluh-DRAS-tis ken-TUK-ee-uh

Bloom Period and Seasonal Colors
Deciduous; soft gold to bright yellow fall foliage; summer blooms in white, usually in alternate years

Mature Height × Spread
30 to 50 ft. × 40 ft.

Another fine native specimen of medium height, yellowwood offers homeowners an alternate choice of shade tree in small or medium gardens. In terms of flowers, yellowwood is not the tree for impatient gardeners. Heavy flowering usually occurs only every two to three years. When in flower, it's a car-stopping experience and, in the opinion of many gardeners, worth every bit of the wait. The flowers are showy, white, fragrant racemes that resemble those of wisteria. Brown seedpods follow the flowers, 2 to 4 inches long. When not in bloom, the broad crown and compound leaves make it a great shade tree with a moderate growth rate. After the leaves have dropped in the fall, the leaf stems often remain, giving it a curious winter texture. It's not commonly found in nurseries; you may have to special-order it.

When, Where, and How to Plant
Yellowwood should be planted in fall. Because it is hard to find, plant whatever size is available, either container grown or balled and burlapped. Trees planted in spring require extra care through the first growing season to maintain moisture. Yellowwood prefers a soil that is moist but well drained and rich in organic matter. It will tolerate slightly alkaline soils. Locate trees in areas protected from strong winds, as the branches can be somewhat brittle. Flowering is best in full sun. See page 130 for planting instructions.

Growing Tips
Once established, yellowwood is drought tolerant. If planted near lawns that are fertilized regularly, additional fertilizer is not necessary. It is a good idea to maintain a 3- to 5-inch layer of mulch around the tree to retain moisture. Increase watering by 25 percent during extreme drought and heat.

Regional Advice and Care
If sited properly in an open area, yellowwood should require no pruning to maintain shape. However, if you are pruning to maintain a desired shape, do it immediately after flowering. Prune dead or damaged wood anytime. Minor problems with wilt are occasionally seen but do not appear to be serious.

Companion Planting and Design
Because this tree has compound leaves, it has a softer texture than other shade trees. Groupings can be used in larger landscapes or parks to provide shade. In smaller landscapes, it looks best as a standalone specimen. Companion plantings include other summer-flowering shrubs and perennials. Because the flowers are white, it blends into any color scheme. Fall color is soft gold to bright yellow and contrasts nicely with maple, black gum, or other trees with red fall color.

Try These
'Rosea' may be found in specialty nurseries. Yellowwood is a Georgia Gold Medal Plant. Retired UGA horticulturist Gary Wade says that the tree provides a strong winter accent with its smooth, pale gray trunk and sinewy branches. Add night lighting and the tree makes a dramatic statement in the winter landscape.

TURFGRASSES
FOR GEORGIA

What would a landscape be without a lawn? Though some prefer a "lawnless landscape," most Georgians prefer grass to grow in front of their homes. A lawn takes more time to care for than any other part of the landscape, yet green turf is seen in front of homes both grand and humble throughout the state.

Many people find lawn maintenance to be a mysterious process. From selection to planting to fertilizing and pest control, lawn work seems to require more knowledge than other landscape chores.

Yet grass grows easily beside the highway with no fertilizer, mowing only once a year, and almost no pests beyond lit cigars and errant SUVs. How so? It's all in the selection—putting the right grass in the right spot.

Springtime lawn bordered by azaleas.

Which Grass Is the Right Grass?

Choosing the right grass for a lawn is initially based on how much sunshine the site receives and how much water you will be able to apply in the summer. Consider also the amount of labor you are willing to invest in your lawn. Tall fescue is classified as a "cool-season" grass. It stays green year-round. Bermudagrass, zoysiagrass, centipedegrass, and St. Augustinegrass are all classified as "warm-season" grasses. They are green most of the year but turn brown (or light green, as in the case of St. Augustinegrass) and stop growing in winter.

Sunlight, Sweet Sunlight

All plants need sunlight, and grass is no exception. Tall fescue is the most shade-tolerant grass, but no grass will grow well in less than four hours of direct sunshine (or eight hours of filtered light under tall trees). Red fescue and bluegrass are somewhat more shade tolerant; however, they are not heat tolerant. Plant them only if you can keep the summer temperatures below 90°F. (In Georgia? Hah!)

When it comes to selecting a grass, use these guidelines for the amount of sunlight tolerated by turfgrasses to grow uccessfully:

Grass Variety	Sun Requirement
Bermudagrass	full sunshine to very light shade
Centipedegrass	full sunshine to very light shade
'Emerald' Zoysiagrass	full sunshine to partial shade
'Meyer' Zoysiagrass	full sunshine to light shade
St. Augustinegrass	full sunshine to partial shade
Tall Fescue	full sunshine to partial shade

Because sunlight levels are hard to define, use these examples as a guideline:

- **Full sunshine:** eight hours of unfiltered sunshine sometime between sunrise and sunset
- **Light shade:** eight hours of sunshine filtered through high pine foliage or scattered hardwood trees or six hours of unfiltered sunshine sometime between sunrise and sunset
- **Partial shade:** six hours of sunshine filtered through high pine foliage or four hours of direct sunshine between sunrise and sunset
- **Shade:** all day sunshine filtered through scattered hardwood trees or direct sunshine at least three hours per day
- **Dense shade:** no direct sunshine touches the grass all day, such as the shade under a Southern magnolia or the shade between two houses whose shadows prevent sunshine from hitting the earth at all

No grass will grow well in shade or dense shade. If you have a shady spot, save yourself some grief and plant groundcovers (see page 61) or cover the spot with mulch.

A buffer of mulch helps keep Bermudagrass out of the flower beds.

To Seed or To Sod? That Is the Question

There are two ways to establish a lawn: by planting seed and then waiting for it to sprout or by laying sod and gaining an instant lawn. Some grasses are better planted from seed, while others can only be planted with sod.

Planting Grass from Sod

Follow these directions to successfully sod your lawn.

1. Kill all weeds by spraying the area with a nonselective weedkiller two weeks before tilling and planting.
2. Till the soil thoroughly to a depth of 6 inches, mixing in the recommended amount of lime and fertilizer (see page 13 for information on soil testing).
3. Rake the area smooth, removing rocks, clumps, and debris.
4. Roll the area with a water-filled roller to reveal low spots.
5. Fill low spots with soil.
6. Starting along the longest straight edge of the area, lay sod pieces end-to-end. Make sure each piece is tightly placed next to its neighbor. Stagger sod pieces in adjacent rows so seams do not line up. Use a small hatchet or sharp shovel to trim pieces to fit around obstructions.
7. Roll the entire area once more, to ensure good sod-to-soil contact.
8. Water the sod thoroughly (see watering information on page 201).

Planting Grass from Seed

Follow these directions to successfully seed your lawn.

1. Kill all weeds by spraying the area with a nonselective weedkiller two weeks before planting.
2. Till the soil thoroughly to a depth of 6 inches, mixing in the recommended amount of lime and fertilizer (see page 13 for information on soil testing).
3. Rake the area smooth, removing rocks, clumps, and debris.

4. Roll the area with a water-filled roller to reveal low spots.
5. Fill low spots with soil.
6. Scatter seed according to rates given in the following chart. Cover very thinly with wheat straw (¾ bale per 1,000 square feet).
7. Follow the watering guidelines provided on page 202.
8. Do not use weed control products on your lawn until at least six weeks (or two mowings) after planting seed.

Seeding Rates for New Lawns

Grass Variety	Pounds of Seed per 1,000 Sq. Ft.
Bermudagrass (hulled)	1 to 2
Centipedegrass	¼ to 1
Tall Fescue	5 to 8
Zoysiagrass	1 to 3
St. Augustinegrass	no seed is available

All bags of grass seed are required to have a label that shows the results of various tests on that batch of seed. Always buy seed that has been tested for its germination rate within the past six months. When deciding which seed to buy, compare the germination percentage and the number of weed seed found in each. You may discover that a higher priced bag of seed is actually a better value because more of the seed will germinate, with fewer weeds.

Water, Water

The best time to water a lawn is in the morning. This allows the grass to dry before nightfall, reducing the risk of disease. Take into account recent rainfall when deciding how much water to apply. Watering restrictions may impact how often you can irrigate. Check www.georgiadrought.org for the latest information. If restrictions mandate watering every other day, the schedules given here may be modified to fit the rules.

In order to accurately water grass, you will need to know just how much water your sprinkler actually "sprinkles" on your lawn. To measure the amount of water applied by your sprinkler, follow these steps:

1. Place six identical containers randomly in the area wetted by your sprinkler. Plastic cups can be used, but weight them down with a heavy washer in the bottom of each.
2. Let your sprinkler run for an hour.
3. Measure the depth of water that has accumulated in each cup.
4. Calculate the average of the depths. That will give you the amount (in inches) of water that the sprinkler has applied in an hour.
5. Next, calculate how long it will take to apply 1 inch of water. Don't be surprised if your sprinkler must run for more than an hour to apply the water your lawn needs.

Watering New Sod

Follow these steps for healthy watering practices for a sodded lawn:

1. Apply 1 inch of water immediately after sod is laid.
2. For the next seven days, apply enough water daily to prevent the top ½ inch of soil from drying out.
3. After that, apply ¼ inch of water every third day for nine days.
4. Next, apply ½ inch of water every fifth day for ten days.
5. After this establishment period, apply 1 inch of water per week for the rest of the growing season.

Note: There is no need to water if rainfall supplies the correct amount.

Watering Newly Seeded Lawns

For lawns newly seeded with such grasses as centipedegrass, zoysiagrass, bermudagrass, and tall fescue, follow these steps for watering:

1. Apply 1 inch of water immediately after planting.
2. Apply enough water daily to prevent the top ½ inch of soil from drying out until seedlings are 1½ inches tall.
3. After that, apply ¼ inch of water every third day for nine days.
4. Next, apply ½ inch of water every fifth day for ten days.
5. After this establishment period, apply 1 inch of water per week for the rest of the growing season.

Note: There is no need to water if rainfall supplies the correct amount.

Zoysiagrass can tolerate a light shade.

Mow, Mow, Mow the Lawn

Every lawn grass has a height at which it should be mowed for best health. The general rule is that only one-third of a grass plant should be removed in one mowing. As an example, if you intend to mow your fescue lawn at a 3-inch height, you can allow it to grow to 4 inches between mowings. If you fertilize moderately, mowing a lawn should only be needed once per week. See the chart for the recommended mowing height for the various types of grasses.

Measure the mowing height by stationing the mower on a flat surface and noting the distance between the blade and the ground. Make sure all four mower wheels are set to the same height.

It is not necessary to bag clippings if you mow regularly. They contain a substantial amount of nutrients and should either be left on the lawn or added to a compost bin.

Mowing Height for Lawn Grasses (in inches)

Centipedegrass	1 to 1½
Common Bermudagrass	1 to 2
Hybrid Bermudagrass	½ to 1½
St. Augustinegrass	2 to 3
Tall Fescue	2 to 3
Zoysiagrass	½ to 2

Aerating—What Do Those Holes Do?

Aeration is the process of mechanically poking thousands of holes in the soil. This allows water, oxygen, and nutrients to better penetrate to the roots of your grass. Motorized aerator machines can be rented. The best aerator is one with hollow tines (spoons) that pull up plugs of earth as the machine travels along. Solid-tine spike aerators pulled by lawn tractors are of little benefit.

Use a crisscross pattern with the aerator. First, direct the machine over the entire lawn, going back and forth in one direction. Second, direct the machine back and forth at right angles to the first trip.

Examine a square foot area of the lawn. It, and every other square foot, should have at least 12 holes in it. If not, crank up the machine again! If the plugs of soil on the surface are objectionable, let them dry a few days, then drag a 5-foot by 5-foot piece of carpet across the lawn to pulverize them.

May and June are good months to aerate lawns with warm-season grasses, such as bermudagrass, centipedegrass, zoysiagrass, and St. Augustinegrass. March and September are the best months to aerate tall fescue.

Even though aeration damages the grass a bit, it is able to recover rapidly. As the soil plugs disappear from the soil surface, they inoculate the thatch layer with organisms that help decompose it more rapidly. Plan to aerate lawns growing on clay soil every two years.

Fertilizing

Lawn fertilizers are manufactured by many companies. Each manufacturer uses a slightly different blend of plant nutrient chemicals to arrive at a final product. Chemicals such as urea, ammonium nitrate, urea formaldehyde, and ammonium phosphate provide the nutrient nitrogen, which rapidly growing lawns need more than phosphorus and potassium.

Granular fertilizers tend to last longer (up to three months) in the soil. Slow-release fertilizers are generally better for a lawn than fertilizers that release their nutrients quickly during the first rain.

Adding Lime

Turfgrasses need soil that is only slightly acidic in order to thrive. In most parts of Georgia, the soil is more acidic than grass prefers. Garden lime neutralizes acidity and should be applied when needed. It is never the wrong time to lime your lawn, but how much lime should you apply?

Forty pounds per 1,000 square feet of lawn area is approximately enough, but an Extension soil test (page 13) will tell you exactly how much you need. Adding too much or too little lime can harm your lawn in the long run. Don't guess—soil test!

Garden lime can be purchased in bags in two forms: powdered or pelletized. Neither form is inherently better than the other. Pelletized lime flows through a lawn spreader more easily, though powdered lime is slightly less expensive.

Weeds, Weeds, Weeds!

One of the most common problems that Georgia gardeners face is managing plants that have grown out of their own place in the environment. In other words, gardeners must constantly fight weeds.

Identification and Controls

Weed control begins with the identification of the weed. They are usually classified as grassy weeds—such as crabgrass—or broad-leafed weeds—such as dandelions. Once the type is determined, the weed is then categorized as an annual weed that grows from seed each year or a perennial weed that grows back from its roots each year. Knowing what kind of weed you are dealing with will help you decide the correct way to manage it. You will have to decide whether you want to use a weedkiller chemical or just pull the weeds by hand. In most lawns, increasing the vigor of the grass with good management will choke out encroaching weeds.

Annual weeds are easiest to control with herbicides. These weeds come up from seed each year, and scientists have developed chemical herbicides called pre-emergents that prevent seed germination and rooting. Of course, these chemicals need to be applied before the weed seeds germinate. To control annual weeds (such as crabgrass) that grow in summer, a pre-emergent should be applied in early to mid-March, before warm weather makes the seeds germinate. Some annual weeds, such as chickweed, sprout in October and grow rapidly in early spring. To control them, a pre-emergent must be applied in mid-September. Read the labels on every product you consider to make sure it will control the weed you want to fight.

Perennial weeds grow from their roots each year. They may spread farther and farther in your lawn or landscape by seeds or by underground roots. To control them, a post-emergent herbicide is used after the weed leaves have emerged. It pays to observe whether the plant is grassy or broad-leafed; chemicals that kill grassy weeds are usually ineffective on broad-leafed weeds and vice versa. Again, read the product label to determine if it will do the job you desire.

Nonselective plant killers are just that. When sprayed on the green leaves of a plant, whether dandelion or dahlia, the plant will be killed. Several nonselective herbicides have been marketed in the last few years. Most of these chemicals do not linger in the soil, so you can spray a weedy lawn one weekend and plant grass seed the next. Because the chemical can't read your mind, use care when employing these herbicides.

Types of Turfgrasses

Zoysiagrass

Zoysiagrass is a slow-growing but extremely thick and durable turfgrass. It spreads by aboveground stolons and by underground rhizomes. Although thick and carpet-like, zoysia is slow to establish from seed or plugs. Bermudagrass and zoysiagrass have a similar appearance. One way to tell them apart is from the feel under your feet. The stiff blades of zoysia make it feel spongy, like walking on padded carpet. Bermudagrass feels harder to your feet. Zoysia is sometimes advertised in "miracle" terms in periodicals. Note: The grass advertised is 'Meyer' zoysiagrass, which is available from local garden centers.

'Emerald' has a very fine leaf texture and good shade tolerance but is less cold tolerant than other zoysiagrass varieties. 'Meyer' has good cold tolerance and a wider leaf but less shade tolerance than 'Emerald'. 'El Toro' grows rapidly and has a leaf width similar to 'Meyer'. 'Zenith' can be readily established from seed. It grows rapidly, with a dense growth habit, and tolerates light shade.

Tall Fescue

Tall fescue is a fast-growing turfgrass that maintains some shade of green year-round. It looks best in fall through spring, but it has problems when grown on hard soil in full sunshine. It is usually planted from seed, but fescue sod is increasingly popular. Seed companies have improved the old standard 'Kentucky-31' fescue with numerous

Fescue grass

introductions of named turf-type tall fescue, which all rate higher than 'Kentucky-31' fescue in comparison trials.

No one turf-type fescue stands head and shoulders above all the others in all situations. Seed blends of several varieties work well in most situations.

St. Augustinegrass

St. Augustinegrass is an excellent choice for the sandy soils of the lower half of the state, but it's not unusual from Macon up to Atlanta, though it is not the predominant turfgrass choice. In upper northern Georgia, only lawn gamblers plant a grass that will suffer cold injury in most winters. Although less cold tolerant than other warm-season turfgrasses, it does stay green longer in fall. St. Augustinegrass is very tolerant of shade. The wide leaves efficiently gather sunshine underneath shrubs and trees. It is also an excellent full-sun turf and will crowd out most weeds.

'Floratam' is an improved variety released by Texas A&M and the University of Florida. 'Bitterblue' has good cold tolerance and shade tolerance. 'Raleigh' was developed for its improved cold tolerance. 'Seville' is a dark green semidwarf variety selected for its fine leaf texture.

Centipedegrass

Centipedegrass ("The poor man's lawn!") can be a very attractive turf, but it has advantages and disadvantages just like any other grass. Centipedegrass is green in summer but goes dormant in winter. Centipedegrass turf is a gray-green color; some people prefer the deep green of a sodded bermudagrass lawn. Centipedegrass certainly has two advantages, though—it spreads rapidly by aboveground runners and it doesn't grow very tall. Mowing is needed but less frequently than with other turf grasses.

'Tifblair' was developed by University of Georgia researchers to have improved cold tolerance.

Bermudagrass

This warm-season grass is green in summer and buff-brown in winter. It is supremely adapted to Georgia, so much so that flower gardeners sometimes curse it, while lawn owners and golfers revere it. Any grass that grows so rapidly has vast potential for improvement. From common bermudagrass, breeders have selected plants that stay low and produce few seedheads. Tifton 419 and Tifton 94 are sterile hybrids, available only as sod. They produce no viable seed, but a sprig will cover a 12-inch by 12-inch square in only one summer. Laid in a checkerboard pattern over bare earth, bermudagrass sod transforms a red-clay eyesore of a lawn into an eye-pleasing greenscape in just a day. Common bermudagrass, however, is a frequent uninvited guest in landscape beds!

'Riviera' and 'Princess 77' are introductions of improved bermudagrass seed. They tend to be a deeper green than common bermudagrass and are reputed to resemble a hybrid bermudagrass lawn.

Lawn College

Does having a nice lawn require a college degree, or can just about anyone achieve an attractive turf? If you follow the recommendations in this chapter, your lawn will look as good as, or better than, your neighbors'—and you will soon find that the "mysteries" of lawn cultivation are quite easy to master.

A well-designed lawn with annual beds

VINES

FOR GEORGIA

Vines are one of the few plants that can be said to "move." If a vine doesn't like where it is, it can actually grow toward the conditions it prefers. Whether evergreen, deciduous, flowering, clinging, twining, scrambling, or rambling, vines offer gardeners the opportunity to take maximum advantage of vertical gardening space. From clematis draped over a fence to a trumpet creeper climbing a tree, vines add another dimension to the garden. Some need supports—such as arbors, pergolas, fences, walls, or trees—while others will grow happily among shrubs or other climbing plants, creating interesting combinations of foliage and flowers.

Choosing the Right Vine for the Right Spot

Annual vines are a good way to experiment with adding certain colors and textures to the garden without making a long-term commitment. Many are easy to grow from seed. Impatient gardeners may want to start with plants that have already grown a year or two in a nursery. All the vines recommended in this chapter thrive in our hot, Georgia summers and fill the garden with color. Most vines will produce the largest leaves and flowers when they are planted in full sun. At the end of the season, many vines set seed, which can be stored and planted the following spring.

Perennial vines reward us with flowers, foliage, and sometimes ornamental bark in the winter. Take care when selecting a spot for them to grow and flower, as many of them do not like to be disturbed.

Training and Pruning

Most vines need a support to twine on or to climb. This support can be as simple as a chain-link fence or as elaborate as a hand-sculpted metal arbor.

When it comes to pruning, there are a few general rules. If the vine flowers on two-year-old wood (as does *Clematis armandii*), prune it back as soon as it finishes flowering. If it blooms on the current season's growth (as does trumpet creeper), prune it in early spring before new growth begins. In some cases, you will need to prune during the growing season to remove wild shoots that go off in all directions or to keep a particular vine inbounds. More pruning specifics are noted in the individual plant entries.

Planting and Caring for Vines

Whether you are planting vines or any other landscape plants, soil preparation is key. A couple of the vines mentioned here grow weakly if they are not given good soil in which to grow, but when placed in a well-prepared home, they explode with healthy growth. Loosen an area of soil at least three times as big as the rootball of the vine

Wisteria garden

you are planting before placing it in the center of the area. Plant so that the top of the rootball is level with the surrounding soil. Water heavily after planting to settle the soil. Be sure to mulch the plant to keep weeds at bay.

Vines can be treated like perennials and shrubs when fertilizing. If you mix a slow-release granular fertilizer into the soil when you plant, you will not need to fertilize as often as you will if you use 10-10-10. Apply fertilizer twice a year, once in March and once in June. If you plant vines in combination with shrubs or trees, the vines won't need to be fertilized separately but will get sufficient nutrients when you fertilize their companions.

Vines are subject to many of the same pest and disease problems that affect other ornamental plants. Aphids, spider mites, scale, and leaf fungus are common, but vines are not usually harmed much by these pests. In the correct growing spot, a vine can grow so fast that it outruns its detractors. To help keep damage from insects or disease to a minimum, select varieties that are well suited for the environment in which you will plant them. Keeping plants watered and mulched will help ward off problems as well.

American Wisteria

Wisteria frutescens

Botanical Pronunciation
wis-TER-ee-a froo-TESS-enz

Bloom Period and Seasonal Colors
Perennial; deciduous; spring flowers
in purple, white

Mature Length
25 to 30 ft.

Sometime in April as you are driving around Georgia, you'll spot massive trees engulfed in vines that are covered with grapelike flower clusters from top to bottom. Sadly, those suffocating vines are not American wisteria. Forest edges across the South have fallen victim to two Asian species of wisteria (*Wisteria floribunda* and *Wisteria sinensis*), both of which are considered noxious weeds by environmentalists and knowledgeable gardeners. Growing unobtrusively closer to the coast is our native American wisteria. Perfectly hardy throughout the entire state, American wisteria blooms a bit later (after the leaves have emerged) and at a much younger age. Flowers come in the standard purple and white but are just a bit shorter than those of its rampant Asian cousins, resembling purple pine cones.

When, Where, and How to Plant
Container-grown American wisteria can be planted either in fall or spring. Full sun is best for prolific flowering, but it will tolerate light shade. Although it will grow in a wide range of soils, it prefers a soil rich in organic matter and moist but well drained.

Growing Tips
Once established, American wisteria is fairly drought tolerant. Water young or newly installed plants once a week during times of drought. Do not overfertilize. Too much fertilizer, especially if high in nitrogen, will promote growth and reduce flowering.

Regional Advice and Care
It is said that you should prune an Asian wisteria every time you walk by it, but American wisteria is not that rampant. This vine must be trained properly to a support while young. After planting, prune back the leader to 2½ to 3 feet high. During the growing season, let the side branches twine through the support you are using. During the winter, remove any secondary growth from the side branches. Once the vine has reached the desired shape and size, remove any undesired growth in late summer and further reduce the side branches to two to three buds during winter. Remove old flowers if you want to prevent seedpod formation. American wisteria is susceptible to crown gall, leaf spots, Japanese beetles, aphids, leaf miners, scale, and mealybugs, but these rarely seem to slow it down.

Companion Planting and Design
American wisteria grows rapidly in full sun and needs a sturdy support. A well-constructed arbor, trellis, or support on a building is required. This plant works well over an arbor to provide spring flowers and summer shade. It can also be trained into a small tree able to stand by itself without support. American wisteria blends well with other midspring bloomers, including salvia, coreopsis, and fringetree. Keep a careful eye on it, as it will reach out and "grab" nearby plants during the growing season.

Try These
There are two very good cultivars: 'Amethyst Falls' with purple flowers and 'Nivea' with white flowers.

Armand Clematis

Clematis armandii

Botanical Pronunciation
KLEM-uh-tiss (klem-AT-iss) ar-MOND-ee-eye

Other Name Evergreen clematis

Bloom Period and Seasonal Colors
Perennial; evergreen; March to April blooms
in creamy white

Mature Length
20 ft. or more

From the northern Atlanta suburbs south, evergreen clematis is a choice vine that perfumes the air with sweetly scented white flowers in early spring. Each flower is 2 to 2½ inches wide and has four to seven petals. The scent of the flowers has been compared to that of almonds. The dramatic foliage of armand clematis looks good almost year-round, except after a severe winter when it has been damaged by cold. Vines grow happily on a chain-link fence or porch support for dozens of years. It does as well or better than Carolina jessamine might in the same spot. Gardeners love spotting the flowers, which signal that, though the weather is chilly, spring is just around the corner.

When, Where, and How to Plant
Plant in late spring, when soil temperatures begin to warm. Flowering is best in full sun. Unlike many clematis that are very particular about soil, the armand clematis will grow in any moderately fertile soil that is moist but well drained. In the coldest parts of Georgia, protect it from winter winds. Dig a hole equal to or larger than the container. To ensure good drainage, add mini pine nuggets or gravel to the soil used to backfill after planting. A light covering of mulch keeps the roots cool.

Growing Tips
Fertilize year-old vines with ¼ cup of 10-10-10 fertilizer in spring and again with a scant handful in fall. No feeding is needed thereafter. Water during extremely dry periods of no rainfall.

Regional Advice and Care
Established vines do not usually require much care. Because the vine flowers on two-year-old wood, prune after flowering, if needed. It vigorously sends out tendrils in all directions, looking for support. Check on the vine often so you can prevent it from taking over your arbor. Prune away cold damage after it occurs. Few pests or diseases attack armand clematis.

Companion Planting and Design
This evergreen climber needs a support—such as an arbor, fence, or wall—to grow on. Galvanized wire attached to a wall with masonry nails will give it something to hold onto initially. It makes a perfect living trellis on which to train another early summer–blooming clematis, such as Jackman clematis (see page 217). As armand clematis matures, it tends to lose its leaves at the base. Plant it behind an evergreen shrub to mask its unsightly "bare ankles."

Try These
'Apple Blossom', with bronze young foliage and pink flowers, is worth trying if you can find it. 'Snowdrift' is covered with masses of white flowers. *Clematis* × *cartmanii* 'Avalanche' is dependably evergreen and has deeply dissected leaves. There are many other wonderful spring-blooming clematis to include in your garden. One is the fast-growing *Clematis montana* var. *rubens*. This vigorous clematis grows to 30 feet and produces a profusion of pale pink flowers.

Carolina Jessamine

Gelsemium sempervirens

Botanical Pronunciation
jel-SEM-ee-um sem-per-VY-renz

Bloom Period and Seasonal Colors
Perennial; evergreen; blooms in yellow February through April

Mature Length
Climbing vine; 10 to 20 ft. on any supportive surface

Carolina jessamine has been cultivated in Georgia gardens for years, and there are good reasons for the popularity of this adaptable native. It offers shiny evergreen foliage, blooms with fragrant yellow flowers in early spring, and grows in sun or shade. It is popular not only in Georgia gardens, but throughout the South. It's seen on trellises, arbors, chain-link fences, and traffic railings and as a groundcover near Interstate highways. While it is a serviceable performer for many gardens, it should not be confused with Confederate jasmine, *Trachelospermum jasminoides*, an evergreen vine with powerfully fragrant flowers. Jessamine is correctly pronounced "jes-a-min" or "jes-a-mine," not "jaz-min."

When, Where, and How to Plant
Plant this vine in early spring or fall. This native will grow in full sun or shade, but it will make a thicker cover when grown in sun. Carolina jessamine prefers a moist, well-drained soil that is moderately fertile, but it will also tolerate less-than-ideal conditions. Dig a hole three times the size of the container in which the vine was purchased. If you plant it as a groundcover, give it plenty of room to spread. Once you recognize the yellow blooms, you'll have a ready answer to friends who inquire if you have seen the beautiful trees with yellow blooms alongside the Interstate. (The trees are just arboreal arbors for jessamine.)

Growing Tips
Few situations warrant fertilizing jessamine after the initial feeding at planting. Water during periods of drought in the first year, but afterward leave it unirrigated.

Regional Advice and Care
Prune Carolina jessamine after it flowers, if needed. Sometimes a hard pruning in April will help rejuvenate an older plant that has become a tangled mess. When used as a groundcover, mow in early summer to allow new flower buds to form before winter. The vine seems free from attack by insects or disease.

Companion Planting and Design
Plant as a groundcover or as a clambering vine on an arbor or fence. The most common use for this plant is as a climbing, twining vine. It has consumed many a mailbox. Only use it as a groundcover where you can let it run wild. It also works well in areas where fall-blooming bulbs—such as red surprise lilies, *Lycoris radiata*—await. Like most vines, the lower stems are quickly shaded by upper growth and become bare over time. Plan to have low shrubs or evergreen perennials in front of it.

Try These
Gelsemium sempervirens 'Pride of Augusta' (a double-flowering form) and *G. rankinii* are not fragrant, but they flower in spring and then again in fall. They are not as cold hardy as the species. 'Margarita' is very cold hardy and has large gold trumpet flowers.

Climbing Hydrangea

Hydrangea anomala ssp. *petiolaris*

Botanical Pronunciation
hy-DRAIN-juh ah-NOM-uh-luh pet-ee-oh-LAIR-iss

Bloom Period and Seasonal Colors
Perennial; deciduous; June to July blooms in white; fall foliage in yellow

Mature Length
Climbing vine; 60 ft. at least

Although it may take a few years to establish itself in a garden, climbing hydrangea is well worth the wait. It offers lustrous green foliage and white, sweetly scented flowers in 6- to 10-inch flat clusters. This showstopper lights up a woodland garden when its white flowers clothe a dark tree trunk, reaching for the sky. It is equally impressive planted against a brick wall in the sun. The dark green leaves, 2 to 4 inches long, persist late into the season. Climbing hydrangea sometimes exhibits outstandingly rich yellow fall color. Its handsome, cinnamon-brown bark creates beautiful patterns in the winter landscape. Though too slow growing for an arbor, this vine and its flowers incite garden lust once they are well established on a tall tree trunk.

When, Where, and How to Plant
Plant container-grown plants in early spring or fall. This allows the root system time to become established before it is stressed by hot or cold weather. Plant climbing hydrangea in full sun or partial shade. Although this vine will grow in shade, it may not produce as many flowers as when grown in sun or part sun. For best results, plant it in evenly moist, well-drained soil. Amend the planting area with organic matter and coarse sand. Till the ground, working an area as deep as the container and three times its width. Water deeply after planting. Grow this vine next to a structure or wall. Use twine, jute, or copper wire to make a loose attachment, making sure the wires will not girdle the vine.

Growing Tips
If you have amended the soil, the plant will get off to a good start. Fertilize in early spring during the first couple of growing seasons with 1 tablespoon of 10-10-10 fertilizer per foot of height. Water deeply once each week in summer when the soil is dry.

Regional Advice and Care
Climbing hydrangea should not require any pruning when first planted, as it is slow to become established. Once it is growing well, prune it after it flowers to the desired height or spread. No serious insects or disease affect it.

Companion Planting and Design
It is both interesting and attractive to plant this vine near hydrangea shrubs. Although climbing hydrangea clings to surfaces with rootlike holdfasts, it may require extra support. This stately vine can transform the ordinary into art when trained to cover a wooden shed or garage. A word of caution: Make sure that the structure on which you grow this vine is strong enough to support it, as it gets very woody when it matures. This is not a vine to plant for tomorrow's quick cover, but for the landscape in your future!

Try These
Although widely appreciated among knowledgeable gardeners, few superior selections of climbing hydrangea have been bred. 'Miranda' has variegated dark green leaves that are highlighted with irregular yellow margins.

Crossvine

Bignonia capreolata

Botanical Pronunciation
big-NO-nee-uh kap-ree-oh-LAH-tuh

Bloom Period and Seasonal Colors
Semideciduous; March through April blooms in peachy-orange with yellow throats; winter foliage in red, purple

Mature Length
30 to 50 ft.

Crossvine gets its common name from the cross-shaped mark in the pith that is visible when you cut a woody stem in half. In bud, the 2- to 3-inch-long flowers resemble long, narrow balloons. Once they open in early spring, they look more like deep funnels with yellow throats. Mostly evergreen, the foliage starts out a bright, light green and becomes dark and leathery as it matures. In winter, it turns shades of red and purple. Even the tendrils and rootlets—the parts of the vine that grab onto structures or other plants—are showy. They twist and curl sinuously in all directions. To distinguish between crossvine and the related trumpet creeper vine, note that trumpet creeper does not have tendrils, but rather aerial roots, like English ivy.

When, Where, and How to Plant

Plant crossvine in spring or fall. This vine will grow in heavy shade, but for best flowering, give it plenty of sun. Plus, the more sun crossvine gets, the better cover it will provide. It tolerates less-than-ideal soil conditions, growing in wet or dry soils. For best results, plant it in a well-drained, moderately fertile soil. Dig a planting hole three times as wide as the container. This vine is also easy to root from cuttings taken in June and July. Although fast growing, crossvine is much easier to keep inbounds than its aggressive trumpet creeper relative, *Campsis radicans*.

Growing Tips

The first year it is planted, apply 1 cup of 10-10-10 fertilizer in early spring to give it an initial boost.

Fertilizer is not needed afterward. During the first year of establishment, water weekly during summer periods without any rain.

Regional Advice and Care

Prune this vigorous native after flowering to shape and train it. On an arbor, it may become so tangled that massive pruning is required. There will be fewer blooms the next year, but the vine will be better for the shearing. Crossvine does not suffer from any serious pest or disease problems and requires no special care.

Companion Planting and Design

This self-clinging vine uses its tendrils to attach to any rough, slightly sloping surface. Plant it against a fence or wall (it requires a support) or let it sprawl over a stump. Tie it up against a structure when it is a young plant to prevent it from growing along the ground. When growing up a tree, crossvine grows flat, forming a beautiful pattern with its leaves. Flower arrangers collect 2-foot sections of vine, crush them into a ball and place them in the bottom of a clear glass vase to provide a grid for holding long-stemmed flowers.

Try These

Try 'Tangerine Beauty'. 'Jekyll' has smaller flowers but increased tolerance to cold. Another good native is *Decumaria barbara*, the hydrangea vine. It has glossy green foliage and small, white, fragrant flowers in early summer.

Cypress Vine

Ipomoea quamoclit

Botanical Pronunciation
eye-poh-MEE-a KWAM-oh-klit

Bloom Period and Seasonal Colors
Annual; summer to fall blooms in scarlet red

Mature Length
12 ft. or more

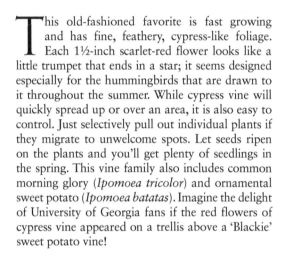

This old-fashioned favorite is fast growing and has fine, feathery, cypress-like foliage. Each 1½-inch scarlet-red flower looks like a little trumpet that ends in a star; it seems designed especially for the hummingbirds that are drawn to it throughout the summer. While cypress vine will quickly spread up or over an area, it is also easy to control. Just selectively pull out individual plants if they migrate to unwelcome spots. Let seeds ripen on the plants and you'll get plenty of seedlings in the spring. This vine family also includes common morning glory (*Ipomoea tricolor*) and ornamental sweet potato (*Ipomoea batatas*). Imagine the delight of University of Georgia fans if the red flowers of cypress vine appeared on a trellis above a 'Blackie' sweet potato vine!

When, Where, and How to Plant
After the last frost, sow seeds directly into the ground. Plant them in groups of two or three, about 1 inch deep and 12 inches apart. After germination, thin the seedlings, keeping only the strongest ones. If you start them indoors, use peat pots and plant the pots directly into the ground. You'll get the best flower production if you plant it in full sun. Consider using a spring-blooming shrub as a support. If you do this, you will get two seasons of bloom in a small space. Cypress vine will grow in almost any type of soil that is not constantly wet. Like its other morning glory relatives, this tropical can become a weed—but it is a welcome weed in most places.

Growing Tips
No fertilizer is needed. Water at establishment and during periods of extreme drought. If the vine becomes too rampant for your taste, don't hesitate to slash foliage.

Regional Advice and Care
This vine needs no special care. In fact, the less care you give it, the better it grows. Let seeds dry on the plant before you collect them. Usually, seeds ripen after we have had at least one frost. Pull up the dead vines in late fall or early spring. A few beetles chew on the leaves, but the vine grows so fast that damage is rarely noticed.

Companion Planting and Design
Plant cypress vine anywhere you want a spot of bright color in your summer or fall garden. Because of its fine texture and bright summer flowers, it's a good companion for spring-blooming vines, such as wisteria and Carolina jessamine. Even without a structure to grow up, cypress vine acts like a delicate veil that creeps along the lawn or climbs over shrubs. Mount a hummingbird feeder to a post and plant cypress vine at the base. You'll have a multitude of hummingbirds in no time.

Try These
Closely related to cypress vine is cardinal flower, *Ipomoea multifida*, but its leaves are not as deeply divided as those of cypress vine.

Hyacinth Bean Vine

Lablab purpureus

Botanical Pronunciation
LAB-lab pur-PUR-ee-us

Bloom Period and Seasonal Colors
Annual; summer blooms in lavender; fall
seedpods in purple to magenta

Mature Length
20 to 30 ft.

A favorite of Thomas Jefferson, the eye-catching hyacinth bean vine is a star in the summer garden when it becomes covered with spikes of lavender flowers. With autumn comes the arrival of show-stopping, 4-inch seed-pods in brilliant magenta. This heat lover is perfect for Georgia gardens, where summers are long and hot. Adding to its ornamental appeal are its purple stems and heart-shaped dark green leaves with purple veins. The seeds are ornamental in their own right: velvet black with a white eye stripe. The beans are considered edible, but one who has tried them admits that frequent borborygmi (stomach rumbling) resulted. Research before eating. If it is happy where it grows, this member of the legume family will reward you with new seedlings every year.

When, Where, and How to Plant
Plant seeds in spring after the last frost. Moderately fertile soil, in a location with plenty of sun, is fine. No special soil preparation is needed. Sow seeds directly where you want the vines to grow. This avoids transplanting delicate seedlings. If you start seedlings indoors to get a head start, use peat pots. Place the pots directly into the ground so that you will not have to disturb individual plants. Plant the seeds 1 inch deep and about 3 to 4 inches apart. After seeds sprout, usually in one to two weeks, thin them to 6 inches apart. Select those exhibiting the most color and discard the rest. Make sure that each plant has a structure to cling to, or hyacinth bean will grab onto nearby plants for support.

Growing Tips
The main requirements for growing hyacinth bean are heat and sun, both of which are easy to come by in Georgia. If you start seedlings indoors, give them a light watering with a liquid fertilizer, such as 20-20-20, when you transplant them. If the soil is moderately fertile, more fertilizer should not be required, although mulch will help keep plants from drying out. Water deeply once a week during drought.

Regional Advice and Care
Once the pods ripen and turn brown, you can collect seed to sow next year. Young seedlings make great presents for gardening friends. Bean rust, Japanese beetles, and Mexican bean beetles occasionally attack hyacinth bean. Call your county Extension office (page 225) for control information. The biggest pests might be deer and rabbits, which love the tender leaves.

Companion Planting and Design
Fast-growing hyacinth bean will cover an arbor or trellis, or twine itself around other plants, almost overnight. It makes an attractive summertime cover for a mailbox.

Try These
There is a selection that has white flowers, but it is not nearly as spectacular as the purple-flowered species. Another colored bean that is fun to grow is 'Jacob's Cattle'. It has brown-speckled seeds and bright red flowers.

Jackman Clematis

Clematis 'Jackmanii'

Botanical Pronunciation
KLEM-uh-tiss (klem-AT-iss) jak-MAN-ee-eye

Bloom Period and Seasonal Colors
Deciduous; summer blooms in various colors, depending on variety

Mature Length
10 to 12 ft.

Big, bold, beautiful, and deep purple, this summer clematis is hard to miss, especially when you see it adorning its usual spot—a mailbox. This is without a doubt one of the most popular clematis species on the market. There are dozens of cultivars. Easier to grow than some of the earlier-blooming varieties, the Jackman clematis is the vine of choice when you need to make a noisy statement with flowers. Growing a bit shorter than other clematis, this clematis can be used in locations where a smaller-statured vine is needed. Like most clematis, this variety is somewhat bland looking when not in bloom and lends itself well as a "mixer" with other vines or shrubs that are more appealing in appearance the rest of the year.

When, Where, and How to Plant

Plant Jackman clematis either in fall or spring. Because of its early summer bloom, spring planting is preferable. Install in a location where the top of the plant receives full sun (although light shade is tolerated) but where the roots and base of the plant are protected by shade. The soil should be fertile and moist but well drained. Amend compacted soil with a 3-inch layer of soil conditioner mixed to a depth of 6 to 8 inches. See page 208 for more planting tips.

Growing Tips

Water young plants weekly until they show vigorous growth. Once established, they can handle mild drought but may need supplemental water in extremely dry weather. Use ½ tablespoon of 10-10-10 fertilizer per foot of height in April, with a secondary dose of "bloom booster" fertilizer about a month later. Mulch 2 to 3 inches thick to protect roots from heat and to retain soil moisture.

Regional Advice and Care

Jackman clematis blooms on the current season's growth and will often bloom better when pruned in early spring before new growth appears. Remove dead or diseased growth anytime. The vine will sometimes wilt for no apparent reason. Prune out the dead parts and it will likely produce new sprouts closer to the ground.

Companion Planting and Design

Jackman clematis, with its showy flowers, makes a great vertical focal point when trained on a wire obelisk. Because it is shorter, it can be used in large containers or on a small trellis. It mixes well with climbing roses, often blooming at the same time as repeat-blooming rose varieties. For a real eye-catcher, mix the dark purple flowers with a softer pink rose. You might also see this vine successfully used to climb through evergreen shrubs, such as holly or loropetalum.

Try These

'Nelly Moser', 'Comtesse de Bouchard', and 'Elsa Spath' are other common cultivars at nurseries. Try them if you are a clematis novice, but look for other cultivars when you perfect your clematis skills.

Japanese Hydrangea Vine

Schizophragma hydrangeoides

Botanical Pronunciation
ski-zo-FRAG-muh hy-drain-jee-OY-deez

Bloom Period and Seasonal Colors
Perennial; deciduous; summer blooms in creamy white

Mature Length
40 ft. at least

In the world of climbing hydrangeas, there exists confusion between at least three plants of similar character yet different parentage. One is actually in the same genus as hydrangea (*Hydrangea anomala*), another is a native vine (*Decumaria barbara*), and the third is the Japanese hydrangea vine. Bearing white flowers in summer that resemble those of a lace-cap hydrangea and sporting bold, heart-shaped, deep green foliage, the Japanese hydrangea vine can be an aggressive grower, attaching itself to structures via aerial roots. Often used as a tree climber, this situation may not always be best for tree or vine either. This vine has the advantage of being able to bloom in a relatively shady location, but it may take several years for it to reach blooming age.

When, Where, and How to Plant

Japanese hydrangea vine can be planted in spring or fall. A sturdy structure is needed to support this woody vine. If being planted to climb a tree, the tree should be large and healthy. The vine should be planted no closer than 2 feet to a host tree. Full sun to light shade will produce the best flowering, but a moderate amount of shade is tolerated. It grows best in moderately rich, fertile soil that is evenly moist. Amend compacted soil by using 40 pounds of soil conditioner or mushroom compost for every 10 square feet, tilled to a depth of 6 to 8 inches.

Growing Tips

This plant may suffer in times of drought; select a location where adequate moisture won't be a problem, either close to a spigot or in a naturally moist area. Soil that has been properly amended will hold moisture longer. Feed established plants with a cup of 10-10-10 fertilizer in spring as new growth begins.

Regional Advice and Care

When the vine is young, attach it to its growing surface with twine or cloth ties. Japanese hydrangea vine blooms on the current season's growth; if pruning is needed, it can be done in early spring. This vine is usually free of pests and disease.

Companion Planting and Design

Few horticulturists recommend that heavy, woody vines be allowed to climb trees. However, this is often the best way to display this plant's handsome foliage and flowers. So, this is a case of *Caveat hortus*! A large, blank brick wall will also host this plant nicely. The creamy white flowers in the summer mix well with other white-flowering hydrangeas, such as 'Annabelle' and 'Peegee'. Try planting it near Florida anise to accent the reddish stems of both plants. Use Japanese hydrangea to brighten areas in partial shade and to add texture with a vertical accent.

Try These

Schizophragma hydrangeoides 'Moonlight' has silvery blue-green leaves and deep green veins; it is showier than the straight species plant.

'Madame Galen' Trumpet Creeper

Campsis × tagliabuana 'Madame Galen'

Botanical Pronunciation
KAMP-sis tag-lee-ah-boo-AH-na

Bloom Period and Seasonal Colors
Perennial; deciduous; June to September
blooms in orange

Mature Length
20 to 30 ft.

One might envision the conception of this plant as a massive connubial tangle of our native trumpet vine (*Campsis radicans*) with its Chinese trumpet creeper cousin (*Campsis grandiflora*). From that union came 'Madame Galen' trumpet creeper. Like many hybrids, this plant has inherited the positive characteristics of both parents along with a couple of their not-so-nice habits. The flowers are larger in size, a trait inherited from its Chinese parent, yet the plant has great hardiness, which comes from its American parent. However, both parents possess an aggressive, if not rampant, growth habit that necessitates their daughter be kept in check with regular pruning. A magnet for hummingbirds, this vine is as versatile as it is tough. It thrives in the hot, humid summers that we regularly experience.

When, Where, and How to Plant

'Madame Galen' trumpet creeper can be planted in fall or spring, but it will likely thrive no matter what time of year it's planted. Flowering and growth will be better in full sun. It tolerates a wide range of soils but prefers moderately fertile, well-drained soil. Amend extremely compacted soil with 40 pounds of soil conditioner or mushroom compost per 10 square feet of planting area, mixed to a depth of 6 to 8 inches.

Growing Tips

Once established, 'Madame Galen' trumpet creeper is drought tolerant and does not need supplemental water or fertilizer. Mulch 3 to 5 inches thick will retain moisture and provide nutrients as it decays. Don't fertilize unless you want to create more maintenance work for yourself.

Regional Advice and Care

'Madame Galen' is a natural climber, using aerial roots that attach easily to most surfaces. Young plants may need to be attached to the growing surface at first. Don't be afraid to prune this vine to keep it inbounds. The flowers appear on new growth each year, so prune it back hard to the height of a few buds in early spring. It is virtually free of disease and pests.

Companion Planting and Design

Plant this lady and stand back! She is a vigorous, if not invasive, grower and will amaze you with how quickly she takes off. This vine is excellent for areas where a vertical accent is needed with nice summer flowers, but where the soil may be poor and the gardener too weak in spirit or flesh to tackle a heavy amending project. Plants also look smart growing on large arbors or walls. Resist the temptation to let 'Madame Galen' climb trees.

Try These

'Crimson Trumpet' has flower clusters that are a pure, glowing red. 'Flava' produces yellow flowers throughout the summer. If you fear the vigor of trumpet creeper, use the closely related crossvine (*Bignonia capreolata*).

Millettia

Millettia reticulata

Botanical Pronunciation
mil-LET-ee-uh reh-tick-yoo-LAY-tuh

Other Name Evergreen wisteria

Bloom Period and Seasonal Colors
Purple blooms in late summer to early fall

Mature Length
Deciduous vine; 12 to 15 ft.

With its intense, wisteria-like red and purple flowers, *Millettia* is sure to arouse envy in gardeners visiting your landscape. *Millettia* is a legume, like beans, kudzu, and redbud trees. Leathery, oval green leaves remain on the vine all year long in mild climates. Flower spikes jut out from leafy stems and the terminal bud from June to September. Each blossom on a cluster is shaped like a pea flower; the red interior surrounds a yellow throat. Flowers are mildly fragrant, reminding some of cedar or camphor. Bees and butterflies pollinate them, leading to seed-containing pods several inches long. *Millettia* is non-invasive and low care. All it needs is an arbor on which to grow and a gardener to admire it!

When, Where, and How to Plant
Millettia should be planted in spring in north Georgia or fall to spring in south Georgia. Flowering and growth will be better in full sun. It tolerates a wide range of soils but prefers moderately fertile, well-drained soil. Amend extremely compacted soil with 40 pounds of soil conditioner or mushroom compost per 10 square feet of planting area, mixed to a depth of 6 to 8 inches.

Growing Tips
Due to its leguminous nature, little fertilizer is needed for *Millettia*. Feed young vines in April with liquid fertilizer. Mature vines need only a yearly application of slow-release granules. Water will be needed in the heat of summer; keep the soil moist,

but never soggy, at all times. Evergreen wisteria is easily propagated from seeds or by partially covering a low branch with soil in late spring. Cut the branch free from the mother plant in October, but don't disturb the root system. It will be ready to transplant in spring.

Regional Advice and Care
Despite its common name, *Millettia* is not evergreen in all locations. In a partially shady spot in South Georgia, it will keep most of its leaves in winter. In full sun there, 50 percent will gradually fall off in winter. In the northern half of the state, vines will lose most leaves annually, but they will re-emerge in spring. Young vines can be frozen to the roots but will usually send up new sprouts in April. The vine may be troubled by whiteflies and spider mites, but they can be controlled with regular blasts from a water hose.

Companion Planting and Design
Millettia needs a sturdy support to climb, like a broad trellis, overhead arbor, or chain-link fence. It can be trained up a stone wall using vine supports epoxied to the wall. Without support, the vine becomes a sprawling, haphazard groundcover.

Try These
There are no named cultivars of *Millettia*, but American wisteria (see page 210) planted nearby would give blooms in spring before *Millettia* flowers emerge.

Moonflower

Ipomoea alba

Botanical Pronunciation
eye-poh-MEE-a AL-ba

Other Name Moonvine

Bloom Period and Seasonal Colors
Annual; summer to fall blooms in white

Mature Length
20 ft. or more

Moonflower lights up the night garden and sweetens the air. Its spectacular flowers start out as twisted tubes and open to long white trumpets that are 6 inches across. Each flower is divided into five points, reminiscent of a giant starfish. This morning glory relative enchants us with its flowers only at night. They will fade to brown after only a few hours of morning sun. Don't be startled at dusk to see large moths visiting the flower. The scent and white color entice them to visit and they help with pollination. This delightful treat will reward you with fragrance and flowers from summer into fall with little care. While many morning glories quickly become invasive weeds, moonflower is a showy, easy-to-grow annual.

When, Where, and How to Plant
After the last frost date, sow seeds directly into the ground where you plan to grow them. Plant in groups of two or three about 1 inch deep and 12 inches apart. After germination, thin out the seedlings, keeping only the strongest. Alternatively, start the seeds in peat pots so that you will not disturb the seedling roots when you transplant them to the garden. A moderately fertile soil plus lots of sunshine are all this vine requires. If you are planting a moonflower that has been grown in a container, dig a hole three times the width of the container and as deep. Like other tropical plants, moonflower grows best when soil and air temperatures are warm, at least 65°F at night.

Growing Tips
Too much fertilizer results in lots of foliage and fewer flowers. Unlike other annuals, once moonflower is planted, it can usually be forgotten—except for a weekly deep watering during dry spells.

Regional Advice and Care
Moonflower requires no special care, but it does need a structure to grow up or over so that the flower display can be appreciated. Wait until after a hard frost before you harvest seeds. The plentiful seedpods enclose gray-white seeds the size of an English pea. Store them indoors in a cool, dry spot and sow them next spring. Begin with one vine and you will find you soon have plenty to share. Pests, other than deer and rabbits, seldom affect it.

Companion Planting and Design
This fast-growing climber twines around any type of structure. Its heart-shaped foliage provides a lush background for its dramatic flowers in late summer. Plant moonflower near windows and doors where you can appreciate its perfume in the evening. Moonflower will grow in a large container or in the ground. Combine it with evergreen vines or roses for a dramatic effect.

Try These
Other easy-to-grow relatives of the moonflower are 'Heavenly Blue' morning glory, with sky blue flowers, and firecracker vine, *Ipomoea lobata*, which has dark red flowers that fade to orange, yellow, and white.

Sweet Potato Vine

Ipomoea batatas

Botanical Pronunciation
ip-oh-MEE-a bat-TAT-as

Bloom Period and Seasonal Colors
Foliage color ranges from lime green to deep purple-black

Mature Length
Annual groundcover vine; 12 in. tall by up to 10 ft. spread

We're lucky UGA's Dr. Allan Armitage didn't turn away from the North Carolina gardener who asked if he'd like to see a sweet potato vine with chartreuse leaves! Allen knew there were a couple of dark-leaved potatoes on the market . . . but light green? That could be a show stopper! Thus was 'Margarita' ornamental sweet potato discovered and subsequently brought to market. Now, with dozens of ornamental sweet potato varieties available, covering cumulative acres of ground, it seems inconceivable that simple happenstance could have opened the eyes of gardeners everywhere. Yet "That's the story, morning glory!" This durable annual is easy to propagate, vigorous in growth, and showy in habit. It grows beautifully throughout the state, providing ground-hugging color to residential and commercial flower beds.

When, Where, and How to Plant
Plant in a sunny spot in spring after all danger of frost. Till the soil beforehand so that roots can easily spread. Sweet potato is typically sold in 4-inch pots, but don't let the small size fool you! Some varieties produce vines 6 to 10 feet long. One lonely plant beside your mailbox will quickly cover several square feet.

Growing Tips
Fertilize at planting with water-soluble fertilizer. After two weeks, begin feeding monthly with general-purpose landscape fertilizer (or Milorganite as noted). Weekly watering will be needed in the heat of summer. Allow the soil to dry somewhat between irrigations; do not let it become soggy.

Regional Advice and Care
Sweet potato vine is just as attractive to deer and rabbits as it is to humans. If these four-legged pests are common in your neighborhood, use Milorganite fertilizer instead of synthetic fertilizer. This product is reputed to repel mammals. Flea beetles and golden tortoise beetles may make numerous Swiss-cheese holes in the leaves. Control them with general purpose garden insecticide. Fancy restaurants now serve sweet potato leaf chips, prepared the same way as kale chips. Some cultivars may produce large tubers, noticed at the end of the growing season. The roots are edible . . . but those who have tried them say they provide 110 percent of your daily roughage needs.

Companion Planting and Design
Leaves vary in shape from cultivar to cultivar, from heart-shaped to deeply lobed. They are primarily foliage plants but will occasionally bloom with pale lavender, morning glory–like flowers. The plant will not climb strongly but will clamber over obstacles, whether a low fence or small perennial flower. Combine the mounding cultivars noted below with vertical plants, such as papyrus or *Sansevieria*.

Try These
'Blackie', 'Margarita', 'Ace of Spades', and 'Tricolor' are among the initial cultivars introduced, and they are still outstanding. All grow vigorously. The Sweet Caroline™ series of cultivars are much more compact and mounding. They are fine for containers, where the leaves can spill over the sides but won't become a trip hazard on your deck.

Virginia Creeper

Parthenocissus quinquefolia

Botanical Pronunciation
par-then-oh-KISS-us kwin-kway-FOH-lee-uh

Other Name Woodbine

Bloom Period and Seasonal Colors
Attractive red foliage in fall

Mature Length
Deciduous vine; 50 ft. easily

Few innocent vines have been maligned as much as Virginia creeper. It inhabits the exact same environment as poison ivy and has an odd number of leaves emerging from a central stem. No wonder an unenlightened gardener might compulsively avoid it or spray it with weed killer. Yet Virginia creeper is one of our most attractive native vines. The deep green leaves have obscured many an outhouse in the South. Several types of butterfly caterpillars feed on the leaves during the summer. The fall foliage yields fiery red fall color similar to the revered Boston ivy, to which it is kin. Still, it gets no respect except from those who know to count the leaflets: "Leaves of five, stay alive; leaves of three, leave it be!"

When, Where, and How to Plant
Plant in spring or fall. This vine will grow in heavy shade but is mostly seen in part sun. It tolerates less-than-ideal soil conditions, growing in wet or dry soils. For best results, plant it in well-drained, moderately fertile soil. Decide initially where you want it to grow and don't hesitate to cut back escaping stems as the vine gets older. Water at planting, but little irrigation is needed afterward. Fertilizer is not needed.

Growing Tips
The plant is rarely found at nurseries, so the best way to get it is by transplanting a small vine from one landscape to another. Anyone with an established woodsy landscape will have plenty of the seedlings to spare. The flowers emerge only on mature vines when they have grown high above your head, but the numerous seedlings tell us that birds find the seeds delectable!

Regional Advice and Care
Once you've determined where to site the plant, train it to grow to the vertical surface using a length of string loosely tied to the base of the vine and to the surface. As the years progress, watch for nearby seedlings, which may sprout from the vine roots or from surface runners. Remove them at their origin. No pests affect Virginia creeper, other than gardeners mistaking it for poison ivy.

Companion Planting and Design
Like Boston ivy, Virginia creeper is sometimes used to cover bare walls. Unlike English ivy, it is not evergreen, so it is not good drapery for a chain-link fence. If allowed onto a wall, don't change your mind—the tendril holdfasts are very difficult to remove. The best use might be to climb bare pillars at a garden entrance, where only a spring shearing might be necessary. The vine also has potential as a groundcover for a slope. It tolerates harsh conditions with aplomb and spreads with enthusiasm.

Try These
Star Showers™' is a variegated form featuring leaves splashed with white, cream, and green. The foliage has a slightly pinkish cast.

GEORGIA PUBLIC GARDENS

Gardeners in Georgia are fortunate to have high-quality public gardens throughout the state that offer inspiration through beautiful gardens, hands-on learning, and basic gardening knowledge. These are some of the major gardens in Georgia that are open to the public.

**American Camellia Society
at Massee Lane Gardens**
100 Massee Lane
Fort Valley, GA 31030
www.camellias-acs.com/MasseeLane

Atlanta Botanical Garden
1345 Piedmont Avenue NE
Atlanta, GA 30309
www.atlantabotanicalgarden.org

Atlanta History Center
130 West Paces Ferry Road, NW
Atlanta, GA 30305-1366
www.atlhist.org

Callaway Gardens
P.O. Box 2000
Pine Mountain, GA 31822-2000
www.callawaygardens.com

Garden of the Coastal Plain
Georgia Southern University
1201 Fair Road (State Hwy. 67)
Statesboro, GA 30460
http://ceps.georgiasouthern.edu/garden/

Gibbs Gardens
1987 Gibbs Drive
Ball Ground, GA 30107
http://gibbsgardens.com/

**Perimeter College
Native Plant Botanical Garden**
3251 Panthersville Road
Decatur, GA 30034
http://gpcnativegarden.org/

State Botanical Garden of Georgia
2450 South Milledge Avenue
Athens, GA 30605
www.uga.edu/~botgarden

UGA Horticultural Trial Gardens
Betty Johnson Horticultural Gardens
(located behind the Pharmacy Building
on the University of Georgia campus)
http://ugatrial.hort.uga.edu

UNIVERSITY OF GEORGIA COOPERATIVE EXTENSION

The University of Georgia Cooperative Extension is an educational organization sponsored by the University of Georgia, Fort Valley State University, and local county governments, with offices scattered throughout the state. All county Extension offices have professional staff members who specialize in agriculture and/or horticulture, home environment, and youth development. Offices provide free educational pamphlets and advice. Many publications are available for immediate download at the Georgia Extension website.

Extension offices can also assist you with soil testing, pest identification, and safe pesticide use. Regardless of whether you are a large farmer or a home gardener, they are very friendly folks who follow the motto of "Putting Knowledge to Work."

University of Georgia Cooperative Extension Service
1-800-ASKUGA1
www.ces.uga.edu

The Master Gardener Volunteer Program is a national educational program offered through local county Extension offices. Through this program, individuals are trained and certified in horticulture and related areas. These individuals, in turn, volunteer their expertise and services, under the direction of their county Extension agent, to help others through horticultural projects that benefit the community.

www.ga.mastergardener.org

BIBLIOGRAPHY

No good gardening book can be completed without references. The following books have been invaluable to us, and we invite you to discover the tremendous amount of horticultural information contained in them.

Armitage, Allan. 2000. *Armitage's Garden Perennials: A Color Encyclopedia.* Timber Press, Portland, OR.

Armitage, Allan. 2001. *Armitage's Manual of Annuals, Biennials, and Half-hardy Perennials.* Stipes Publishing, Champaign, IL.

Armitage, Allan. 2008. *Herbaceous Perennial Plants: A Treatise on Their Identification, Culture, and Garden Attributes.* Stipes Publishing, Champaign, IL.

Armitage, Allan. 2010. *Armitage's Vines and Climbers.* Timber Press. Portland, OR.

Brooklyn Botanic Garden. Plants and Gardens Handbooks, many different subjects. List available from Brooklyn Botanic Garden, 1000 Washington Ave., Brooklyn, NY.

Copeland, Linda, and Allan Armitage. 2001. *Legends in the Garden: Who in the World is Nellie Stevens.* Wings Publishers. Atlanta, GA.

Darke, Rick. 2004. *Timber Press Pocket Guide to Ornamental Grasses.* Timber Press. Portland, OR.

Dirr, Michael. 2009. *Manual of Woody Landscape Plants.* Stipes Publishing. Champaign, IL.

Dirr, Michael. 2011. *Dirr's Encylopedia of Trees and Shrubs.* Timber Press. Portland,OR.

Gardiner, J. M. 1989. *Magnolias.* Globe Pequot Press. Chester, PA.

Gates, Galen et al. 1994. *Shrubs and Vines.* Pantheon Books. New York, NY.

Halfacre, R. Gordon, and Anne R. Shawcroft. 1979. *Landscape Plants of the Southeast.* Sparks Press. Raleigh, NC.

Harper, Pamela. 2000. *Time-Tested Plants: Thirty Years in a Four-Season Garden.* Timber Press. Portland, OR.

Hipps, Carol Bishop. 1994. *In a Southern Garden.* Macmillan Publishing. New York, NY.

Lawrence, Elizabeth. 1991. *A Southern Garden.* The University of North Carolina Press. Chapel Hill, NC.

Lawson-Hall, Toni, and Brian Rothera. 1996. *Hydrangeas.* Timber Press. Portland, OR.

Loewer, Peter. 1992. *Tough Plants for Tough Places.* Rodale Press. Emmaus, PA.

MacKenzie, David. 1997. *Perennial Groundcovers.* Timber Press. Portland, OR.

Mikel, John. 1994. *Ferns for American Gardens.* Macmillan Publishing. New York, NY.

Ogden, Scott. 1994. *Garden Bulbs for the South.* Taylor Publishing. Dallas, TX.

Still, Steven. 1994. *Manual of Herbaceous Ornamental Plants, 4th edition.* Stipes Publishing. Champaign, IL.

Wilson, Jim. 1999. *Bullet-Proof Flowers for the South.* Taylor Publishing. Dallas, TX.

INDEX

MEET
ERICA GLASENER
& WALTER REEVES

Erica Glasener

Erica Glasener, horticulturist, author, lecturer, and award-winning host of HGTV's *A Gardener's Diary* for 14 years. As the host for this popular TV show, she introduced her audience to gardeners, horticulture professionals, specialty plant growers, landscape architects, and more from across the country. In July of 2011 she received a Garden Media Award from the Perennial Plant Association for her promotion of perennials through writing and lectures. Currently she provides online content for the Southern Living Plant Collection (http://southernlivingplants.com/) and for Fiskars where she is a garden expert (http://www2.fiskars.com/Activities/Gardening/Gardening-Experts). She also writes a bimonthly blog for Gibbs Gardens, located in Ball Ground, Georgia.

For over ten years she wrote a column on plants and garden design for the *Atlanta Journal-Constitution*. She has also written about gardening for *Southern Lady Magazine* and served as a contributing editor for *Fine Gardening*. Her articles have appeared in *The New York Times, The Farmer's Almanac*, and *The Green Guide*. A frequent guest on regional and national lifestyle radio programs, she enjoys helping people solve garden problems. A popular speaker, she presents lectures at garden shows across the country from Seattle to Epcot. In 2010 she was invited to Homer, Alaska, as a speaker. The author of several books, her latest is *Proven Plants: Southern Gardens*. She lives with her family in Atlanta, Georgia, where her garden serves as a test site for many of the plants she writes about. To keep up with her garden activities, you can subscribe for free updates at www.ericaglasener.com or follow her on Twitter @ericaglasener.

Walter Reeves

Walter Reeves is retired from the University of Georgia Cooperative Extension, where he worked for 29 years. He grew up on a farm in rural Fayette County, Georgia, where he learned to garden from his parents and his grandmother, Bubber.

He hosts *The Lawn and Garden Show* radio call-in show on NewsTalk WSB every Saturday morning from 6 to 10 a.m. and has hosted gardening radio shows for 25 years.

Walter also writes a weekly column of garden questions and answers for the Thursday Living section of the *Atlanta Journal-Constitution* and has just completed his twentieth year of this effort. He hosted *Your Southern Garden* on Georgia Public Television for 10 years.

In his spare time, Walter manages www.walterreeves.com, which contains over 6,000 articles and answers to garden questions. He also edits and publishes *The Georgia Gardener*, a bi-weekly email newsletter.

He's the author of *Month by Month Gardening in Georgia; Georgia Gardener's Guide; Georgia Vegetables, Fruits, Herbs, and Nuts;* and *501 Garden Questions and Answers for Georgia,* all published by Cool Springs Press.

Walter has served on the board of Southface, the sustainability organization, for 16 years. He is an honorary master gardener and an enthusiastic promoter of environmentally responsible landscaping.

PHOTO CREDITS

William Adams: pp. 34, 57, 82, 104, 148, 202

Alamy: pp. 156 (Klaus Lang), 174 (blickwinkel)

Liz Ball and Rick Ray: pp. 24, 35, 49, 71, 76, 94, 95, 114, 132, 159, 170, 176, 182, 190, 192, 195, 198, 213

Mike Dirr: pp. 57, 197

Thomas Eltzroth: pp. 10, 13, 14, 18, 25, 26, 29, 31, 36, 37, 42, 43, 44, 50, 54, 55, 56, 58, 66, 67, 69, 72, 73, 74, 78, 79, 83, 85, 89, 92, 96, 101, 103, 105, 109, 122, 123, 126, 129, 134, 138, 140, 149, 155, 161, 167, 168, 171, 173, 175, 181, 185, 200, 205, 207, 212, 215, 219

Katie Elzer-Peters: pp. 154, 172

Erica Glasener: pp. 22, 30, 32, 33, 46, 52, 59, 62, 65, 80, 88, 93, 98, 100, 107, 110, 111, 113, 115, 117, 121, 125, 131, 141, 144, 152, 163, 169, 184, 186, 191, 216, 220, 222, 223

Lorenzo Gunn: pp. 145

Pam Harper: pp. 133, 143, 151, 160, 165, 177, 179, 188, 193, 196, 214, 221

Dency Kane: pp. 162

Dave MacKenzie: pp. 146

Charles Mann: pp. 28, 52, 81

Jerry Pavia: pp. 9, 27, 38, 47, 51, 60, 63, 64, 68, 70, 75, 84, 86, 87, 90, 91, 97, 99, 102, 106, 108, 112, 116, 119, 124, 127, 128, 136, 137, 139, 142, 150, 153, 157, 158, 164, 178, 180, 187, 189, 210, 218

Felder Rushing: pp. 39, 135, 194, 211

Shutterstock: pp. 41

Ralph Snodsmith: pp. 147

Neil Soderstrom: pp. 40

Andre Viette: pp. 118, 183, 209, 217

© Lee Anne White: pp. 6